The Spirit
and Science
of Holistic Health

More than Broccoli, Jogging, and Bottled Water
...More than Yoga, Herbs, and Meditation

Jon Robison   Karen Carrier
Foreword by L. Robert Keck

authorHOUSE

1663 LIBERTY DRIVE, SUITE 200
BLOOMINGTON, INDIANA 47403
(800) 839-8640
www.authorhouse.com

First published by AuthorHouse 09/23/04

ISBN: 1-4184-1353-4 (e)
ISBN: 1-4184-1352-6 (sc)
ISBN: 1-4184-1351-8 (dj)

Library of Congress Control Number: 2003097324

Printed in the United States of America
Bloomington, Indiana

This book is printed on acid-free paper.

In loving memory of our mothers
Marjorie Funderburk and Mona Robison

CONTENTS

Part One

FAILING FOUNDATIONS

Part Two

EMBRACING THE NEW SCIENCES

Part Three

"GETTING" PEOPLE TO CHANGE

Part Four

MORE THAN EXERCISE, NUTRITION, AND INCENTIVES

Part Five

THE MOTHER OF ALL CHANGES

Part Six

BREATHING SPIRIT INTO HEALTH PROMOTION

A NOTE ABOUT THE BOOK COVER

The creation of a better and healthier world is highly dependent on the decline of patriarchy and the creation of balance between feminine and masculine perspectives in future societies. This book is committed to promoting this belief. Therefore, as female and male coauthors, we gave extensive thought to the way our names would be listed on the cover. As a contradiction to the tradition of patriarchy, our names have been listed side by side, reflecting the fact that the content of the book is based on equal amounts of input from us both. We would like it to be noted that Jon's name is listed first not because he is the man but because he was able and willing to devote a greater amount of time to finishing the book.

world as a forest
↳ trees of health promotion

text & texture

FOREWORD

L. Robert Keck

The book you hold in your hands is a work of genius. In its original Latin roots genius means *the distinctive characteristics of a place, person, or era*, and Karen Carrier and Jon Robison are not only persons of distinction in their field of expertise, they have shown us, with substantive insight and wisdom, how health promotion fits within the distinctive characteristics of our era, the deep-values shaping our time in history.

This book is a work of genius, first of all, because the authors are able to see the big picture, the cultural and historical "forest" as well as having a great deal of experience with the individual "trees" of health promotion. They are historians, philosophers, and visionaries, yet are well acquainted with the practical and the pragmatic. They know that the historical and evolutionary context of humanity's deep-value system influences, to a great degree, both the text of our lives and the texture of our experience with health or illness.

The deep-value research that I have been engaged in suggests that evidence of human values emerged about 35,000 years ago — what I have called Epoch I in the history of the human soul. The first transformation of humanity's deep-values began about 10,000 years ago with an entirely different value system, and Epoch II was launched. We currently find ourselves within the second major chrysalis time in the history of the human soul, as the value system of the Epoch II caterpillar is dying and the new and very different values of the Epoch III butterfly are emerging. It is a transformation of soul, both literally and metaphorically — a great deal of empirical evidence suggests a substantive change in deep-values, and the Greek word for butterfly is the same word as for soul (psyche).

Robison and Carrier recognize that modern scientific medicine, and how most of us have historically thought about health and illness, and what we thought was efficacious to do when we got sick, were all products of the Epoch II value system. They perceive the ways in which our separation from nature (the organic and archetypal

xiii

feminine side of soul) led inevitably to the emergence of patriarchy, reductionism, hierarchical power, and a great deal of violence. And, they recognize how those values led to both the contributions and the drawbacks of modern medicine.

Looking through their contextual wide-angle lens they also understand the extent to which the current transformation of deep-values is creating an entirely new way of thinking and acting regarding health promotion, disease prevention, and the possibilities of healing. The tension today is created by a reductionistic biomechanical medical model which all too often wants to alter the human soul to fit its Epoch II values, whereas Robison and Carrier understand that modern medicine must alter itself in order to fit into the Epoch III human soul. When one analyzes the evolutionary history of the human soul and the rise and fall of cultural institutions, there is no question that, in a transitional time such as ours, institutions either change to conform to the soul's current values, or they die. Although there is inevitably a great deal of chaos within the chrysalis — the caterpillar people are always wanting to return to their familiar and comfortable past, while the butterfly people are wanting to experience the joy of flying — the evolutionary energies of the soul are always reaching for the stars.

Secondly, this book is a work of genius because Carrier and Robison are exceptional visionaries who are able to see beyond the horizon. What is particularly impressive is the degree to which they understand the subtleties of how holism is transcending the restrictions of reductionism, how cooperative partnerships are liberating health promotion in ways that patriarchy could never imagine, and so much more. These authors understand intellectually the subtle nuances, and they also feel it in their bones, as only long-term practitioners in a field can do. To a remarkable degree, Robison and Carrier are both grounded in the contributions of the past and capable of flying high enough to envision the future.

The term "holistic health" is, of course, a redundancy — albeit a necessary one. There is an ancient and important insight in the etymological relationship between whole, health, and holy — a relationship that has been largely ignored in mainstream medicine. The biomechanical medical model has been unabashedly reductionistic. But what is particularly interesting has been to watch several decades of the evolution of the so-called holistic health movement. Many people sensed intuitively both the limitation of the old medical model and how holism must balance out the traditional reductionism. They saw, appropriately, that many "alternative" approaches and modalities could be helpful. But, all too often, they became reductionistic themselves — narrow-minded, tunnel-visioned evangelists for this or that alternative. "It's all in what you eat," some would say. "No," others would say, "the secret is in energy work." "No," said others, "it's all in the spiritual work." In contrast, the essential meaning of "holistic" is that no one piece, no one modality, no one specialty has all of the secrets for health and well-being. The "all" is not in any part, but in an exponential synergy wherein the whole is more than the sum of the parts.

Robison and Carrier are among the rare health professionals who truly understand the wonders of holism and its potential for empowerment. They are also rare in their grasp of how simplistic thinking and an emotional need for black and white answers are the result of the Epoch II Cartesian goal of certainty, whereas holism involves embracing a great deal of humility and the wonderful shadings and textures of mystery.

I don't believe any book in the field of health promotion can match the one you hold in your hands for a comprehensive understanding of the changes taking place in our time in history, and how they will influence our thinking in this important vocation. Do yourself a great big favor — read carefully and savor the wisdom within the following pages. This book has the capacity to change your life in wonderful and serendipitous ways.

GRATITUDES

Karen

I have had the privilege of knowing some very fine and intelligent people. I would like to acknowledge these people in the order in which they came into my life.

Let me start first with my family. I would like to thank my parents for their enormous support while I was writing this book. They helped me with my children, maintained computers, took care of accounting issues, and even provided some home cooked meals! I would also like to thank my husband Max for his hard work, which gives me the financial freedom to do projects such as this book. And last, I want to acknowledge my daughters: Lindsey for her enthusiasm about having a mom who creates controversy and Madison for her efforts to nurture me with shoulder massages and quiet time while I was writing (although the quiet time was sometimes mischieviously interrupted by kazoo playing as well).

Beyond my family I would like to recognize my college roommate and colleague Mary Steinhardt. Mary and I worked closely in the 1980s on the development of some of the new paradigm ideas you will see in this book. Also very important to me were my creative co-workers on the wellness staff at Conoco, especially Bob Ealing, my first boss and a dear friend. During the eleven years I worked with Bob at Conoco, he always championed my work, even when conservative aspects of the organization tried to discount my contributions as a young female. And, of course, Jane Hirschmann and Carol Munter were the women who showed me an entirely new way to think about food, eating, "beauty," and my body. They opened my eyes to women's issues just as I became a mother to two young daughters. I also want to express my gratitude to Linda Bedre, who introduced me to Re-evaluation Counseling theory and helped me understand how different types of trauma and oppression lie at the root of most human suffering and illness. Linda has been my closest personal ally in my own healing work.

There have been so many other mentors over the years: Elaine Sullivan who introduced me to Harville Hendrix's Imago Therapy work; Terry Golden, who opened my eyes to quantum physics and the book *Turning Point;* Walter Elias and his alternative views of evaluation and cost containment; and Bob Keck, who so bravely speaks out on spirituality, religion, and violence. I want to thank them all for their work and support.

Believe it or not the most recent person to enter my life is my co-author Jon Robison. I can never thank Jon enough for the patience he has displayed while giving me the time and space required to write this book together. Writing is my least preferred method of communication, and I dislike computers, scanners, printers, and so on. His gentle but persistent encouragement kept us moving forward and led to the completion of this book. Jon is both a powerful colleague and a lifelong friend.

Jon

Although we have tried to keep our balance by not giving up on the rest of our lives while writing this book, there have certainly been times when I was in my office working when I could have been spending time with my family. I want to thank my wife Jerilyn and my son Joshua for giving me the space I needed to work. I also want to thank Jerilyn for opening my eyes to the critical importance of trauma to health, healing, and helping and for always being there to, among other things, tell me when I am not being "Zen" enough about what I am writing. And I want to give special thanks for my son Joshua just because he is such a gift and because he instructs me every day about the wonderful, innate capabilities of children. Finally, I want to thank my parents for always allowing me to be who I am even when they were not happy with who that was.

I want to thank my coauthor Karen Carrier for her passion and for helping me to get a foot in the door in my profession by introducing me to *all* of the sixteen hundred or so participants at the first National Wellness Conference that I attended. I also want to give special thanks to my friend Karen Gagnon for tirelessly donating her time and transcribing my presentation tapes, which made it possible for me to finish my part of the book during this millennium. Special thanks also go out to our editor, Jan Opdyke for spending so much time making things look like we knew what we were doing and always patiently answering my questions on the phone.

I want to express my gratitude to my colleagues, friends, and mentors around the country who have helped me in so many ways over the years. I hesitate to make a list for fear of leaving somebody important out but certainly want to mention Cheri Erdman, Pat Lyons, Brian Luke Seaward, Karin Kratina, Esther Park, Bob Keck, Glenn Gaesser, and Lisa Edwards. Special thanks also go to friend and colleague Walter Elias, who shared his expertise, allowing us to write an accurate and up-to-date chapter on evaluation and cost containment.

I also want to extend the warmest appreciation to the extraordinary women of Mercy Medical Center in Mason City, Iowa, for successfully implementing our approaches in a real world situation and particularly to my friend and co-conspirator Kelly Putnam for her tremendous creativity and for agreeing to contribute to the perfect finish for our book—a chapter describing their Kailo program.

AN INVITATION

After a time of decay comes the turning point.

I Ching

Since the early 1990s we have given many presentations based on the material in this book. We have suggested that it is critically important to view health education and promotion in the larger context of the huge upheavals humanity is currently experiencing. Both of us feel that these upheavals are creating vast changes in every aspect of human existence.

It has always been difficult in lectures and workshops to provide examples that convey the magnitude of the changes we humans are experiencing. Startling findings in the sciences, global movements such as feminism and deep ecology, and seemingly spontaneous events such as the fall of the Berlin Wall and the breakup of the Soviet Union were early indicators of what we might expect.

Then came the fall of 2001. The horrific, terrorist violence of September 11, the greed-driven collapse of Enron, and the astounding revelation of pedophilia and cover-up in the Catholic Church have given us all a chilling, new, and "close to home" sense of the chaos that is occurring.

As you read this book, we hope that the message will be clear. These disturbing, unprecedented events are interconnected—and there are reasons why they are now occurring with greater frequency. These seemingly unrelated incidents are, in fact, all sirens blaring the message that our current way of living on this planet needs to change—that in fact it is in the process of collapsing.

The resulting chaos is disturbing and unsettling. Yet, if we listen carefully, we can hear in this same chaos the quiet emergence of a new and better way of being human. It will allow us to move forward as a species into more cooperative, diverse societies with equality for men and women, diminished human on human violence, reduced worship of material wealth, and a more harmonious and sustainable relationship with our planet. This journey will be by no means an easy one. Every aspect of the "realities" to which we have become so accustomed will be challenged during this exciting crossover time in human history.

In this context, we propose that the major health crises in the United States are not about heart disease, cancer, osteoporosis, or obesity. Instead they are about violence, prejudice, social isolation, and runaway materialism. They are about children shooting children, about greedy corporate executives making millions while their employees lose their life's savings, and about our trusted religious leaders committing and covering up the most abhorrent of crimes against the most innocent and vulnerable members of our society. For growing numbers of people in this country, the real health crisis is about a gnawing hunger for meaning and purpose and an overwhelming feeling of disconnection and disempowerment.

Unfortunately, traditional health education and promotion continue to "attack" our problems by declaring war on disease, obsessing about epidemiologically based risk factors and frightening people about what they eat, how much they weigh, and what they like to do or not do. Using increasingly Orwellian means of persuading, cajoling, and pressuring people to change their behaviors "in the name of health," these approaches create an atmosphere of anxiety and confusion that rarely helps and that often leads to a loss of professional credibility.

This book is an invitation to health professionals (and all others interested in the health of our nation and the world) to rethink our current understanding of health, illness, and the process of healing. It is time to re-create our profession and set a daring new course to improve the quality of the human experience.

INTRODUCTION

Many years of nontraditional training, reading, networking and experience have gone into creating this book. It is our hope that the information and people that inspired us and profoundly changed our lives can now touch the lives of even more people through our readers.

Who Is This Book For?

At the most inclusive level, *The Spirit and Science of Holistic Health* is for anyone who is interested in world change and a better future for humanity and our planet. At a more specific level, this book is written for professionals and students involved in health education and promotion. We recognize that some professionals identify with the term *health education* while others identify with the term *health promotion*. For the sake of efficiency, we will use the term *health promotion* to refer to both fields throughout the book.

We believe that nurses, dietitians, physicians, exercise professionals, alternative medicine practitioners, social workers, psychologists, personal trainers, coaches, teachers, clergy, and others will all find this book relevant and helpful. In short, it is appropriate for anyone who is working to help people improve their social, emotional, spiritual, and physical quality of life—anyone whose occupation involves promoting the health of others. And because promoting the health of others is inextricably tied to promoting the health of self, this book is also appropriate for those people, professionals and laypersons alike, who are searching for a different way of understanding and creating their own health.

What Does the Book Cover?

The first two parts of the book contain information that is rarely addressed in traditional health promotion literature: the sociocultural history of the human species, the nature of paradigms, the significance of the Scientific Revolution, and new information on quantum physics, chaos theory, and psychoneuroimmunology. While it may seem at first as if this information is only marginally related to health promotion, we believe it provides a critical foundation for understanding the limitations of traditional health promotion efforts and introduces the rationale for adopting the dramatically different holistic approach that we discuss later.

The third and fourth parts of the book take an in-depth look at the biomedical approach to health promotion. The limitations of this traditional model are examined. The components of an alternative approach, Holistic Health Promotion, are thoroughly explored, and the professional process of preparing to work with this approach is presented.

Parts five and six provide detailed information about how to apply the philosophy and beliefs of Holistic Health Promotion in a variety of settings. All three of the chapters in part five address the complex issues surrounding eating and weight. We have devoted so much attention to these issues because it is the area in which health professionals have the most difficulty embracing "new paradigm" information. The chapters in part six cover ideas for all other aspects of programming as well as how to evaluate programs and how to create management support for holistic approaches.

Chapter 21, "Kailo: An Organizational Case Study," provides a fitting final chapter for the book. It is written by a passionate, creative woman from a very conservative city and workplace in the Midwest who embraced Holistic Health Promotion and created a successful, award-winning employee health promotion program. We believe that the story she tells of her five-year experience with creating, marketing, and implementing this program will be an inspiration and a practical guide for people who are considering taking a similar leap of faith.

At the end of the book, we have included a special section entitled "Reflections: People Who Have Helped to Clear the Way." This is a collection of stories from people who have explored the use of holistic approaches in corporations, hospitals, academic institutions, and the community. We have included this section in the book because, as we have spoken around the country, students and professionals in a wide variety of health-related fields have expressed the following concern:

> The holistic approach sounds wonderful and validates what I have believed for some time, but I can't imagine how it will fly in my conservative town, city, or workplace. I don't know how I would do this where I work!

We hope that it will be inspirational and reassuring to read about the actual experiences of holistic "paradigm pioneers." Their stories demonstrate that it is possible to successfully use this approach in a variety of settings.

In closing, we would like to note that the chapters in this book vary somewhat in terms of structure and presentation. Some are heavily referenced to provide the reader with a comprehensive list of places to go to more fully explore the foundational literature being cited. Other chapters have fewer references, as the information they contain is either synthesized from a few major sources or is mostly comprised of our own original material. Regarding resource information, there is also a section at the end of the book devoted to listing organizations, conferences, and journals that will be helpful.

We hope this book will stimulate your mind, touch your heart, inspire your spirit and support your efforts to improve the human situation.

Part One

FAILING FOUNDATIONS

Chapter 1

HIS-STORY

A One-Sided View of the Human Experience

The art of writing emerged on the human scene about the same time that patriarchy was becoming firmly established...virtually all of recorded history...was written by men, for men, and from a patriarchal perspective of the world.

L. Robert Keck
Sacred Quest

The Question

Those of us living in the early twenty-first century are faced with a provocative and critically important dilemma. How are we to think about and evaluate our progress as a species? As we will explore in the chapters to come, how we answer this question will have a profound impact on how we go about pursuing our roles in the field of health promotion.

There are two coexisting yet very different perspectives regarding this question. The view that is currently most visible is that we humans have brought about remarkable progress for ourselves. As Richard Tarnas, author of the best-selling book *The Passion of the Western Mind,* writes:

We can recognize a certain dynamism, even nobility—a kind of brilliant heroic impulse—at work in Western civilization and in Western thought. We see examples in the symphonies of Beethoven, the plays of Shakespeare, Greek philosophy and tragedy, the Sistine Chapel, or something as unbelievably intellectually pro-

3

found as the Copernican revolution. . . . In our own time, landing human beings on the moon, or even the extraordinary images of the vast cosmos coming from the Hubbell telescope, express this heroic impulse.[1]

As seen from this perspective, humans, especially in the last three hundred years, have harnessed the power of nature to produce the progress in technology and economic growth that has led to improved living conditions and increased knowledge, freedom, and well-being across humanity.

An entirely different view, however, is also receiving attention. This view has been around all along but is just now emerging for consideration in our contemporary consciousness. This alternative perspective holds that these same modern human advances have brought us to a point of extreme crisis in every dimension of society, creating a "tragic story of a radical fall and separation from an original state of relative unity—from a sense of interconnectedness between humankind, nature and the spiritual dimension of existence."[2] In this view, our hunger for power and control has led humans to the brink of a multidimensional crisis—politically, socially, ecologically, economically and spiritually. We have polluted and damaged the planet; violence, war and ethnic cleansing continue unabated and millions of people around the world still live in conditions of extreme famine and poverty.

So how are we to understand our current situation? How do we plan a path forward that makes sense? L. Robert Keck, author of *Sacred Eyes: An Invitation to View the Entire Human Journey and Your Own Life,*[2] and Riane Eisler, author of *The Chalice and the Blade,*[3] point out that we can best understand the significance of our current crisis, and the possibilities for our future, by carefully reviewing our past. In order to do this we must look back across human history, starting long before the emergence of the technological "progress" of the last few centuries.

Epoch I:

The Earliest Humans

Deep-value research examines "the deepest, most fundamental, and causal values that shape mainstream human cultures."[4] According to this research, the first known archaeological records of human societies indicate that the earliest humans lived in peaceful, cooperative societies. Keck refers to this first time period in human history, which began around 30,000 years ago (during the Paleolithic Era), as Epoch I. During this period, our "childhood" as a species, we lived in hunter-gatherer societies and the focus of humanity was on our physiological growth and development. The major "deep values" of this epoch were (1) a closeness with nature and a sense of unity and cooperation with all living things, (2) nonviolence, and (3) celebration of the feminine, leading to a profound cultural focus on respecting and worshipping life giving and life nurturing activities.

Eisler describes the human cultures of this time period as "partnership societies."[3] She points out that these early societies were matricentric (mother centered) and matrilinear (with descent traced through the mother's side of the family). Women and men lived in harmony, and both feminine and masculine characteristics were valued equally. Female deities and the "mother goddess" were worshiped because they represented the life-giving and nurturing qualities so highly esteemed in these cultures. In these partnership societies there were no hierarchies of power and *no record of human on human violence.* Eisler summarizes the archaeological and anthropological findings pertaining to this time period as follows.

As a general rule, descent was probably traced through the mother. The elder women or heads of clans administered the production and distribution of the fruits of the earth, which were seen as belonging to all members of the group. Along with common ownership of the principal means of production and a perception of social power as responsibility or trusteeship for the benefit of all came what seems to have been a basically cooperative social organization. Both women and men . . . worked coop-

5

eratively for the common good. Greater male physical strength was not the basis for social oppression, organized warfare, or the concentration of private property in the hands of the strongest men. Neither did it provide the basis for supremacy of males over females, or of "masculine" over "feminine" values. On the contrary, the prevailing ideology was gynocentric, or women-centered, with the deity represented in female form.[3]

In these societies descent was traced through the mother and women played major roles in all aspects of life as both priestesses and heads of clans. However, there is no evidence to suggest that there was any social subordination of men similar to that to which women are commonly subjected in present day cultures. Eisler suggests that this is a major factor distinguishing partnership models of human social organization. Thus, "in a partnership model of social organization, difference is *not* automatically equated with inferiority or superiority, with in-groups versus out-groups, with dominating or being dominated."[5]

A detailed analysis of the tremendous implications of these revelations for our culture and our species is beyond the scope of this book and has been exquisitely pursued in *The Chalice and the Blade* and *Sacred Pleasure,* also written by Eisler. We will see later that this new information has powerful implications for our understanding of health and disease as well as for the role of the health promotion professional.

Epoch II:

Our Adolescence

Epoch II was our "adolescent stage" of ego development and development of our mental abilities. During this time period, starting about ten thousand years ago, we began domesticating plants and animals and forming what are known as Neolithic agriculturally based cultures. But harnessing and controlling the power of animals and "Mother" Nature led us to separate or individuate from nature as well, much as developing adolescents seek to create an ego identity and separate from their parents. This separation from nature was synonymous with the beginnings of our withdrawal from the woman-centered focus of Epoch I, what Keck refers to as our "feminine side of soul."[3] Accordingly, Epoch II deep values came to focus on: (1) a separation between humanity and nature, which led to an emphasis on control over nature; (2) hierarchies of power based on strength and violence; and (3) patriarchy, the fundamental valuing of masculine over feminine values. In essence, what ensued along with the changes in our relationship with Mother Nature was the "domestication" of women by men.

This great change was solidified around 4500 B.C. when the first of many waves of violent, nomadic groups began to overrun the peaceful partnership societies that had existed for so many thousands of years during Epoch I. These invading groups were headed by male warrior priests who worshiped a masculine god and placed supreme value on the taking rather than the giving of life. Eisler points out that the social organization of these "dominator societies" was based on enforced hierarchies maintained through male aggression and violence. These societies were characterized by rigid control of religious and social belief systems and adolescent notions of power through control "over" others.

It is important to take note that these patriarchal, dominator cultures first emerged on the European continent about 6,000 to 7,000 years ago. This means that from 30,000 B.C. to about 4500 B.C. (about 25,000 years) a female, goddess-worshiping, peace-seeking partnership society was the model for human civilization. This is, in fact, about *four times longer* than the time during which our current patriarchal model has been the norm. The drastic changes in all aspects of human society brought about by the transition from Epoch I to Epoch II are summarized in figure 1.1.

Partnership Model

- Females and males are equally valued in governing ideology. Stereotypically feminine values (nurturance, compassion, nonviolence) can be given operational primacy.

- Violence and abuse are not structural components of the system. Boys and girls are both taught nonviolent conflict resolution, resulting in a low degree of social violence.

- Social structure is more generally egalitarian and differences (races, color, etc.) are not automatically associated with superior/inferior or social/economic status.

- The primary functions of sex are bonding between male and female through the give and take of mutual pleasure and the reproduction of the species.

- The life-giving and life-sustaining powers of nature and the feminine are highly valued. The divine is imaged through myths and symbols of unconditional love.

- Caretaking, lovemaking, and other activities that bring pleasure are considered sacred.

- The highest power is to give, nurture, and illuminate life, symbolized by the holy chalice or grail. Love is recognized as the highest expression of evolution on our planet as well as the universal unifying power.

Dominator Model

- The male is ranked over the female, and traits and social values associated with masculinity are valued over those associated with femininity.

- There is a high degree of institutionalized violence, from wife and child beating to warfare and psychological abuse by superiors.

- The social structure is predominantly hierarchic and authoritarian to a degree roughly equal to the degree of male dominance.

- The primary functions of sex are male procreation and sexual release.

- Man and spirituality are ranked over women and nature, justifying exploitation and domination. The powers that govern the universe are seen as punitive entities.

- The infliction and/or suffering of pain are sacralized.

- The highest power is to dominate and destroy. Love is often used to justify violent and abusive actions by those who dominate, from men killing women suspected of sexual independence to holy wars fought in the name of a deity.

Figure 1.1. Partnership versus dominator models of human culture. (Based on Eisler, *Sacred Pleasure.*)

Epoch III:

Spiritual Maturation

Deep-value research suggests that we are living in the last stages of Epoch II, and the early stages of Epoch III, a time of human spiritual maturation. This is a "crossover" time of profound transformation, the second large, cataclysmic shift in human culture to date. As we move into Epoch III we will again see dramatic changes in the deep values and social organization of human cultures. Keck believes that Epoch III will be a time in which we begin "re-membering" how we naturally were as humans during Epoch I. It is also expected to be a time for re-creating a sacred relationship with nature and reconnecting with the "feminine side of soul" across all aspects of our culture.

There are many indications that the shift to Epoch III is already under way. In 1940 there were 13 democracies in the world. Today there are 119.[1] Although there have certainly been setbacks, the feminist movement has led to improved status and conditions for women worldwide. Other global efforts are under way to improve conditions for animals and to help humans learn to live more "lightly" on the planet. In 1995, a large study identified nearly one-quarter of the adult population of the United States, more than 44 million people, as "cultural creatives" interested in "values focused on spiritual transformation, ecological sustainability, and the worth of the feminine.[6]

One of the most significant indicators that we are well on our way into Epoch III is the exploding interest in alternative medicine and holistic health. There has been enormous interest, especially in Western culture, in the reintegration of ancient concepts of life, spirituality and healing. As Rob Lehman, in his article "Love and Money: Our Common Work," reports:

A recent study sponsored by the Fetzer Institute and the Institute of Noetic Sciences shows that about 20 million Americans are part of a growing constellation of people who link their own spiritual growth with their life in service and social action. During the last five years alone sales of spiritually oriented books have increased by 800 percent. Dan Yankelovich reports that the percentage of the public who see spiritual growth as a critical value in their lives has grown from 53 percent to 78 percent in just the last three years. And only 6 percent of this group consider themselves "New Age." This is a mainstream movement.[7]

Even depressing events such as chronic corruption and downsizing in organizations and escalating human on human violence around the world may actually be signs that we are moving toward a more "humane humanity" in Epoch III. Deep-value Research suggests that these events signal the last, desperate gasps of autocratic, male-dominated organizations and social systems based on the dying Epoch II values of patriarchy, hierarchal coercion and power through control over others.[4]

This possibility takes on almost immeasurable importance given the tragic events of September 11, 2001. The horrors committed on that day as well as most human on human violence have occurred as a direct result of the continued dominance of Epoch II values. Religious wars, ethnic cleansings, hate crimes, and terrorism all have at their roots the "separation" of groups or individuals from the whole (followed by the assumption that difference implies inferiority) that is inevitably used as a justification for violence.[1] Keck and Eisler remind us that this process is not innately human. Peaceful, cooperative, partnership societies existed as the norm for human culture for twenty-five thousand years. Indeed, Deep-value Research suggests that one of the major shifts in Epoch III will be the reclaiming of our more peaceful and cooperative human nature.

Back to the Future

In order for the emergence of Epoch III to become a reality, the values and institutions of Epoch II must undergo crisis, experience chaos and fully recede. One of the most significant values and underlying foundations of Epoch II has been unquestioned faith in the objectivity and infallibility of science. It is therefore not surprising that, as we inch toward Epoch III, science has undergone and continues to experience radical transformation.

The next few chapters will examine the nature of scientific "paradigms" and explore how dramatic shifts in these paradigms are indicators of the changes in humanity that scholars such as Keck and Eisler are predicting. We will see that many of the *new* revelations are not new at all but rather represent a return to previous understandings that have been forgotten. We believe that these changes will dramatically alter what we do in health promotion.

References

The material in this chapter is based largely on the work of Riane Eisler and Robert Keck. We are deeply in their debt for helping us to gain the perspective needed to begin to think about reshaping health promotion in a direction more attuned to the true nature of humankind. For more in-depth explorations of the issues presented in this chapter, we strongly recommend Eisler's *The Chalice and the Blade, Sacred Pleasure,* and *The Power of Partnership* and Keck's *Sacred Eyes, Sacred Quest,* and *Healing as a Sacred Path.*

1.   Tarnas, Richard. "The Great Initiation." *Noetic Sciences Review* 47 (winter 1998): 24–31, 57–59.

2.   Keck, L. Robert. *An Invitation to View the Entire Human Journey and Your Own Life with Sacred Eyes.* Boulder: Synergy Associates, 1992.

3.   Eisler, Riane. *The Chalice and the Blade: Our History, Our Future.* San Francisco: HarperSanFrancisco, 1988.

4.   Keck, L. Robert. *Sacred Quest: The Evolution and Future of The Human Soul.* West Chester, PA: Chrysalis Books, 2000.

5.   Eisler, Riane. *Sacred Pleasure: Sex, Myth, and the Politics of the Body—New Paths to Power and Love.* San Francisco: HarperSanFrancisco, 1996.

6.   Ray, P. "The Rise of Integral Culture." *Noetic Sciences Review* 37 (spring 1996): 2–13.

7.   Lehman, Rob. "Love and Money: Our Common Work." *Noetic Sciences Review* 47 (winter 1998): 20–24.

Chapter 2

PARADIGMS

The Myth of Scientific Objectivity

The proponents of competing paradigms . . . see different things
when they look from the same point in the same direction . . . what
cannot even be demonstrated to one group of scientists
may seem intuitively obvious to another.

Thomas Kuhn
The Structure of Scientific Revolutions

Imagine for a Moment

You are riding home from work on the train on a still, hot, August
afternoon.[1] The air conditioning is broken, and the train is very full.
People are crowded against each other, and everyone is sweaty, sul-
len, and cranky. To make matters worse, two young children are crying loudly, pushing and shoving each other and bumping into people
in an attempt to hang on to a man who appears to be their dad. This
man, who happens to be standing next to you, is looking down at the
floor and making no effort to control his children. The hotter it gets,
the angrier you get. Doesn't he see what is going on? Why can't he
control his children? Doesn't he realize they are annoying people in
what is already an intolerable situation? Finally you are able to contain yourself no longer. You turn to the man and say: "Isn't there
something you can do about your children? They seem to be out of
control." After a brief pause, he looks up at you with sad, tear-filled
eyes and says in a quiet voice: "I'm sorry, you are right. We are returning from the hospital where their mother just died unexpectedly."

Take just a minute to feel what you are feeling. What do you think would happen to your original assessment of the situation? What would happen to your anger and rage? Most likely they would turn to sadness and remorse, perhaps even shame—and your initial assessment of the situation would change dramatically. You might even turn to the man in the next instant and say something like: "I am so sorry, is there anything I can do to help?" What you have experienced in this encounter is a "paradigm shift." Although this may seem like a dramatic example, most of us have at one time or another experienced this kind of profound shift in thinking and feeling.

The Power of Paradigms

A paradigm is a model or frame of reference from which we determine how we feel about and interact with our surroundings. Think of it as "a set of rules and regulations that (1) defines boundaries; and (2) tells you what to do to be successful within those boundaries."[2] Our personal paradigm is a result of the total sum of our life experiences. It is, most simply, the way we look at the world, or, as the late Willis Harmon, former president of the Institute of Noetic Sciences, put it, "the basic way of perceiving, thinking, valuing, and doing associated with a particular vision of reality."[3] Each of us actually has "layers" of these "ways of perceiving, thinking, valuing and doing" that help create our particular vision of reality. Thus, our personal vision of reality is likely to be influenced concurrently by a human paradigm, a Western civilization paradigm, an American paradigm, a particular religious paradigm, a community paradigm, an age-specific paradigm, and so on. As we have just experienced with the train story, our personal paradigms do not describe reality *as it is* but merely create a picture or representation of reality *as we have learned to see it.*

What is most critical to understand about the role paradigms play in our lives is that they act as powerful filters of information. In essence, our paradigms actually determine what we perceive. Something that may be perfectly obvious to a person with one paradigm may be invisible to a person with a different paradigm. This striking power of different paradigms to create different realities for different people has been called the "paradigm effect." In his book *Discovering the Future: The Business of Paradigms,* Joel Barker discusses the nature and power of paradigms.[2] Here are three major characteristics of paradigms as summarized from his work.

1. ***Paradigms are common.*** They exert their powerful influences in all areas of life from science, to politics, to organizations, to social customs, etc. In all these areas, paradigms set up rules and regulations that guide behavior and set standards for the "rules of the game."

2. ***Paradigms are functional.*** Paradigms are, in fact, necessary to help us to live in a highly complex world. They help us to continually determine what information is important and what is not and in doing so prevent information overload.

3. ***Paradigms too strongly held lead to "paradigm paralysis."*** Blindly holding on to old paradigm thinking inhibits innovation and seriously threatens the ability to adapt to change. Barker refers to this serious, chronic condition as "hardening of the categories."

This last point is extremely important, and it holds true for all fields of endeavor. There are countless examples in technology, business, science, and culture in which individuals, businesses, and institutions have paid dearly for their inability to recognize and take advantage of the emergence of new paradigms. Few are more striking, however, than the story of the invention of the quartz watch.

A Case of "Paradigm Paralysis"

Before the invention of the quartz timepiece, Swiss watchmakers enjoyed a world market share as high as 90 percent.[2] With the invention of the electronic watch, that share dropped to a level as low as 10 percent in just a relatively few years. The sad but powerful irony is that this "new paradigm" watch was actually invented by the Swiss! That's right, the Swiss Watch Federation Research Center, the research arm of the Swiss watch manufacturers, actually presented a prototype of the first quartz watch to Swiss manufacturers in 1967. Although we don't know exactly what was said at that presentation, we can probably imagine the response of the watch manufacturers.

It doesn't tick. It looks too clumsy. It has no gears, no springs. How can it even be considered a watch? It's too radical a change. We don't do things that way! Who do you think you are?

What we do know is that Texas Instruments and Seiko of Japan were not stuck in the Swiss watch paradigm. They snatched up the new technology, and today virtually everyone has a watch with quartz timing. As is so often the case, the new paradigm offering was initially met with scorn and rejection. This is not because the Swiss manufacturers were inherently narrow-minded or short-sighted. New paradigms by their very nature are anxiety producing for those operating under the old paradigm. The longer people practice in the old paradigm, the more they have invested in maintaining the status quo and the more difficult it is for them to see things any other way. While this is certainly natural and understandable, the consequences can be devastating. In this instance, the result was the destruction of Swiss domination of the watchmaking industry and the loss of tens of thousands of jobs!

Paradigms, Science, and Objectivity

Much of the basis for the new health promotion approaches proposed in this book will be outside of traditional scientific paradigms. It is therefore critical to understand that all health care professionals, just like scientists, are strongly influenced by the prevailing paradigms of their time. As with the case of the quartz watch, this is not so much a result of personal egos and narrow-mindedness (although this can certainly enter into the equation) but more likely a result of the fact that, as Harmon reminds us, "Objectivity is a function of the prevailing (partly unconscious) assumptions about the nature of reality."[3] Therefore, while it may be difficult (and perhaps painful) to accept, the concept of an "objective" scientist defined as "uninfluenced by emotion, surmise or personal prejudice"[4] is in reality an illusion.

In the same context, and for similar reasons, scientific theories are actually not objective descriptions of reality. As the internationally renowned physicist Fritjof Capra reminds us in his groundbreaking book, *The Turning Point:*

> Scientific theories can never provide a complete and definitive description of reality. They will always be approximations to the true nature of things. To put it bluntly, scientists do not deal with the truth; they deal with limited and approximate descriptions of reality.[5]

This is precisely because all sciences as well as all scientists have paradigms that provide a framework for investigation, focusing attention and guiding inquiry in certain areas to the exclusion of others. In *The Structure of Scientific Revolutions*, T. S. Kuhn describes the nature and significance of paradigms in relation to science.

> Paradigms are constituted from the concepts, assumptions and rules that guide workers in their pursuit of knowledge and the solution of problems in a given field. . . . Paradigms gain status to the extent that they are successful in solving problems and they lose status as paradoxes multiply.[6]

These paradigms or models are, like our individual paradigms, made up of the sum of a vast constellation of experiences. Like our own personal paradigms, therefore, they are not in fact reality but merely a particular representation of reality, which is subject to change as new information becomes available. Throughout history, scientific revolutions have been brought about when this emerging information demanded explanations that could not be made within existing paradigms.

Paradigms and Science:

An Example from History

Before the sixth century B.C., the earth was assumed to be flat. In the course of their scientific inquiry, the ancient Greeks encountered a number of phenomena that could not be explained by the prevailing flat earth paradigm.

- When they traveled away from Greece they noticed that different stars were visible from different points on the earth.

- When they watched their ships sail out to sea the ships didn't grow smaller and smaller until vanishing as mere points in the distance but rather disappeared while still perceptibly larger than points, always hull first with sails still visible and irrespective of the direction in which they traveled.

Through their contemplation of the failure of the existing flat earth paradigm to explain these and other phenomena, the Greeks hypothesized that the earth was not flat but spherical. This paradigm shift provided a new framework for their scientific inquiry, not only suggesting answers to these and other philosophical dilemmas of the time but also leading ultimately to discoveries involving a more accurate understanding of the solar system.

Paradigms and Medicine:

The "Tomato Effect"

By the middle of the 1500s tomatoes had become a staple of the continental European diet. Yet it took almost three hundred years for Americans to accept this fruit! Why? Because Americans believed that tomatoes, like several other plants in the nightshade family (belladonna, mandrake) were poisonous. Only when a brave individual publicly ate this dreaded fruit on the courthouse steps in Salem, New Jersey, and survived did Americans begin to embrace the tomato, which is now one of our largest commercial crops.

The "tomato effect" in medicine is said to occur when an effective treatment is shunned because it does not fit within the prevailing paradigm of disease mechanisms and drug action.[7] One example of the tomato effect involves the use of aspirin for the treatment of rheumatoid arthritis. As far back as the late 1800s, controlled trials reported in major medical journals such as the *Journal of the American Medical Association* (JAMA) and the *Lancet* demonstrated the effectiveness of aspirin in treating the disease. Yet with the acceptance of the "germ theory" of disease in the early twentieth century the use of aspirin to treat "infectious" rheumatoid arthritis "made no sense." The prevailing paradigm was so powerful that medical textbooks of the early 1900s made no mention of this effective treatment. In fact, it wasn't until the late 1950s that aspirin began to be recommended by the medical establishment for this condition. As the paradigm shifted, and we learned that rheumatoid arthritis was not an infectious but an autoimmune disease, it "made sense" that aspirin could be an appropriate treatment!

The power of paradigms to shape and mold scientific research and interpretation as well as health promotion theory and practice will be reflected over and over again in the material that we discuss in the chapters to come.

Paradigms and Change

One of the most important reasons for exploring the paradigm concept is that it enables us to appreciate the tremendous difficulties involved in embracing paradigmatic shifts such as the ones discussed in this book. Throughout history, paradigm shifts in science have not only been discredited and rejected but have often been met with violent opposition. Indeed, many of those involved in suggesting such shifts have been hung, burned at the stake, or at the very least ostracized and excommunicated, even when they could scientifically prove what they were suggesting! In the sixteenth century the Italian scientist Giordano Bruno was the first to suggest that the earth might not be the center of the universe. He was promptly burned at the stake for his scientific curiosity. A hundred years later Galileo said the same thing, and he too was forced to recant, on penalty of excommunication, in spite of the fact that he invented the telescope so that people could see the truth for themselves!

We certainly don't expect any such repercussions from this book. However, because paradigms are so fundamental to our very existence, questioning them is often unsettling at a very basic level. Many of the approaches to health promotion and behavior change suggested in this book will conflict with what we have learned from our teachers, our parents, and our culture as a whole. The initial reaction may therefore include strong emotions and resistance. This is to be expected. Rather than ignoring these emotions, the essential task for each person will be to seek to understand and incorporate them into a realistic and dynamic evaluation of the information presented, perhaps guided by an old Buddhist saying: "Don't bite the finger, look to where it is pointing."

Paradigm Pioneers

One of the most exciting things about paradigms is that because they deal primarily with perception they can be changed. People can and often do choose to look at their world through a different set of filters—to change their paradigms. Yet moving to a new paradigm always involves risk. There is, as we have seen, the almost guaranteed and sometimes extremely distasteful disapproval of old paradigm advocates. Then there is the stress and anxiety that accompanies letting go of old ways of doing things that carry with them significant personal investment. And, to make matters even more difficult, there is often only limited quantitative evidence available for the efficacy of the paradigm shift being proposed. So choosing to embrace a new paradigm often must be done largely on the basis of faith and intuition, from the heart and not the head, if you will. Kuhn says that individuals who choose this path must "Have faith that the new paradigm will succeed with the many large problems that confront it knowing only that the older paradigm has failed with a few. A decision of that kind can only be made on faith."[6] Yet with risk comes the potential for substantial gain. Particularly in times of great stress and turmoil, it is those individuals most open to trying new ways of doing things—the *paradigm pioneers*[3]—that fare the best and make the most significant contributions to their world. We invite you to consider becoming one of those pioneers!

Summary

Paradigms help us operate in the world by providing structure and establishing guidelines for defining reality. Paradigms formed in the sciences are especially important because they trickle down to create the foundations for all of the values and institutions of our larger culture. To be paradigm pioneers in health promotion, we first need to have a clear understanding of the new paradigms emerging in today's sciences and how they differ from the increasingly outdated views of the old sciences. Let's begin this process by examining the seventeenth century worldview that emerged from Newtonian physics and the Scientific Revolution.

References

For readers interested in additional information on the topic of paradigms, we strongly recommend the work of Thomas Kuhn. Kuhn was the first person to conceptualize the idea of paradigms and reading his book, *The Structure of Scientific Revolutions*, is very helpful. More recently, the work of Joel Barker has also helped to move the understanding of paradigms forward. We highly recommend Barker's book, *Discovering the Future: The Business of Paradigms.*

1.   Covey, Stephen R. *The Seven Habits of Highly Effective People.* New York: Simon and Schuster, 1989.

2.   Barker, J. A. *Discovering the Future: The Business of Paradigms.* St. Paul: ILI Press, 1989.

3.   Harmon, W. *Global Mind Change: The Promise of the Twenty-first Century.* San Francisco: Berrett-Koehler, 1998.

4.   *American Heritage Dictionary of the English Language.* Boston: Houghton Mifflin, 1978.

5.   Capra, F. *The Turning Point: Science, Society, and The Rising Culture.* Toronto: Bantam, 1983.

6.   Kuhn, T. S. *The Structure of Scientific Revolutions.* Chicago: University of Chicago Press, 1962.

7.   Goodwin J. S., and J. M. Goodwin. "The Tomato Effect: Rejection of Highly Efficacious Therapies." *Journal of the American Medical Association* 251, no. 18 (1984): 2387–90.

Chapter 3

THE MECHANISTIC UNIVERSE

Newtonian Physics and the Scientific Revolution

The notion of an organic, living, spiritual universe was replaced by that of the world as a machine and the world-machine became the dominant metaphor of the modern era.

Fritjof Capra
The Turning Point

The waves of invasions that established dominator societies and values across human cultures took place thousands of years ago. However, the momentous upheaval that propelled humanity from our Epoch I childhood to our Epoch II masculine adolescence reached its pinnacle during the Scientific Revolution of the seventeenth century, a time period Keck refers to as our "late adolescence." Although this was a time of great change and progress, particularly in the scientific arena, Keck points out that the Epoch II deep values remained unchanged.

> We simply switched our worship from God and the Church to the scientific capacity to make sense of the world. We turned our loyalty from the Church's priesthood to the "priesthood" and "saints" of modern science.[2]

The deep values of Epoch II—patriarchy, separation from nature, and control through violence—were actually reinforced and scientifically validated as a result of the rapid accumulation of knowledge during the Scientific Revolution. For almost four hundred years, literally every aspect of our Western culture has been dominated by the paradigm or worldview handed down from the Scientific Revolution.

In this chapter and the one that follows, we will examine this world-view and its impact on our culture, our science, and particularly our approach to health and disease in order to provide the appropriate historical and cultural context to the need for change.

The Way We Were:
The Organic Worldview

In his landmark book *The Turning Point,* Fritjof Capra describes life in Europe and most of the rest of the world before the Scientific Revolution of the seventeenth century.[2]

> People lived in small, cohesive communities and experienced nature in terms of organic relationships, characterized by the interdependence of spiritual and material phenomenon and the subordination of individual needs to those of the community. The scientific framework of this organic world view rested on two authorities—Aristotle and the Church.

Indeed, medieval science, based on the reason of Aristotle and the faith of the Church was very different from the science of today. Medieval scientists believed in an organic, living, spiritual universe. The earth itself was considered to be a living organism within a living cosmos, as Carolyn Merchant describes in her book, *The Death of Nature:* "The living character of the world organism meant not only that the stars and planets were alive, but that the earth too was pervaded by a force giving life and motion to the living beings on it."[3] Furthermore, from the beginning of civilization the purpose of science had been to understand the meaning and natural order of this living cosmos in order to be able to live in harmony with nature. Thus, medieval science regarded inquiry into God, spirituality, ethics, and the human soul as critical for the understanding of natural phenomena. But all of that was about to change!

The Scientific Revolution:

A Mechanistic Universe

The seventeenth-century paradigm or worldview developed largely as a result of revolutionary changes in physics, astronomy and mathematics emerging from the work of Galileo Galilei, René Descartes, Sir Isaac Newton, Sir Francis Bacon, and others. So influential were these great thinkers that this period is referred to as the age of the Scientific Revolution and the description of reality they formulated is commonly called the Cartesian or Newtonian paradigm. For these men, the universe was not a living entity but a great machine. Although they believed in a male God of Creation, they believed that this god had long since left the daily functioning of the universe to the fundamental mechanical and mathematical laws he had also created. As scientist and visionary Willis Harmon put it they believed that: "It is essentially a dead universe, constructed and set in motion by the Creator, with subsequent events accounted for by mechanical forces and lawful behaviors."[4] Thus, Nature itself was compared to a huge clock composed of dead, inert particles and devoid of purpose, spirituality, or life. Understanding the workings of any of the components of the universe and all natural phenomena no longer necessitated exploration of spiritual or ethical matters but only of those things that could be measured and quantified. The organic view of nature was thus rapidly replaced by the "world as machine."

Reductionism:

The Whole Is Equal to the Sum of Its Parts

The concept of reductionism is derived from classical Newtonian physics, the most important assumption being that all complex phenomena in this "mechanistic universe" can be understood only by reducing them to their smallest component parts. As most of us probably remember from our high school science classes, classical physics describes matter as being composed of discreet particles that can be broken down into their primary atomic and subatomic building blocks. This reductionist approach to determining the nature of reality has become the gold standard for scientific investigation in the physical sciences as well as medicine and the social sciences. In fact, in virtually every aspect of our society the legacy of reductionism has resulted in a focus on breaking down whatever is being examined into smaller and smaller component parts, discovering how the parts relate, and then reassembling them in order to understand the workings of the whole. Reductionist science views nature and all of nature's components and phenomena, including all living things, as sophisticated machines that can be examined and understood only in this manner.

Dualism:

Separating Matter from Spirit

and Humanity from Nature

One of the major consequences of this mechanistic, reductionist approach to reality was the separation of the universe into two parts. The material universe (anything composed of matter) was viewed as objective, quantitative, and measurable and therefore subject to human comprehension. The immaterial universe, including thoughts, feelings, emotions, and human consciousness, was seen as subjective and qualitative and beyond the realm of understanding. Thus, the seventeenth-century worldview was founded on the separation of matter from spirit and humanity from nature. Only that which could be measured and quantified was considered to be real. The resulting rational, mathematical, analytical approach to defining reality through science is perhaps best expressed by one of its main architects, René Descartes.

> All science is certain, evident knowledge. . . . We reject all knowledge which is merely probable and judge that only those things should be believed which are perfectly known and about which there can be no doubts.[3]

The focus on the scientific method and the mathematical description of nature led to tremendous advances in physics, mathematics, chemistry, biology, astronomy and medicine. It is becoming more and more apparent, however, that we have also paid a significant toll for the restriction of science to the study of phenomena that are measurable and quantifiable. Psychiatrist R. D. Lang describes the problem pointedly.

> Out go sight, sound, taste, touch, and smell, and along with them have since gone esthetic and ethical sensibility, values, quality, soul, consciousness, spirit. Experience as such is cast out of the realm of scientific discourse.[5]

We will discuss the tremendous impact of the legacy of the Scientific Revolution on medicine and health care in the next few chapters and on health promotion later in the book.

Meanwhile, the separation of man from the rest of nature had other far-reaching implications. Searching for control over nature, and no longer considering himself to be a part of it, man was now free to concentrate on scientific domination. Therefore, he felt entitled to utilize whatever force, or indeed violence, might be necessary.[2]

> Man could observe matter, tinker with it, mutilate it, experiment with it, and himself remain untouched and untouchable. Inert matter could not reciprocate or revenge man's depredations.

In fact, the creators of the seventeenth-century worldview deemed mastery over the natural world to be the highest purpose of science. What a change from the age-old pursuit of wisdom to achieve peaceful coexistence with nature! Scientists were now exhorted to take whatever steps were necessary to achieve this domination. For, in the words of Sir Francis Bacon, the purpose of science was now to "torture nature's secrets from her so she can be forced out of her natural state and squeezed and molded."[2] The implications for our culture have been monumental, and we are now facing the potentially species-threatening consequences of this license to exploit the environment under the guise of scientific investigation.

The Patriarchy:
A Man's World

Throughout history, nature has always been associated with the feminine aspects of humanity. In discussing the role of this association in the organic worldview that existed prior to the Scientific Revolution, Merchant states that "Central to the organic theory was the identification of nature, especially the earth, with a nurturing mother: a kindly, beneficent female who provided for the needs of mankind in an ordered, planned universe."[3] However, nature as female has traditionally had an additional, opposing association. This is the image of nature as a wild and uncontrollable female producing violence and chaos through storms, droughts, and other natural disasters. As the Scientific Revolution progressed, the image of the *nurturing mother* was gradually lost and the association with *disorder* became the foundation for the call to exert control over and dominate nature.

It is therefore no mere coincidence that in his redefinition of the purpose of science Sir Francis Bacon described a "feminine" nature needing to be squeezed and molded, even tortured by a "masculine" science. The licenses to manipulate and exploit nature and women go hand in hand. Bacon referred to nature as a "common harlot" who "takes orders from man and works under his authority." If this seems like a stretch, it may be helpful to recall that Bacon was attorney general in England under King James I, when untold thousands of women were accused of being witches and subsequently burned to death. As attorney general, Bacon was certainly no stranger to these proceedings. In fact, he often incorporated images of the torture chamber in his descriptions of nature, as when he suggested that she could best be studied when "straitened and held fast, so nature exhibits herself more clearly under the trials and tribulations of art (mechanical devices) than when left to herself."[4] As we discussed at length in chapter 1, the patriarchy was certainly not an invention of the Scientific Revolution. However, the belief in the natural superiority of men and masculine values over women and feminine values was scientifically reinforced and sanctioned by the emerging mechanistic, reductionist, dualistic worldview. Once again, Merchant summarizes the tremendous shift that occurred at this time.[3]

> An organically oriented mentality in which feminine principles played an important role was undermined and replaced by a mechanically oriented mentality that either eliminated or used female principles in an exploitative manner. As Western culture became increasingly mechanized in the 1600's, the female earth and virgin spirit were subdued by the machine.

Patriarchal cultures value the "masculine" traits of aggression, competition, and rationality over feminine nurturing, cooperation, and intuition, often, in fact, devaluing the latter. Therefore, such societies are ruled by men through an elaborate hierarchy based on physical, political, and economic power. Religious institutions are governed by another male hierarchy, with both hierarchies answering to an all-powerful male god.

The patriarchal worldview depicts man as strong, brave and intelligent while woman is viewed as passive, weak, and lacking in intelligence. In his *Origin of Species,* Charles Darwin provided the scientific validation for this underlying foundation of patriarchal culture when he stated that "Man is more courageous, pugnacious, and energetic than woman, and has more inventive genius."

Summary

The major assumptions of the seventeenth-century worldview are listed below. It was thought that the universe was:

1. Mechanistic; the universe functioned as a great machine
2. Reductionist; the whole equaled the sum of its parts
3. Dualistic; matter and spirit were separate

4. Patriarchal; man and masculine values were naturally superior

It is critical to emphasize that these assumptions continue to form the foundation for almost every aspect of contemporary Western society, from politics to economics, education, religion, and our legal and health care systems. Let us take some time next to examine more closely the tremendous influence these assumptions have had on the development of our traditional Western medical system.

References

We would like to pay special tribute to the person and book that got us both started on the "holistic" path many years ago. The person is physicist Fritjof Capra and the book is titled, ever so appropriately, *The Turning Point.* We would recommend this as the best introduction to the tremendous changes that humanity must undergo in order to fulfill our human destiny. We have also drawn from and highly recommend his other books: *The Tao of Physics* and *The Web of Life.*

1. Keck, L. R. *Sacred Eyes.* Boulder: Synergy Associates, 1995.

2. Capra, F. *The Turning Point: Science, Society, and the Rising Culture.* Toronto: Bantam, 1983.

3. Merchant, C. *The Death of Nature: Women, Ecology, and the Scientific Revolution.* San Francisco: HarperSanFrancisco, 1980.

4. Harmon, W. *Global Mind Change: The Promise of the Twenty-first Century.* San Francisco: Berrett-Koehler, 1998.

5. Laing, R. D. *The Voice of Experience.* Pantheon: New York, 1982.

Chapter 4

THE HUMAN BODY AS MACHINE
The Biomedical Model

The biomedical model, like an X ray, is ultimately a representation, one so powerful and pervasive that we often mistake it for fact.

David Morris
Illness and Culture in the Postmodern Age

René Descartes:
Separating the Mind and Spirit from the Body

Of all the great thinkers of the Scientific Revolution probably none had a greater impact on Western medicine and our current views of health and disease than René Descartes. Descartes took the concept of the mechanistic universe and applied it directly to all living things including human beings.

> I do not recognize any differences between the machines made by craftsman and the various bodies that nature alone composes. . . . I consider the body as a machine . . . my thought . . . compares a sick man and an ill-made clock with my idea of a healthy man and a well-made clock.[1]

Descartes also extended the reductionist, dualistic concept of separation of material and immaterial phenomena to include the belief that the human mind and the body are separate entities, stating that "There is nothing included in the concept of the body that belongs to the mind; and nothing in that of the mind that belongs to the body."[1] In fact, Descartes used this argument to convince the Catholic Church to permit the first dissection of human cadavers in a medical school. The story goes that the reigning Pope was adamantly opposed to this proposition but finally relented when Descartes argued that since the spirit or soul was housed in the mind no harm would come to them from such procedures performed on the body. In return for the Pope's blessing, Descartes promised that medicine would leave all matters of the soul and spirit to the Church, concerning itself only with the body.

So, following the prevailing reductionist dogma of the day, the "human machine" was essentially divided into three disconnected parts and the care of each part was awarded to a different profession. The end result was that care of the soul or spirit was given to the Church, care of the body to medical science, and care of the dispirited mind eventually to the domain of psychiatry.

A Seventeenth-Century Understanding
of Health and Disease

By applying the old paradigm, seventeenth-century worldview to medicine, Descartes in essence created the biomedical model that remains to this day as the foundation of Western approaches to health and disease. Following in this tradition (which is often referred to as Cartesian in honor of the contributions of Descartes), biomedicine views human beings basically as sophisticated machines that can be analyzed in terms of their parts. Sickness and disease are considered to be "malfunctions" of the biological "mechanisms" of the machine. The role of the doctor as repairman is to find the underlying cellular or molecular malfunctions and/or causative organisms and to "fix" the machine. Issues related to the mind or the spirit are considered to be separate from and irrelevant to health concerns. After all, machines have neither minds nor spirits! The underlying foundation of the biomedical model can be summarized as follows.

Human being	=	Machine
Disease	=	Malfunction of the machine
Doctor	=	Repairman
Focus	=	Physical determinants of disease

Also consistent with the basic tenets of the old paradigm, biomedicine has been characterized by a historic neglect of women's health issues.[2] From menopause to autoimmune diseases and breast cancer, mainstream medicine has failed to adequately invest in and research issues that affect women's health, and women have been routinely excluded as research participants in many important areas of study. In the study of heart disease, for example, "medicine's most fundamental assumptions—such as the role of cholesterol and diet and the efficacy of certain treatments for heart attack patients—have been predicated on data from studies exclusively involving men."[3]

Furthermore, as we will discuss in more depth in a later chapter, when women's health issues have been addressed it has often been from a controlling, patriarchal perspective reminiscent of Sir Francis Bacon. As just one example, Victorian Era medical science actively promoted women's use of corsets to achieve the plump, hourglass figure deemed desirable, though this often resulted in constricted lungs, squeezed bladders, and dislocated stomachs.[4,5] We shall see that this was only the beginning of a pattern of prescribing dangerous and sometimes fatal treatments to help women "control" their shape and size "in the name of health," a pattern that continues unabated to the present day.

Determining Cause and Effect:
The "Germ Theory of Disease"

By the time the nineteenth century arrived, the mechanistic, reductionist, scientific approach to medicine had become firmly entrenched. Almost all the basic structures of the human body had been discovered, and great progress had been made in understanding the body's physiological processes. With the work of Louis Pasteur and

Robert Koch, the "germ theory," in which bacteria were seen as the single cause of all disease, became widely accepted. While this may seem unreasonable given our knowledge today, the idea of a disease being caused by a single factor fit perfectly into the existing Cartesian paradigm: the human body as machine whose breakdown could be traced to the malfunctioning of a single part or mechanism, which could be replaced or repaired.

Strengths and Weaknesses of Biomedicine

There is no question that the biomedical model has resulted in remarkable advancements in medicine. Particularly in the areas of acute injury, infectious disease, and surgical and pharmaceutical interventions, we have created a medical technology second to none. Although traditional approaches based on the medical model have resulted in great advances in our understanding of health and disease, we will see that the underlying mechanistic, reductionist view of reality has also placed significant limitations on this understanding. As in many other areas of scientific endeavor:

> When scientists reduce an integral whole to fundamental building blocks—whether they are cells, genes, or elementary particles— and try to explain all phenomena in terms of these elements, they lose the ability to understand the coordinating activities of the whole.[1]

For contemporary Western medicine, the problem is that 85 percent of health care costs in the United States today result from chronic medical conditions related to lifestyle. For many of these so-called "diseases of civilization" (cancers, heart disease, depression, chronic fatigue syndrome and osteoporosis) and particularly for behaviorally oriented issues (alcoholism, smoking, sedentary lifestyle) traditional biomedical approaches are much less effective. This is because, more than ever before, these problems necessitate understanding the individual from a systems point of view, that is, as a dynamic, integrated whole, including not only the physical but the emotional, social, and spiritual components of the human experience. These are precisely the factors that have long been ignored and even belittled under the seventeenth-century worldview and the biomedical model.

Furthermore, for the vast majority of these complex illnesses the germ, single-cause theory of disease simply does not work. Even when germs are involved, they are usually only one of many potential contributing causes. The end result is that the mechanistic, reductionist, dualistic view of health and disease often interferes with our understanding of health and illness by blocking our vision of the whole person and the bigger picture.

Heart Disease

Let us use as an example coronary heart disease. We know a tremendous amount about the pathophysiology of this disease. Almost everyone is aware of the major biomedical, lifestyle "risk factors" linked to it. Yet it is common medical knowledge that all of these risk factors (smoking, high blood pressure, high cholesterol, diabetes, etc.) combined with family history explain only about half the cases of the disease.[6] What explains the other half?

Actually, our knowledge of risk factors for disease comes mostly from epidemiological studies in which large groups of people are followed over a period of years to determine the existence of relationships between lifestyle risk factors and causes of death. For example, we gained much of our original understanding of biomedical risk factors for heart disease from the Coronary Pooling Project, research that combined and analyzed results from the first six big epidemiological studies of coronary heart disease. Scientists looked at the relationship between mortality and the three major risk factors (cigarette smoking, high blood pressure, and high cholesterol levels) in a total group of about 7,300 men who were followed for almost ten years. (Note that the first six big studies to examine the epidemiology of heart disease included only men!) What they found was surprising. Fully 80 percent of the men with all three risk factors and 90 percent of the men with two risk factors did not have heart attacks during the period. In fact, most of the men who did have heart attacks did not have any of these risk factors![7]

Furthermore, even for the best-known of the traditional biomedical risk factors actual causes are often anything but clear. High blood pressure is a good example. It is well known that upward of 90 percent of the high blood pressure cases seen in the physician's office are of the "essential" type. This means that there is no known physiological cause for the condition. Cholesterol is another example. We hear so much about the relationship between exercise (and especially diet) and the control of cholesterol levels and ratios. Yet there is substantial evidence that stress may play as large if not a larger role in determining levels of cholesterol in the blood. In one study, the average cholesterol levels of medical students increased by more than one hundred points during the course of studying for and taking an important exam![8] What exercise program or dietary intervention can provide that kind of a change? It is indeed a testament to the profound, ongoing influence of the seventeenth-century legacy of the mind/body separation that only a few years ago a review of the hundreds of identified risk factors for coronary heart disease in the *Journal of the American Medical Association* included no mention of emotional, social, or spiritual factors.[9]

This is not to suggest that people should ignore their blood pressure, cholesterol, and other traditional biomedical risk factors for heart disease. What it does suggest is that these risk factors are not very accurate predictors of who will or will not contract a particular disease; they cannot function as the "specific etiology" described by the germ theory of disease. In fact, it is becoming evident that these biomedical risk factors are more likely to be "symptoms" of underlying emotional and or psychological issues that are the true, though extremely complex and difficult to quantify, causes of most of today's common illnesses. Recent research indicates, for example, a strong relationship between emotional, physical, and sexual abuse in childhood and health risk behaviors and disease in adulthood.[10] Unfortunately, these are just the kinds of issues that have been ignored as a result of the Cartesian legacy because they cannot be easily measured and quantified and therefore are not considered to be valid subjects for scientific investigation. We will discuss the important implications of this for health promotion practice in a later chapter.

What we are suggesting here is that continued adherence to the seventeenth-century Cartesian paradigm has severely hampered our ability to understand and treat heart disease as well as many of the other chronic, complex medical conditions of our time. Our inability to look beyond the measurable physical risk factors of Descartes's material universe has caused us to ignore a rapidly growing body of evidence that suggests that, unlike machines, human beings have personalities, thoughts, feelings, and emotions, all of which appear to contribute significantly to our resistance to illness and our ability to heal ourselves.

Culture, Science, and Medicine: The Big Picture

Worldview
Mechanistic
(nature as machine)

Science
Reductionist
(whole = sum of its parts)

Culture
Dominator
(patriarchal)

Medicine
Biomedical
(fix the machine)

So far, we have examined our culture, science, and medicine from the perspective of the dominant worldview of the last four hundred years, what we are calling the old paradigm. Looking at a summary of this information (see sidebar to the left), what is most important to note is that the vertical categories flow logically and naturally from each other. Thus, a mechanistic worldview naturally informs a reductionist science (machines are best understood and fixed by attending to their constituent parts). Similarly, a reductionist science that emphasizes separation from and control of nature leads logically to a control-oriented, patriarchal, dominator culture. Combined with a reductionist science such a culture naturally creates a medical model focused on "fixing" and controlling the human machine by altering measurable physical factors that are seen as the specific determinants of disease. We believe that looking at the big picture in this way is critically important for helping us to put into perspective the changes in health promotion that we will discuss later in the book.

Summary

Four hundred years ago the Scientific Revolution created a mechanistic, reductionist worldview that further amplified the cultural concepts of patriarchy and control over nature. In the last hundred years, however, new developments in the sciences have challenged nearly all of the assumptions of this seventeenth-century paradigm. It is perhaps ironic that the new emerging worldview is largely a result of startling discoveries in the same discipline that almost four hundred years ago spawned the mechanistic worldview—physics! Let us now explore how the *quantum* revolution in the *hardest* of the sciences is changing our understanding of the universe in which we live and broadening our perspectives on health, illness, and the process of healing.

References

1.   Capra, F. *The Turning Point: Science, Society, and the Rising Culture.* Toronto: Bantam, 1983.

2.   Inlander, C. B., L. S. Levin, and E. Weiner. *Medicine on Trial: The Appalling Story of Ineptitude, Malfeasance, Neglect, and Arrogance.* New York: Prentice-Hall, 1988.

3.   Dreher H. "Mind-Body Medicine for Women: New Data and Directions." *Advances* 13, no. 1 (1997): 68–74.

4.   Rothbloom, E. D. "'I'll Die for the Revolution, but Don't Ask Me Not to Diet': Feminism and the Continuing Stigmatization of Obesity." In P. Fallon, M. Katzman, and S. Wooley, eds.,

Feminist Perspectives on Eating Disorders. New York: Guilford Press, 1994.

5.   Bennett, W., and J. Gurin. *The Dieter's Dilemma: Eating Less and Weighing More.* New York: Basic Books, 1982.

6.   Rosenman, Ray H. "The Questionable Role of the Diet and Serum Cholesterol in the Incidence of Ischemic Heart Disease and Its Twentieth-Century Changes." *Homeostasis* 34, no. 1 (1993): 1–44.

7.   Pooling Project Research Group. "Relationship of Blood Pressure, Serum Cholesterol, Smoking Habit, Relative Weight, and ECG Abnormalities to Incidence of Major Coronary Events: Final Report on the Pooling Project." *Journal of Chronic Disease* (special issue) 31 (1978): 201–306.

8.   Thomas, C.B., and E.Z. Murphy. Further Studies on Cholesterol Levels in John's Hopkins Medical Students: The Effect of Stress at Examination. *Journal of Chronic Disease* 8 (1958): 661-68.

9.   Joeg, J. M. "Evaluating Coronary Heart Disease Risk: Tiles in the Mosaic." *Journal of the American Medical Association* 277 (1997): 1387–90.

10. Felliti, V. J., R. F. Anda, D. Nordenberg, and D. F. Williamson et al. "Relationship of Childhood Abuse and Household Dysfunction to Many of the Leading Causes of Death in Adults: The Adverse Childhood Experiences (ACE) Study." *American Journal of Preventive Medicine* 14, no. 4 (1998): 245–58.

Part Two

EMBRACING THE NEW SCIENCES

Chapter 5

QUANTUM PHYSICS

What Do Subatomic Particles
Have to Do with Health?

We need to be prepared to question every single aspect
of the old paradigm. Eventually we will not need
to throw everything away, but before we know that
we need to be willing to question everything.

Fritjof Capra
The Web of Life

Reevaluating the Assumptions

In the first three decades of the twentieth century, beginning with the pioneering work of Albert Einstein and continuing through the collaboration of an international group of scientists, developments in the sciences have changed our understanding of reality in ways nobody could have imagined. This new information has forced scientists to rethink the foundations of classical physics as well as our assumptions about the nature of the material world.

Why should those of us in health promotion care about these discoveries? Because physics has always been the "gold standard" of rational, empirical science and the measuring stick by which all other scientific disciplines are judged. These discoveries in physics suggest an entirely new view of reality and a completely new set of assumptions about why people get ill and how they heal. This emerging worldview is having profound effects on all of the sciences and throughout our culture.

Before embarking on a discussion of the major principles of quantum physics it is important to stress that much of this information may at first appear to be difficult to understand and perhaps even downright weird! You may wonder why we have devoted an entire chapter to this topic in a book on health promotion. The more you read, however, the more the relevance of this information will become clear to you. Although the information is complex, do not feel too frustrated by this. Nobel Prize winning physicist Richard Feynman, one of the architects of quantum physics, said it best.

> No one understands quantum mechanics. Do not keep saying to yourself, how can it be like that? Because you will go down the drain into a blind alley from which nobody has yet to escape. Nobody knows how it can be like that.[1]

We do not claim to understand quantum physics, and neither will you after reading this chapter. Don't feel too badly about that. Einstein didn't understand it either. He describes his frustrations as follows.

> All my attempts to adapt the theoretical foundation of this old physics to this knowledge failed completely. It was as if the ground had been pulled out from under one with no firm foundation to be seen anywhere.[2]

Much of what we discuss in this chapter will be outside the sphere of that measurable, quantifiable "material universe" described earlier. And much of it will not fit our traditional view of physical reality. As Feynman says, "Quantum mechanics describes nature as absurd from the point of view of common sense. And it fully agrees with experiment. So I hope you can accept nature as she is — absurd."[3] Although we may not understand quantum physics, there is much we can learn from it!

Quantum Reality:

The "Stuff" We Are Made Of

We begin this discussion of quantum physics with a brief overview of its four major tenets: complementarity, uncertainty, connectedness, and nonlocality. Although quantum physics pertains mostly to the microscopic, subatomic world, it also has important implications for the macroscopic, everyday world of which we are a part. Later in this chapter we will discuss some of the implications for our culture; our understanding of health, illness, and healing; and the field of health promotion.

Tenet 1: Complementarity—A Both/And Universe

The old, Newtonian view of physical reality is based on the existence of tiny, solid, separate building blocks of matter that cannot be further broken down into smaller constituent parts. These particles were thought to occupy definite places in space and time that could be measured and quantified. From quantum physics, however, we now know that this understanding is incomplete. It turns out that these subatomic entities exist not only as particles (like little billiard balls) but also and at the same time as waves (like electricity). For this reason physicists often refer to them as "wave packets." This wave-particle duality, known as the *Principle of Complementarity*, was introduced by Niels Bohr, one of the founding fathers of quantum physics. Electrons, protons, neutrons, photons (the smallest quantities of light), in fact, all subatomic entities, are at the same time both particles and waves. Therefore, a description of matter in terms of its particle nature or its wave nature is only partially correct. Both descriptions actually *complement* each other, and only together do they represent an accurate picture of physical reality.

Tenet 2: Quantum Uncertainty

In order to have a valid understanding of these subatomic entities, therefore, it is necessary to know about both their particle and wave natures. Unfortunately, it is impossible to measure both at the same time! This mind-blowing revelation is the second major tenet of quantum physics, known as the *Heisenberg Uncertainty Principle*, named after another of the founding fathers of the new physics, Werner Heisenberg. According to this principle, it is possible to measure the position (particle nature) of a subatomic entity such as an electron and it is also possible to measure its speed (wave nature), but it is not possible to measure both accurately at the same time. As Danah Zohar says in her book *The Quantum Self*:

> While we can measure wave properties, or particle properties, the exact properties of the duality must always elude any measurement we might hope to make. The most we can hope to know about any given wave packet is a fuzzy reading of its position and an equally fuzzy reading of its momentum.[4]

The reasons for this are beyond the scope of this book, but a good and understandable explanation can be found in *The Elegant Universe* by Brian Greene.[5] Suffice it to say here that the inability to accurately quantify matter in this way appears to be built into the universe and is not due to a lack of scientific knowledge or technique!

It is precisely because of this essential "fuzziness" that physicists do not refer to subatomic entities as existing at definite places but rather as showing "tendencies to exist," which they describe in terms of mathematical probabilities. Therefore, events such as the movement of electrons in an atom, commonly discussed in high school chemistry classes, can never be predicted with certainly. It is only possible to suggest the likelihood of an event happening. Zohar discusses the significance of this in relation to our traditional conception of physical reality.

> This essential fuzziness . . . replaces the Old Newtonian Determinism, where everything about physical reality was fixed, determined, and measurable, with a vast "porridge" of being where nothing is fixed or fully measurable. Here everything remains indeterminate, somewhat ghostly, and just beyond our grasp.[4]

Tenet 3: Quantum Connectedness—A Universe of Relationships

The solid, measurable, material objects of classical physics are actually fuzzy, wavelike patterns of probabilities! Thus, the classic Newtonian description of the "building blocks" of matter that we learned about in high school is obsolete. These subatomic entities are not things but interconnections between "things" that can only be accurately described in terms of their relationships with other "things." Physical matter is therefore a dynamic network of interconnected particle/waves that have no existence by themselves. In the words of the Danish physicist Niels Bohr, "isolated material particles are abstractions, their properties being definable and observable only through their interaction with other systems."[6]

But there is more! According to traditional Newtonian thinking, the scientist as the "objective" observer stands outside of (separate from) and is impartial to the measurable, material "reality" being explored. However, quantum physics defines quite a different relationship between the observer and the observed. The Cartesian idea of a purely objective scientist is an illusion. Quantum physics has shown us that "what is being studied is inseparable from the scientist, who devises mental constructs of his/her experiences with it as a means of characterizing his/her understanding of its properties and behavior."[7]

Furthermore, recent experiments prove that not only is the scientist as observer not separate from what is being observed but in fact, *the very act of observing* alters the properties of what is being observed. Whether an electron exists as a particle or a wave therefore depends on how we look at (measure) it. If we try to measure it as a wave, it will appear as a wave, and if we try to measure it as a particle it will appear as such. There seems to be some sort of "connection" between the electron and the scientist that alters the reality of the situation. Not only is the scientist not a separate and detached observer, but the act of observation itself becomes part of and has a profound effect on the outcome. As physicist Fritjof Capra puts it, "subatomic particles have no meaning as isolated entities but can be understood only as interconnections, or correlations between various processes of observation and measurement."[6]

Tenet 4: Nonlocality—Action at a Distance

The concept of the interconnectedness of all things leads to the last and perhaps the most bizarre tenet of quantum physics—nonlocality. It has now been proven that subatomic particles have some "connection" or means of "communication" between them that is instantaneous and does not diminish with distance. If two paired electrons, for example, are separated and one is taken to the other side of the room or the country (or theoretically the universe), alterations in the spin of one of the electrons will instantaneously affect the spin of the other! Capra sums up the striking implications of this finding.

> The behavior of any part is determined by its nonlocal connections to the whole, and since we do not know those connections precisely, we have to replace the narrow classical notion of cause and effect by the wider concept of statistical causality . . . whereas in classical mechanics the properties and behavior of the parts determine those of the whole, the situation is reversed in quantum mechanics; it is the whole that determines the behavior of the parts.[2]

Quantum Weirdness:

The Double-Slit Experiment

This might be a good time to repeat Richard Feynman's warning about not developing a "quantum headache" by trying to *understand* all of this. There is however, a relatively simple procedure called the double slit experiment that can be helpful in attaining a sense of the wondrous nature of these principles. In fact, Feynman himself has stated that "all of quantum physics can be gleaned from carefully thinking through the implications of this single experiment."[5] In this experiment a special machine is used to project photons of light (though it could be any subatomic entity) through a piece of cardboard that has two slits in it. On the other side of the cardboard is placed a recording device that detects light or subatomic particles as they strike it (fig. 5.1). Let us say that we turn on the machine, close off one of the slits and start projecting light. What do we expect would happen on the recording surface (fig. 5.2)? Now let's say that we close that slit and open the other one. What would we expect to happen now on the recording surface (fig 5.3)? Now what would we get if we open both slits (fig. 5.4)? Unfortunately, this is not what happens. As bizarre as it may seem, here is what we get when both slits are open (fig. 5.5).

Figure 5.1. In the double-slit experiment, a beam of light is shone on a barrier in which two slits have been cut. The light that passes through the barrier is recorded on a photographic plate when either or both of the slits are open. *(Adapted with permission from Greene, The Elegant Universe)*

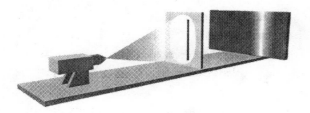

Figure 5.2. Only the right slit is open, leading to an image on the photographic plate as shown.

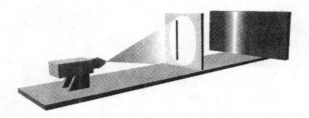

Figure 5.3. Only the left slit is open, leading to an image on the photographic plate as shown.

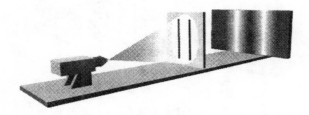

Figure 5.4. When both slits are open we might expect a merger of the images in figures 5.2 and 5.3 as shown.

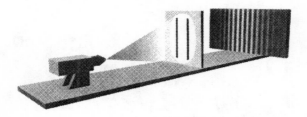

Figure 5.5. However, this is the pattern that actually emerges when both slits are open.

Before we go any further, it is important to reflect on the wonder of this result. The following explanation is from *The Elegant Universe* by world-renowned physicist Brian Greene.[5]

If you're not bowled over by this fact of nature it means that either you have seen it before and you've become blasé or the description so far has not sufficiently been vivid. So in case it's the latter, let's describe it again but in a slightly different way. You close off the left slit and fire the photons one by one at the barrier. Some get through, some don't. The ones that do create an image on the photographic plate dot by single dot, which looks like the Figure in 5.2. You then run the experiment again with a new photographic plate, but this time you open both slits. Naturally enough you think that this will only increase the number of photons that pass through the slits in the barrier and hit the photographic plate thereby exposing the film to more total light than you did in the first experiment. But when you later examine the image produced, you find that not only are there places on the photographic plate that were dark in the first experiment and are now bright, as expected, there are also places on the photographic plate that were bright in your first experiment but are now dark as in Figure 5.5. By increasing the number of individual photons that hit the photographic plate you have decreased the brightness in certain areas. Somehow, temporally separated individual particulate photons are able to cancel each other out. Think about how crazy this is. Photons that would have passed through the right slit and hit the film in one of the dark bands in figure 5.2 failed to do so when the *left* slit is open (which is why the band is now dark). But how in the world can a tiny bundle of light that passes through one slit be at all affected by whether or not the *other* slit is open. . . . It's as strange as if you fire a machine gun at the screen and when both slits are open, independent, separately fired bullets somehow cancel one other out, leaving a pattern of unscathed positions on the target—positions that *are* hit when only one slit in the barrier is open.

So when one slit is open and one is closed we get a particle. When both slits are open we get a wave. To make matters even more fantastic, if we keep both slits open and use a special device that measures particles we get a particle and the photon passes through only one slit. If we do the same thing and use a device that measures waves, the photon goes through both slits and we get waves! The photon or other subatomic entity seems to "know" how many slits are open. In fact, it has been suggested that the electron or the photon may be, in a manner of speaking, *conscious*![4,8]

Cause and Effect:

Everything Is Affected by Everything Else

Quantum physics also forces us to reexamine traditional views concerning cause and effect. Using the movement of electrons in an atom that most of us studied in high school illustrates the situation. Remembering the models of atoms with their electrons orbiting the nucleus, we learned that these electrons can "jump" to different energy levels (orbits around the atom), either giving off or absorbing energy. What we know from quantum physics is that these movements are in large part random and spontaneous. There is no prior warning, no cause and no way to predict the outcome of events; no way of knowing if the electron will move to a lower or higher energy state.

Furthermore, some physicists believe that the electron may move in all directions simultaneously, acting as if it is "smeared out" all over space and time and is everywhere at once. Before moving, it actually puts out "feelers" in every possible direction that in essence "try out" all the possible new orbits in which it might settle. If this is difficult to comprehend, think about how you might solve a problem by examining all of the possible solutions in your mind before attempting any. Although you would eventually arrive at and act on a decision, certainly the different scenarios you investigate could have an effect on determining which course of action you finally take. In quantum physics, these feelers are called *virtual transitions*, and it turns out that they too can have lasting effects, even though the electron eventually "makes a decision" to go in only one direction. The implications of this phenomenon are again summarized by Zohar.

If all potential "things" stretch out infinitely in all directions, how does one speak of any distance between them, or conceive of any separateness? All things and all moments touch each other at every point. The oneness of the overall system is paramount.[9]

From the Microscopic to the Macroscopic World

Quantum physics thus tells us that the concept of linear cause and effect in the subatomic world is an illusion. Because everything is connected, everything affects (rather than causes) everything else.[10] Like the fuzzy measurements we take of the wave packet, our understanding of cause and effect is, by nature, vague and imprecise. But how does this relate to the everyday world in which we live?

We recall that Descartes taught that the elimination of uncertainty was the only path to true knowledge and Bacon insisted that eliminating uncertainly could only be accomplished by conquering and controlling nature. In his powerfully insightful novel *Ishmael,* Daniel Quinn satirizes our Western obsession with the illusion of control, writing that we believe that:

> Only one thing can save us. We have to increase our mastery of the world . . . we have to go on conquering it until our rule is absolute. Then, when we're in complete control, everything will be fine. We'll have fusion power. No pollution. We'll turn the rain on and off. We'll grow a bushel of wheat in a square centimeter. We'll turn the oceans into farms. We'll control the weather—no more hurricanes, no more tornados, no more droughts, no more untimely frosts. . . . All the life processes of this planet will be where they belong—where the gods meant them to be—in our hands.[11]

How was this to be accomplished? For the traditional reductionist scientist, all natural processes could be understood only by assembling and disassembling them, just like a watch. Once the component "cogs, levers, springs and gears" were examined sufficiently and the appropriate universal laws applied, it would be possible to both predict and control future changes. This linear understanding of change (linear causality) is represented in mathematics by "linear equations." Linear equations can be used to describe many types of processes in the macroscopic world, from the flight of a cannonball to the growth of a plant, the burning of coal, and the performance of a simple machine. They are familiar to us in that small changes in one variable produce small effects in outcomes and larger effects can be predictably produced by adding up many small changes. Linear equations are not, however, the only kind of equations that exist; there are also nonlinear equations.

Complexity and Chaos:
A New Understanding of Change

Scientists have known about "nonlinear" equations for more than one hundred years, but it is only in the last thirty that they have begun to understand them. It turns out that change in complex systems—from the behavior of an airplane in flight to the pattern of cars clustering on a freeway, the flow of blood in our arteries, the fluctuations in the stock market, and the formation of snowflakes—are primarily nonlinear processes governed by nonlinear equations. For our purposes, the most important point is that with nonlinear systems and their equations small changes in any particular variable can have a tremendous effect on the final outcome.[12,13]

Why should we be interested in complex nonlinear systems? Because, contrary to traditional scientific wisdom, they are by their very nature both unpredictable and uncontrollable. The new science of Chaos is concerned with the study of such systems, perhaps most easily illustrated by the weather, which is where the initial discoveries in the science were made.[13] Even with all of our sophisticated techniques and computers, it is impossible to accurately predict the weather for more than a few days in advance. Just like the inability to accurately measure the wave and particle nature at the same time, chaos theory tells us that this limitation is not due to the inadequacies of our knowledge or technology but is an inherent characteristic of the weather as a "complex system." Change in such systems occurs through myriads of negative and positive feedback loops that result in "nonlinear" effects that twist and turn them in ways that are impossible to measure and predict accurately. Like the myth of scientific objectivity, the old paradigm concept of linear cause and effect in such systems is an illusion.

Just as quantum physics has shown us that we can only speak of probabilities and not certainty when it comes to what orbit within an atom will be the next home for any particular electron, chaos theory informs us that the same is true for prediction in most of the real world. As professor of English John Briggs and physicist David Peat write in *Turbulent Mirror: An Illustrated Guide To Chaos Theory and the Science of Wholeness*: "In the nonlinear world—which includes most of our real world—exact prediction is both practically and theoretically impossible. Nonlinearity has dashed the reductionist dream."[12]

Systems Theory:
From the Parts to the Whole

All matter is made up of quantum wave packets. The universe and all of nature itself are therefore not composed of isolated material elements but rather appear as a complicated web of relations between the various parts of a unified whole. This radical departure from the Cartesian, Newtonian model of reality sent shock waves throughout the scientific world during much of the twentieth century. From physics to biology, chemistry, psychology, medicine, and organizational development, this new approach manifests itself in what is generally referred to as systems thinking or systems theory. According to systems theory, "the essential properties of an organism, or living system, are properties of the whole, which none of the parts have. They arise from the interactions and relationships among the parts. These properties are destroyed when the system is dissected, either physically or theoretically into isolated elements. Although we can discern individual parts in any system, these parts are not isolated, and the nature of the whole is always different from the mere sum of its parts."[6]

Roll over René Descartes!

Quantum Science:

A Holistic, Ecological Alternative

Holistic and *ecological* are the terms most often used to describe the new systems thinking about the nature of reality. They are often used interchangeably, although they differ slightly in their meanings. A holistic view of something means that it is seen as a functional whole with a number of interdependent parts. An ecological view includes this holistic perspective but adds information about how the object is embedded in its social and natural environment. In the case of a bicycle, these perspectives would look like this.

The *holistic perspective* acknowledges the interdependence of the parts of the bicycle and their relationship to the function of the whole.

The *ecological perspective* includes the holistic perspective but is also concerned about where the raw materials for the bicycle come from, how and where it is manufactured, what the effect of its usage is on the environment, and so on.

The distinctions between these two perspectives become clearer when they are applied to living systems because connections to the environment are so much more important. For simplicity sake, we will use these terms interchangeably, with each including the perspective of the other. The new vision of reality that emerges out of these perspectives has been referred to as "deep ecology." As described by Capra, deep ecology:

Sees the world not as a collection of isolated objects, but as a network of phenomena that are fundamentally interconnected and interdependent. Deep ecology recognizes the intrinsic value of all living things and views humans as just one particular strand in the web of life.[6]

What modern physics shows us is that scientific thinking does not have to be mechanistic and reductionist and that holistic, ecological approaches to science are also scientifically sound. As Capra says:

> Scientists will not need to be reluctant to adopt a holistic framework, as they often are today, for fear of being unscientific. Modern physics can show them that such a framework is not only scientific but is in agreement with the most advanced scientific theories of physical reality.[2]

Quantum Implications

For almost four hundred years, physics has formed the foundation for our beliefs about the nature of physical reality and remains the cornerstone on which all of our sciences are based. The beliefs and values that evolve from these sciences trickle down and shape the "softer" social sciences as well as our cultural institutions. It is therefore critical on both a personal and professional level that we consider the implications of these scientific findings for our understanding of health and illness and for our role as health professionals. As we move through the remaining chapters of the book, we will often refer to this information. Therefore, we would like to summarize some of the most important implications of the concepts that have been presented.

Complementarity

Complementarity tells us that we live in a *both/and* and not an *either/or* universe. Physical reality is not only about things but also about process. Within one year 90 percent of the atoms within our bodies go someplace else and are replaced.[14] Within five years all of them are replaced. Where do they go? They might go to make up another person or they might become part of a tree or a rock. So, our body is a work in progress. Like a river that is constantly flowing and changing, never the same at two different points in time, we are constantly changing "shape" as a result of our experiences and our interactions with our surroundings. Physician Larry Dossey says that because of this realization we may need to modify the golden rule to "Do unto others because they are you."[1]

Figure 5.6 illustrates some other powerful implications of the concept of both/and for our understanding of health and illness and for our culture at large. The ancient Chinese symbol in the middle is known as the T'ai-chi T'u, or the "Diagram of the Supreme Ultimate," and it represents the concept of the dynamic interconnectedness of all things, even those that seem to be opposites. We want to suggest that while items listed in the left column may seem to be opposites of the items in the right column, quantum physics tells us that they are in fact intimately connected.

Particle		**Wave**
Disease		Health
Body		Spirit/mind
Masculine		Feminine
Rational science		Intuition
Science		Religion

Figure 5.6. Complementarity: A both/and versus either/or universe

Just as the particle and wave are not separate and opposite but part of the same whole, so disease is not the absence of health and health is not the absence of disease. Both are part of the bigger whole we call life. Further, contrary to Cartesian thinking, the body, spirit, and mind are not separate entities but inextricably interconnected. (We will explore this in the next two chapters.) Similarly, masculine and feminine are not opposites but part of a bigger whole. Both men and women have masculine and feminine traits. Unfortunately, in our present culture we don't value the feminine, with many devastating consequences. Rational science and intuition, too, are not mutually exclusive. Many of the beliefs and concepts discussed in this book are based on age-old intuition. But testing these beliefs and concepts scientifically can add to our understanding of them.

Quantum Uncertainty

Remember what Descartes said nearly four hundred years ago during the Scientific Revolution? If it is not precisely measurable and quantifiable, it cannot be important because it is part of the immaterial, subjective universe. Our knowledge of quantum science tells us something quite different. Physicist Fritjof Capra notes that "Twentieth-century physics has shown us very forcefully that there is no absolute truth in science, that all our concepts and theories are limited and approximate."[2]

Quantum physics suggests that rather than ignore those things that we can't measure we might begin to see them as the true foundation of our being and our health. As we shall see in the next few chapters, the literature strongly supports the importance to our health of many factors from the "immaterial universe" that can't be measured. We are often so focused on the numbers, on having something quantifiable to measure, that we miss the chance to involve ourselves in the all-important process. The uncertainty principle reminds us that this obsession with measurement is an illusion. Just like unsuccessfully trying to pin down the exact location of an elementary particle, we will never truly know the exact causes of most of peoples' illnesses or the true outcomes of most of our work. That doesn't mean that we should avoid measuring things or looking at outcomes. It is an illusion, however, to believe that what we see is all or even necessarily the most important part of what really is.

Quantum Connectedness

We have seen how our quest for certainty and control has led us to a fascination with linear cause and effect. As we might expect, this fascination is also fundamental to our traditional understanding of the nature of health and illness. We have developed lists of "risk factors" for most diseases, and we often base much of our judgment about the degree of health of an individual on the absence or presence of these factors. We continue to do this, even though these factors are not very good predictors of who does and doesn't get a particular disease. We will discuss in chapter 9 the perils of misusing these risk factors in health promotion.

Quantum physics tells us that because everything is interconnected everything affects everything else. Chaos theory adds that it is the nature of complex, nonlinear systems, like the weather and human beings, to be unpredictably sensitive to small changes. It is not possible for us to be aware of all the connections, and even if it were we would not be able to accurately predict the path of such systems. Therefore, just as with subatomic particles, prediction and control of these systems become impractical and impossible. Chaos theory demands that we modify our traditional understanding of causality because:

> The simple laws of cause and effect do not sufficiently explain the life changes one experiences. We do not totally understand the complex feedback mechanisms at work in men and women. Nevertheless, we can learn to rely more on our intuitive, creative capacities in the face of disorder and uncertainty, even though we may not "know" the mechanisms of cause and effect.[14]

We will talk more in chapter 12 about the effects of our current *measurement mania* and *outcome obsession* in medicine and in health promotion. But for now it is important to remember that they are the logical extension of our outdated understanding of the nature of physical reality. What happens when we are so focused on determining linear cause and effect is that we miss the uncertainty, chance and chaos that appear to play a crucial role in all aspects of our physical universe.

The Nonlocal Universe

It has been suggested that the concept of nonlocality may be the single most important discovery in the history of science.[15] If the nonlocality that has been proven to exist at the most basic levels of matter holds true for human consciousness as well, phenomena such as healing from a distance, intercessory prayer, precognitive and shared dreams, intuitive diagnosis, and telesomatic events, which are often spoken of as being paranormal or supernatural may be far more than unscientific, New Age, touchy-feely fluff.

We have proof that the universe is nonlocal. We have seen that the stuff of which we are made acts nonlocally. Because electrons act nonlocally does it mean that human thoughts, feelings, and so on can also act nonlocally? In fact, there is an impressive body of research that strongly supports this conclusion. Thousands of double-blind, well-controlled studies conducted by respected researchers in eminent institutions over many years have clearly demonstrated the existence of such "psychic phenomena." The best in-depth examination of this paradigm-busting research can be found in Dean Radin's, *The Conscious Universe: The Scientific Truth of Psychic Phenomena.*[16] Although it is certainly premature to suggest that the mechanisms of nonlocality for human consciousness are similar to those in quantum physics, to say that nonlocality should not be studied because it is unscientific is in fact unscientific![17]

Quantum Health Promotion?

What is the relationship between this new scientific information and health promotion? If you believe, as we do, that the most serious "health" problems in this country are not, at the most basic level, about exercise, obesity, or heart disease but about the loss of a sense of belonging, connection, and meaning, then the relationship to health promotion begins to seem like a powerful one indeed. We will be referring back to quantum principles throughout the rest of the book. For now, the following examples illustrate aspects of traditional health promotion that need to be reconsidered in light of the new scientific understandings we have discussed in this chapter.

- *Health Observance Months that address health issues separately.* The hypertension addressed in February is likely to be related to the stress addressed in June, which could certainly be connected to the high cholesterol featured in September!

- *Medical, employee assistance (EAP), and wellness programs that function separately in organizations.* Often these departments are literally in different parts of the company complex and information on employees is not shared among them. Sometimes the three departments don't talk or even know each other. How can you treat a person's ulcer in the medical department without knowing about the panic attacks and depression being treated in EAP and the compulsive eating behavior being addressed in the wellness program?

- *Mechanistic, reductionist exercise programs.* We continue to try to solve our culture's sedentary lifestyle problem by having people sit down on a machine, move one body part at a time, in only one range of motion, at a certain speed, for a certain number of repetitions and a certain number of sets, or by having them ride on stationary bicycles on a gym floor. What happened to dancing, playing with the kids, and chopping wood?

- *Negative judgments, attitudes, and beliefs about clients who smoke, overeat, or don't exercise.* The latest science would suggest that even our unspoken expectations and perceptions can affect clients' reality and health status, not to mention the way we relate to them.

- *Health recommendations to individuals that do not take into consideration the systems in which they live.* How can we accurately assess and compassionately advise people on health matters while ignoring work, family, racial, ethnic, religious, political, and spiritual influences; geographic location, and socioeconomic class?

- *Measurement of risk factors for the purpose of predicting who will and won't get sick.* There is randomness and unpredictability naturally built into complex systems such as human beings. There are only probabilities for what may or may not happen.

- *Documentation of the outcomes of our interventions with clients.* Our work with a client is part of the vast constellation of factors that interact to produce change. Our obsession with outcomes can distract us from the process and can interfere with healing.

Science and Spirituality: Healing The Rift

Perhaps not surprisingly, the emerging quantum vision of reality has a decidedly spiritual flavor. The idea of the interconnectedness of all things is a major component of the "perennial philosophy" that forms the basis for all of the world's great spiritual traditions. This philosophy is based on the understanding that spirituality for human beings has to do with feeling of belonging, of connectedness to each other, to nature, and to the cosmos as a whole. Many of the pioneers of quantum physics were struck by the similarities between their findings and the wisdom of the great spiritual teachings of antiquity. In fact, it is often difficult to distinguish statements made by these scientists from the teachings of these great traditions as the following excerpts demonstrate.[18]

The world thus appears as a complicated tissue of events, in which connections of different kinds alternate or overlap or combine and thereby determine the texture of the whole. (physicist)

The material object becomes . . . something different from what we now see, not a separate object on the background or in the environment of the rest of nature but an indivisible part and even in subtle ways an expression of the unity of all that we see. (Eastern mystic)

Things derive their being and nature by mutual dependence and are nothing in themselves. (Eastern mystic)

An elementary particle is not an independently existing unanalyzable entity. It is, in essence, a set of relationships that reach outward to other things. (physicist)

Reductionist science separated facts from faith by demanding that knowing and believing were two separate entities, one the authentic domain of science, the other of religion or spirituality. Quantum physics suggests to us that the artificial separation of science and spirituality is just as much an illusion as either/or Cartesian dichotomies that we discussed earlier in this chapter. We only have one universe, and all of it is interconnected.

Summary

Few people who pick up a book on health promotion expect to be reading about quantum physics. Yet, we want to emphasize that this information from the new sciences provides a foundation for creating a broader, more holistic understanding of the nature of health, illness, and the process of healing. In the next chapter we will explore this new understanding in more detail.

References

Once again, we wish to acknowledge our debt to the work of Fritjof Capra as a major inspiration for this chapter. Through his books, *The Turning Point, The Web of Life,* and *The Tao of Physics,* he has made the new sciences and their impact on our lives understandable for all people, not just physicists!

1. Dossey L. "Healing and Modern Physics: Exploring Consciousness and the Small-Is-Beautiful Assumption." *Alternative Therapies in Health and Medicine* 5, no. 4 (1999): 12–18.

2. Capra, F. *The Turning Point: Science, Society, and The Rising Culture.* Toronto: Bantam, 1983.

3. Feynman, R. *QED: The Strange Theory of Light and Matter.* Princeton: Princeton University Press, 1985.

4. Zohar, D. *The Quantum Self: Human Nature and Consciousness Defined by the New Physics.* New York: Quill/William Morrow, 1991.

5. Greene, B. *The Elegant Universe: Superstrings, Hidden Dimensions, and the Quest for the Ultimate Theory.* New York: Norton, 1999.

6. Capra, F. *The Web of Life: A New Scientific Understanding of Living Systems.* New York: Doubleday, 1996.

7. Engel, G. L. "How Much Longer Must Medicine's Science Be Bound by a Seventeenth-Century World View?" *Psychother Psychosom* 57 (1992): 3–16.

8. Zukav G. *The Dancing Wu Li Masters: An Overview of the New Physics.* New York: Quill/William Morrow, 1979.

9. Zohar D., and I Marshall. *The Quantum Society: Mind, Physics, and a New Social Vision.* New York: Quill/William Morrow, 1994.

10. O'Murchu, D. *Quantum Theology: Spiritual Implications of the New Physics.* New York: Crossroad, 1997.

11. Quinn Daniel. *Ishmael.* New York: Bantam, 1992.

12. Briggs J., and D. Peat. *Turbulent Mirror: An Illustrated Guide to Chaos Theory and the Science of Wholeness.* New York: Harper and Row, 1989.

13. Gleick, James. *Chaos: Making a New Science.* New York: Penguin, 1987.

14. Gelatt, H. B. "Chaos and Compassion." *Counseling and Values* 39, no. 2 (1995): 82–160.

15. Stapp, H. P. "Quantum Physics and the Physicist's View of Nature: Philosophical Implications of Bell's Theorem." In R. E. Kitchener, ed., *The World View of Contemporary Physics.* Albany: State University of New York Press, 1988.

16. Radin, D. *The Conscious Universe: The Scientific Truth of Psychic Phenomena.* San Francisco: Harper Edge, 1997.

17. Dossey L. "How Healing Happens: Exploring The Nonlocal Gap." *Alternative Therapies in Health and Medicine* 8, no. 2 (2002): 12–16, 103–10.

18. Capra, F. *The Tao of Physics*. Boston: Shambhala, 1991.

Chapter 6

HEALTH, ILLNESS, AND HEALING
A Dramatically New View

The loss of emotional, psychological, and spiritual power
is at the root of all disease.

Caroline Myss
Natural Health

From Fighting Disease to Creating Health

Our most prominent public health campaign slogans boast of "winning the war" against heart disease and "fighting the battle" against cancer. The emphasis on the development of "weapons" of war to solve health problems clearly indicates how the philosophy of Epoch II–Dominator humanity has shaped the biomedical model's response to illness. However, from the perspective of the new emerging humanity this way of thinking about disease is outdated, ineffective, and potentially dangerous.

Consistent with the deep-value system out of which it developed, the priority of the biomedical model is to use medication, invasive surgery, or other technology to dominate, control, and eradicate diseases and their symptoms. This is often carried out at great economic cost and sometimes at the expense of quality of life as well. For instance, hundreds of thousands of coronary bypass surgeries (at costs of up to $70,000 each) are performed every year in this country, "despite the fact that the scientific research does not support the claim that for most people the survival rate is higher for those who have surgery than for those who do not."[1] Perhaps even more significant are the ways in which these medical "weapons" may cause problems of their own. World-renowned proponent of integrative medicine Dr. Andrew Weil suggests why this is so.

> Weapons are dangerous. They may backfire, causing injury to the user, and they may also stimulate greater aggression on the part of the enemy.[2]

Indeed, we have seen this prophecy come true in recent years in the form of drug-resistant bacteria, which are becoming more and more of a problem in the treatment of many conditions. Some strains of both staphoccocus and tuberculosis are now literally immune to any currently known antibiotics. This is thought to be the result of years of rampant overuse of antibiotics across the medical community.

Disease Is Not the Enemy

To work "holistically" requires no longer viewing disease as the enemy. In contrast, from a holistic perspective the priority is to understand what the disease represents, with the emphasis on working "with it" to help people heal and reestablish health. The following passage from *Health with a Chinese Twist* (1991) is a beautiful illustration of this delicate concept. The author, Dean Black, recounts the following conversation with a Chinese friend.[3]

> "The problem," said the Chinese friend, "is your approach. You think you can become healthy merely by fighting being sick, but that's not the way life works." "What do you mean?" said Dean Black. The Chinese friend responded . . . "Does fighting bad habits create good ones? Does fighting war create peace? Obviously not. And fighting illness doesn't create health."

Black goes on to say that:

> We spend those billions of dollars studying diseases, which we then take on as if they were enemies in a war. The Chinese, by tradition, walk a more peaceful path. They study health, and seek

merely to create it. They do not see the body under siege, nor do they adopt a warlike state of mind. They understand that fighting illness and creating health are two entirely different activities and that in the long run, fighting illness doesn't work. Why? Because there's a rule of life that says we can't create what we want by opposing what we've got. The spirit of opposition is not a creative spirit. Acts of opposition are not creative acts. The goal of healing is not to oppose, which comes from fear, but to create, which comes from hope.

Holistic Health:
More Than Alternative/Complementary Therapies

There is much confusion about what exactly the term *holistic health* means. Most laypeople and many health professionals equate this term with herbal remedies, acupuncture, meditation, and other forms of alternative or complementary therapies. While these types of treatments are part of the picture, it is important to understand that the term *holistic health* refers to a whole lot more. *Holistic health* refers to a philosophy and set of beliefs (a paradigm) about how people get sick and what they need in order to heal. As the internationally renowned British physician David Reilly says:

> People should be aware that there are many practitioners within the field of alternative medicine who are every bit as mechanistic, power-oriented, interventionist, and invested in "the therapy" as elsewhere. One of the things that moved me fifteen years ago was that people were going to the psychiatrist and the cardiologist and the general practitioner. Now they are going to the aromatherapist, the homeopath and whatever. Sometimes that's good. But for the group of patients I see there's a missing ingredient.[18]

What is missing is a truly holistic perspective. For medicine this means approaches that don't seek to just medicate suffering and disease away but to explore how these physical manifestations are connected to underlying social, emotional, and spiritual pain. As we will see in later chapters, for health promotion it means not suppressing symptoms by pressuring people to change their lifestyle habits but helping them to explore the issues underlying their behavioral struggles.

A New Set of Assumptions

No longer viewing illness as the enemy is a significant philosophical shift. In fact, the overall philosophy and *all the underlying assumptions* about why people get sick—and how they heal—shift when moving from a biomedical to a holistic view of health and illness. In this chapter we will outline the major new assumptions associated with a holistic philosophy. All the underlying assumptions are supported by findings in the new sciences. Therefore, although these new assumptions may conflict with more traditional scientific explanations, they are very much in tune with the most recent scientific understandings of the nature of physical reality.

Assumption One

The potential for health or illness in humans (as complex systems) is the result of a complicated interaction among many variables. These variables include genetics, personality, environment, and access to social/spiritual support as well as lifestyle choices. Furthermore, as with all other aspects of complex systems human health is significantly influenced by chance.

Genetics. Genetics play an important role in determining the ways in which we are likely to be either resilient against or vulnerable to illness. Whether or not these strengths and weaknesses are expressed depends on a complex interaction among many aspects of a person's life experience.[4–7] For example, a person with a genetic predisposition toward cancer who grows up in a family that discourages emotions, ends up living in social isolation, and has been exposed to industrial toxins in his or her geographic location may go on to develop cancer. Another person with the same genetic propensity for cancer who experiences different emotional/social/environmental circumstances may not develop the disease.

Personality. Thoughts, attitudes, and beliefs can boost or deplete the function of our immune system and create positive or negative changes in the physical body. We will discuss the scientific research that demonstrates this in chapter 7. We also know that a person's ability to experience emotions and express emotions to others influences health. Both suppression and overexpression of feelings appear to diminish immune function and make us more vulnerable to disease.[8] Furthermore, the specific types of illnesses we get may be, at least in part, a reflection of our personalities and emotional styles.[4,5,6,9] People who are chronically angry or hostile suffer more heart attacks and greater coronary artery blockage, and research also points to relationships between personality and other diseases, including cancer and rheumatoid arthritis.[10]

Environment. The types of organizations and communities in which we live and work have an ongoing impact on each of us. Ideal environments provide access to safe, clean, living and working spaces free from violence. They also offer supportive and diverse social and spiritual interactions, economic resources, intellectual stimulation, contact with nature, an abundant variety of foods, and opportunities for rest, movement, pleasure, and play. When access to any of these important factors is absent, the resulting imbalance can contribute to physical and/or emotional illness.[4,5,11,12]

Social and Spiritual Influences. Close relationships at home, at work and in the community are important determinants of health. People with many social contacts live longer and have better health than people who have few social ties.[4,5] Social connection through membership in religious groups as well as pursuing a sense of spirituality through individual meditation or prayer also affect health and mortality. In fact, regardless of whether a person participates in organized religion or explores spirituality in his or her own context (e.g., through a connection to nature), research shows that individuals who report a deep sense of spiritual values report less frequent use of medical services, fewer minor illnesses and more complete recovery from minor illness than the national average.[13]

Lifestyle Choices. This aspect of health has been the primary focus of biomedical health promotion efforts. For the last thirty years it has been stressed that illness can be prevented and health can be created primarily by adopting a healthy lifestyle: low-fat eating, aerobic exercise, smoking cessation, stress management and control of blood pressure and cholesterol. While the holistic approach supports the idea that individual lifestyle choices affect health, it views this as only one part of the complex "equation" (a decidedly nonlinear one!) that determines a person's health experience. A holistic philosophy takes a systems perspective in emphasizing that the "lifestyle choices" a person makes must be understood in the context of his or her genetic propensities, personality, relationships, and the environment. Caroline Myss, author of *Why People Don't Heal and How They Can,* has a somewhat irreverent quotation that sums up this concept.

> You can be a vegetarian and run 6 miles a day, but if you are in an abusive relationship, or hate your job, or have daily fights with your parents, you are losing energy and you will get sick. On the other hand, if you call back your energy from negative beliefs, you can eat cat food and stay healthy![14]

Chaos and Chance. Last, but certainly not least, the laws of the new science of chaos tell us that complex systems are always to an important degree unpredictable and subject to random and sometimes explosive changes. Human beings as complex systems are subject to the same laws. While we know that all of the above-mentioned factors influence our state of health at any one time, it is important to remember that it is scientifically impossible to know for certain exactly why one person gets sick while another does not or why one heals while another does not. Therefore, blaming people for their illnesses because they did not exercise enough, ate the wrong foods, or did not think positively is not only unethical but unscientific. Chaos teaches us to be both humble and compassionate in the face of the complex and "wonder-full" universe in which we live.

Assumption Two

There is meaning embedded in health problems. Pain, illness, behavioral struggles, and injuries don't "just happen." They are always at least partly a reflection of life imbalance; physical manifestations of our emotional/spiritual struggles.

We can learn valuable information about ourselves and our lives by paying close attention to *when* we get sick and *where* in our body our sickness manifests itself. It is also important to ask ourselves what illness, pain, an injury, or a behavioral struggle *invites us to do differently*. Significant health struggles can propel us to take risks and change our lives in ways that we were too timid to do before. The following passage from an article by Alan Cohen in *Recovery Today Journal* (September 1998) illustrates this concept.[15] In this passage, Cohen is having a conversation with a client about an accident that injured her hand.

> "My whole life changed when I injured my hand," Judy told me. "I lost my career, my house, and I found myself alone for many hours a day . . . it was really a rude awakening."
>
> Judy's choice of words struck me. "You've told me about the rude part," I responded. "What about the awakening?"
>
> "Well, there were some major blessings," she admitted. "I quit running around like a crazy woman; I was always on call before. I would be driving home after my shift at the hospital, my beeper would go off, and I would turn right around and go back. I began to think about what I really wanted to do with my life, and I went back to college. And I had more quality time with my kids. In the long run, I'm better off."
>
> As my friend Judy described the changes resulting from her hand injury, she reported, "The thing that drove me most crazy was when my 'spiritual' friends asked, 'How did you create this?' If my hand was healthy I would have punched them! While I was hurting physically and emotionally, the last thing I wanted to feel was guilty about doing something stupid."
>
> "I would like to ask you the same question with a different twist," I told Judy. "How in wisdom did you create the event?

How, through loving yourself, did you draw such an experience into your life?"

"The truth be told," Judy answered, "I was quite unhappy with my life the way it was, but I didn't want to confront my fears about making a change. I needed a dramatic event to get my attention. If I were challenged in a lesser way, I probably would have just gone on clinging to my old security blankets, but feeling empty inside."

It is easy to see how Judy's hand injury created suffering and difficulties in her life. At the same time it provided her with the opportunity to make very important and dramatic changes that she had previously been too frightened to face. From a holistic perspective all physical and emotional struggles in life present a person with this kind of opportunity.

In pursuing this line of thought a bit further, it is important to acknowledge that there are many holistic health professionals and healers who believe there is more than just a "connection" between pain or illness in the body and life struggles. These individuals believe that there is also a direct correlation between where in the body a person gets ill or injured, and the specific life struggle that needs to be addressed.[6,7,9,16,17]

For example, well-known psychologist and best-selling author Louise Hay has an entire section in her one of her earliest books that lists the different areas of the body, various illnesses, and the correlating life struggles that accompany each illness. She also lists an affirmation that a person can explore as a contradiction to the life situation that contributed to developing a specific illness. For examples, see table 6.1.[17]

TABLE 6.1. Life Struggles and Illness

Illness	Life Struggle	Affirmation
Arthritis	Feeling unloved. Criticism, resentment.	I am love. I now choose to love and approve of myself. I view others with love.
Asthma	Smother love. Inability to breathe for oneself. Feeling stifled. Suppressed crying.	It is safe now for me to take charge of my own life. I choose to be free.
Hypertension	Long-standing emotional problem not solved.	I joyously release the past. I am at peace.
Sinuitis	Irritation toward one person, someone close.	I declare peace and harmony will dwell in me at all times. All is well.
Sore throat	Holding in angry words. Feeling unable to express the self.	I release all restrictions, and I am free to be me.

(Adapted from *Heal Your Body*, by Louise Hay)

Assumption Three
Each of us is inherently good and we all have a deep internal wisdom to guide us on a natural process toward health and healing. The holistic perspective assumes that people are always striving to improve themselves and their health.

People often participate in behaviors that are hurtful to themselves or to others. This is not because they are "undisciplined or immoral." It is because they are overwhelmed with distress which is a result of previous trauma or oppressive experiences. This distress then leads to unhealthy behaviors and the development of illness.

Childhood trauma is one of the main sources of the distress that underlies behavioral struggles. We would now like to explore how childhood trauma can lead to the chronic patterns of behavior that lead to physical and emotional illness.

Trauma and the Manifestation of Illness

There is an entire field of holistic study known as "body-based psychotherapy," which explores how life difficulties and traumas predispose a person to specific types of acute and chronic illness.[19,20] Healers working in this field believe that these distresses are acquired over a person's lifetime and stored as "distress recordings." Distress recordings interrupt the homeostasis of the mind and body and interfere with our natural ability to be healthy and live well.

Body-based psychotherapy differs significantly from more traditional forms of psychotherapy. Individuals are encouraged to experience emotions and talk about difficulties as they do in traditional therapy. In body-based psychotherapy, however, special healing techniques are also used to help the client access and release distress stored in different areas of the physical body. Body-based therapists use skillful touch and assist clients with special postures and movement of body segments to help them bring to the surface old trauma recordings embedded deep in the body. Two of the best-known forms of body-based psychotherapy are Radix and Hakomi. (For more information on these therapies, see "Holistic Resources" at the end of this book.)

The following information from the field of body-based psychotherapy outlines in more detail the concepts regarding how we get hurt, how we store our distress, and how this distress affects our basic patterns of health or illness.

Childhood Trauma

Traumas and deprivations during childhood overload the body with stress, and childhood stresses predispose a person to acute and chronic illnesses during adulthood. Parenting practices in most, if not all, industrialized countries are drastically out of touch with children's basic needs, so the type of early life stress and trauma that creates a predisposition to acute and chronic illness is widespread.[12] The traumas and deprivations that commonly lead to illness include the following.[12]

- An inadequate amount of touching and holding during childhood

- Suppression of the child's need for emotional contact and expression

- The failure of adults to recognize the child as a separate and significant person with needs that are just as important as any adult's

- Exposure to violence and violent behavior, especially violence that occurs among the child's family members

- Misinformation and lack of support for the child's developing sexuality

Tragically, research indicates that these types of childhood trauma and their damaging consequences are all too common in our culture. A recent study of a large HMO population (more than 10,000 adults) in California collected data on the relationship between health risk behavior and disease in adulthood and exposure to childhood emotional, physical, and sexual abuse.[21] It is important to remember that the numbers represent *reported* experiences of abuse and trauma that do not include occurrences that people did not want to reveal in writing or those (particularly in the case of sexual abuse) that they may not have remembered. It is also important to recall that this is a relatively normal segment of the population, not a sample composed of clinical patients of one kind or another who may be more likely to have suffered childhood trauma. Given these caveats, in this study:

- 28 percent of women reported sexual abuse

- 16 percent of men reported sexual abuse

- 25.6 percent of the whole group reported that they had lived with a substance abuser

- 10.8 percent of the whole group reported physical abuse

What makes these data all the more poignant is that fully one-half of the population reported experiencing at least one category of childhood trauma, 25 percent reported at least two categories and 6 percent reported at least four categories! Furthermore, the researchers found a strong, graded relationship between exposure to childhood trauma and the presence of adult health risk behaviors and disease.

Manifestation of Illness

Children react to trauma and deprivation by experiencing unbearable levels of terror, rage, heartbreak, and grief. They long for closeness, comfort, and understanding. In order to survive these intolerable emotions, the entire body, including involuntary and voluntary muscle systems, becomes chronically tense. Breathing is inhibited, and there is a numbing of emotional responses. This tension eventually permeates all of the body's organs and tissues. This process, known as *emotional armoring,* suppresses the vitality of the child and disrupts the normal, healthy function of the body in three ways.[12,22]

By stopping the discharge of painful emotions armoring causes the stress of these emotions to become trapped in the body. The body continuously reacts as if it is in an ongoing life or death situation. This cycle is very destructive to all the systems of the body and continues until the painful emotions are discharged and the need for closeness and emotional nurturing are met.

Maintenance of emotional armoring uses an enormous amount of the body's energy. Energy is diverted from the normal maintenance of physical and emotional health and is used to maintain the emotional armor. This leaves the cells of the body in a state of energy starvation. Diseases such as cancer, heart disease, chronic fatigue, and others can eventually manifest themselves as a result of chronic, ongoing, energy starvation.

The emotional armoring that protects us from painful emotions as a child also prevents closeness and meaningful emotional contact with others when we become adults. The emotional closeness offered by other people cannot penetrate the armor that saved us when we were young. We become chronically isolated, starved by our own defenses.

It is very important to note that the physical manifestation of illness in the body is partly a *degenerative breakdown* in normal function and partly an active, *creative adaptation* that helps the person survive the stress and trauma. The body literally develops disease and symptoms of illness in an effort to partially discharge the toxicity of emotions trapped by armoring. It is a way of physically "letting off steam," so to speak. Interestingly, the symptoms and nature of each illness often closely imitate the emotional expression they partially discharge. For example, coughing uses the same muscles as sobbing. Watery eyes and a runny nose mirror the activity of the body when crying.[12,22]

Healing the Wounds

In order to facilitate the body's natural wisdom and healing process three things must occur.[12]

First, the person needs the support of a holistic counselor to help them express his or her feelings and discharge the stored emotions that have been trapped in the body for so long. This facilitates a dissolving of the emotional armor that has kept the person trapped in chronic patterns of distress.

Second, it is important to help the person create meaningful, close relationships within which emotional and sexual needs can be met.

Third, traditional and alternative medical- and health-related treatments must be used to help the body heal and repair the damage done by years of storing toxic emotions.

A Place to Learn about Trauma, Oppression and Healing

For anyone interested in learning more about trauma, social oppression and healing, Re-evaluation Counseling can be an excellent resource. Re-evaluation Counseling is practiced by an international community of people committed to improving conditions for humanity worldwide. The philosophy and intent of Re-evaluation Counseling are remarkably similar to the holistic information we are presenting in this book. Reading the organization's description below, it is easy to see how it can support anyone who wants to become more involved in holistic health and creating Epoch III humanity.

Re-evaluation Counseling is a process whereby people of all ages and of all backgrounds can learn how to exchange effective help with each other in order to free themselves from the effects of past distress experiences.

Re-evaluation Counseling theory provides a model of what a human being can be like in the area of his/her interaction with other human beings and his or her environment. The theory assumes that everyone is born with tremendous intellectual potential, natural zest, and lovingness, but that these qualities have become blocked and obscured in adults as the result of accumulated distress experiences (fear, hurt, loss, pain, anger, embarrassment, etc.) which begin early in our lives.

Any young person would recover from such distress spontaneously by use of the natural process of emotional discharge (crying, trembling, raging, laughing, etc.). However, this natural process is usually interfered with by well-meaning people (who say things such as "Don't cry," Be a big boy," etc.) who erroneously equate the emotional discharge (the healing of the hurt) with the hurt itself.

When adequate emotional discharge can take place, the person is freed from the rigid pattern of behavior and feeling left by the hurt. Their basic loving, cooperative, intelligent, and zestful nature is then free to operate. Such a person will tend to be more effective in looking out for his or her own interests and the interests of others, and will be more capable of acting successfully against injustice.

In recovering and using the natural discharge process, two people alternate counseling and being counseled. The one acting as the counselor listens, draws the other out, and permits, encourages, and assists emotional discharge. The one acting as the client talks, discharges, and re-evaluates. With experience and increased confidence and trust in each other, the process works better and better.

Re-evaluation Counseling provides conferences, workshops, classes, journals, articles, pamphlets, and video- and audiocassettes on hundreds of topics related to the human experience of oppression (around race, class, gender, age, religious or ethnic heritage, sexuality and more). Materials address healing approaches for responding to the distress that results from these

81

types of oppression. For more information on the Re-evaluation Counseling community, see their Web site at www.rc.org.[23]

Please be aware that the primary focus of the Re-evalutation Counseling Organization is creating world change. Its members are interested in joining with people committed to the emergence of a better humanity. By participating in Re-evaluation Counseling activities, most people find that they work very intensely on their own hurts and distress patterns as they learn how to be more effective healing allies for others.[23]

Summary

Becoming conscious of the new assumptions about health, illness, and healing can help us all support people in a more holistic fashion. Fortunately, there is a great deal of new medical research and scientific data that can help us understand how and why working from these holistic assumptions is important in helping people heal. In the next chapter we will take a look at findings from one of the most exciting areas generating this new research: the field of psychoneuroimmunology.

References

For this chapter we would like to acknowledge the work of Caroline Myss and Louise Hay. Both of these women have beautifully illustrated the metaphorical relationship between life struggles and the manifestation of specific illness in the mind and body. Both have published many books, but we highly recommend starting with Myss's *Why People Don't Heal and How They Can* and Hay's *You Can Heal Your Life.*

1.   Alderman, E.L., et al. "Ten-Year Follow-Up of Survival and Myocardial Infarction in the Randomized Coronary Artery Surgery Study (CASS)." *Circ.* 82 (1990): 1629–46.

2.   Weil, Andrew. *Spontaneous Healing.* New York: Knopf, 1995.

3.   Black, Dean. *Health with a Chinese Twist.* 1991.

4.   Blair, Justice. *Who Gets Sick: How Beliefs, Moods, and Thoughts Affect Your Health.* Los Angeles: Jeremy P. Tarcher, 1987.

5.   Ornstein, Robert, and David Sobel. *The Healing Brain: Breakthrough Discoveries about How the Brain Keeps Us Healthy.* New York: Simon and Schuster, 1987.

6.   Myss, Caroline. *Why People Don't Heal and How They Can.* New York: Random House, 1997.

7.   Myss, Caroline. *Anatomy of the Spirit: The Seven Stages of Power and Healing.* New York: Random House, 1996.

8.   Pennebaker, J. W., and H. C. Traue. "Inhibition and Psychosomatic Processes." In Harold C. Traue and James W. Pennebaker, eds., *Emotion Inhibition and Health.* Seattle: Hogrefe and Huber, 1993.

9.   Hay, Louise. *You Can Heal Your Life.* Carlsbad, CA: Hay House, 1987.

10.   Karren, K. J., B. Q. Hafen, N. L. Smith, and K. J. Frandsen. *Mind/Body Health: The Effects of Attitudes, Emotions, and Relationships.* San Francisco: Benjamin Cummings, 2001.

11.   Ornstein, Robert, and David Sobel. *Healthy Pleasures.* Reading, MA: Addison Wesley, 1989.

12.   Marks, Linda, and Brian Schultz. Handouts from Fourth International NICABM Conference on the Psychology of Health Immunity and Disease, vol. B, December 11–12, 1992.

13. Koenig, Harold George, and Harvey J. Cohen, eds. *The Link between Religion and Health: Psychoneuroimmunology and the Faith Factor.* Oxford: Oxford University Press, 2002.

14. Caroline Myss. *Natural Health.* January-February 1997.

15. Alan Cohen. *Recovery Today*, September 1998. Newsletter for licensed chemical dependence counselors.

16. Hay, Louise. *Love Yourself, Heal Your Life Workbook.* Carlsbad, CA: Hay House, 1990.

17. Hay, Louise. *Heal Your Body: The Mental Causes for Physical Illness and the Metaphysical Way to Overcome Them.* Carlsbad, CA: Hay House, 1988.

18. Reilly, D. "Research, Homeopathy, and Therapeutic Consultation." *Alternative Therapies in Health and Medicine* 1, no. 4 (1995): 70.

19. Kurtz, Ron. *Body-Centered Psychotherapy: The Hakomi Method.* LifeRhythm, 1990.

20. Marks, Linda, and Brian Schultz. "The Use of Touch in Psychotherapy." 1992. Manuscript.

21. Fellitti V. "Relationship of Childhood Abuse and Household Dysfunction to Many of the Leading Causes of Death in Adults." *American Journal of Preventive Medicine* 14, no. 4 (1998): 245–58.

22. Schultz, Brian. "Symptoms as Compensatory Mechanisms of Discharge." 1990. Manuscript.

23. *Present Time: Quarterly Journal for the Re-evaluation Counseling Community* 32, no. 2 (2000).

Chapter 7

PSYCHONEUROIMMUNOLOGY

The Physiology of Attitudes, Beliefs, and Emotions

The immune system, like the central nervous system has memory and the capacity to learn. Thus it can be said that intelligence is located not only in the brain but in cells that are distributed throughout the body, and that the traditional separation of mental processes, including emotions, from the body is no longer valid.

Candace Pert
Molecules of Emotion

One of the major criticisms of the holistic view of health and illness is that there are no scientific data to support it. However, the new science of mind/body/spirit medicine, also known as psychoneuro-immunology (PNI), is helping to change that. PNI is providing us with a large and ever expanding body of research that documents the ways in which attitudes, beliefs, and emotions impact our health. These new data strongly support the importance of holistic approaches for understanding health, illness, and the process of healing.

In this chapter and the next we will explore the basic components of this new mind/body/spirit science. We will examine some of the studies that support the ways in which our thoughts, beliefs, emotions, and relationships affect our health. We will see that clinging to an outdated, mechanistic worldview and its narrow focus on biomedical risk factors limits our understanding of some of today's most pressing health problems. We will suggest that a new set of variables (i.e., attitudes, beliefs, emotions, and relationships) may be the "missing links" in our understanding of many of these common problems.

The New Field of Psychoneuroimmunology

How is it possible that our thoughts, beliefs, and emotions can have profound effects on our physical health? Until recently we have had only our own intuition and very little in the way of scientific evidence to even begin to suggest answers to this question. Now, however, the young but exciting science of PNI is helping us find some of the answers. The term *psychoneuroimmunology* can be better understood by breaking it down into its constituent parts (being careful to remember that the whole is always greater than the sum of its parts).

psycho	→	the mind and the emotions
neuro	→	the nervous system
immuno	→	the immune system

Traditionally we were taught that these were three separate bodily systems. PNI has shown conclusively that this is not the case. In fact, these systems are inextricably intertwined and interconnected. Although going into detail on this complicated science is beyond the scope of this book, a brief overview of what we have learned from PNI is important because it has tremendous ramifications for the way we view health and illness and for what we do as health professionals. A great reference for further reading (as well as the main source for the next few pages) is Candace Pert's *Molecules of Emotion*.[1] Dr. Pert is one of the great pioneers in the field of mind/body/spirit science. She has done a marvelous job of translating an extremely complex science into a thoroughly enjoyable text that is both informative and readable.

The "Electrical" and "Chemical" Brains

Many of us remember being taught that the brain and central nervous system are primarily an elaborate telephone complex. Electric charges (action potentials) travel along trillions of miles of wires (axons and dendrites) and cause cells to release substances (neurotransmitters) that travel across spaces between cells (synapses). Depending on the type and number of these substances, the electronic message either continues or stops at the neighboring cell, signaling feelings, emotions, thoughts, and so on.

While this type of "electrical" communication is certainly part of brain activity, the latest research supports the existence of an older and more widespread communication system, often referred to as the "chemical brain." This system involves chemical substances called neuropeptides. While this may be an unfamiliar word, most of us are familiar with serotonin, dopamine and endorphins, all of which have been in the news in recent years. These and other neuropeptide chemicals (collectively referred to as ligands) are released by nerve cells and travel back and forth to different parts of the brain through extracellular spaces in the blood and cerebrospinal fluid. All cells in the brain contain receptors that are especially designed to recognize these chemicals. Once recognized, the neuropeptides are incorporated into the new cell where they set in motion a chain of biochemical events that causes all sorts of changes to occur within the cell. It now appears that this is how the majority of messages are passed back and forth within the brain, resulting in what we refer to as thoughts, feelings, and emotions.

Bodymind

Until a few years ago, it was commonly believed that this process of "chemical" communication took place only within the brain. Thanks to pioneering work in PNI, however, we now know that many cells in the body produce these neuropeptides and that receptors for these chemicals are found throughout the body. If these chemicals are responsible for thinking and feeling, the logical extension is that cells other than those in the brain may be capable of thinking and feeling!

While this may be a difficult concept to grasp given four hundred years of training to the contrary, it has been understood on an intuitive level for some time. It is well known, for instance, that the center for emotions in the brain is located in an area known as the limbic system. This area is loaded with neuropeptides and their receptors. We now know that these same neuropeptides and receptors are also found in large numbers throughout the lining of the gut. So when we say "I'm having a gut feeling" that's exactly what we are having. And when we say that somebody is a "pain in the neck" it's very likely to be the case as well!

PNI shows us that the reductionist distinctions we have been making between the various systems of the body are artificial ones. There is more and more research supporting the interdependence of the psychological, neurological, and immune systems. One of the most exciting areas of recent PNI research involves the role that thoughts and emotions play in the immune system and thus our ability to prevent disease and heal ourselves.

Research Supporting PNI

One of the first places where we began to learn about the interconnection between our thoughts and emotions and the immune system was in multiple personalities (more technically referred to as dissociative identity disorders or DID). Multiple personalities result from serious trauma in childhood such as physical and sexual abuse. In order to survive, children wall off the torturous memories and create a new personality or personalities (the proper scientific term is *ego states*). It is well known that these personalities have different names, voices and so on. What is really fascinating is that they can also have different immune responses. One personality may be allergic to dogs, and another may not. Even more amazingly, one personality can have type II diabetes and show elevated blood glucose levels while another will not.[2] How is this possible? There aren't two immune systems. There aren't two brains. Once again, something is going on that does not fit the old "mind separate from the body" paradigm.

Over the past thirty years or so the evidence for this mind/body link has been steadily growing (see the references at end of this chapter for further reading). Some examples include the following.

"Pessimistic" animals and humans.[3,4] When rats and mice are placed in a situation where they receive a periodic small electric shock from which they cannot escape they become "pessimistic" and their immune function is suppressed. When they are allowed to learn to escape from the shock, their immune systems are unharmed. As we will see later in this chapter, people who look at the world in a pessimistic way also tend to have suppressed immune function.

Stress and the common cold.[5] Individuals exposed to a variety of respiratory viruses in the form of nasal drops were then quarantined and monitored for the development of infection and cold symptoms. Rates of respiratory infection and clinical colds increased in a dose-response manner with the degree of psychological stress experienced in the previous year.

Stress and wound healing.[6] People who were caring for parents suffering from Alzheimer's disease received a small puncture wound in the finger. Healing time was then measured as well as a number of immune function parameters. Compared to a matched group of people who did not have parents with Alzheimer's this group experienced slower wound healing and suppressed immune function.

Salivary Immunoglobulin A.[7–10] People who were shown films of Mother Teresa consoling the poor and the sick experienced increased levels of Salivary Immunoglobulin A, one of the body's first lines of defense against invading pathogens. Children have been shown to be able to increase levels of this substance through relaxation and self-hypnosis, and humor has been shown to increase levels in adults.

Meditation.[11–14] Different forms of meditation and relaxation have been shown to have a wide range of benefits for mental and physical health at least partially through enhancement of immune function. These mind/body approaches have been used effectively to treat anxiety and panic disorders and reduce a variety of types of pain. They may even be effective in reducing the risk of heart attack and stroke.

In his typically eloquent manner, Deepak Chopra sums up these eye-opening findings.

Sad or depressing thoughts produce changes in brain chemistry that have a detrimental affect on the body's physiology, and likewise, happy thoughts, loving thoughts of peace and tranquility, of compassion, friendliness, kindness, generosity, affection, warmth, and intimacy . . . each produce a corresponding state of physiology via the flux of neurotransmitters and hormones in the central nervous system.[15]

In fact, it now appears that these chemicals are producing effects not just in the central nervous system but also throughout all the systems of the body. The implications of these findings are tremendous. For example, it is common medical knowledge that the mutations that lead to cancer are occurring in our bodies every day of our lives. Yet some people get cancer while others do not. What if we could learn to use positive thoughts and feelings to strengthen the immune system? Then perhaps more people would avoid experiencing illnesses like cancer or at least boost their bodies' natural ability to respond and heal. This is not to say that sophisticated radiation and pharmacological interventions would lose their place in medicine, but perhaps these toxic interventions (which are often only partially successful) could eventually be used only as treatments of last resort.

The Placebo Effect

Perhaps the best-known example of the power of the mind to create physical changes in the body is the placebo effect. Most health professionals have heard of placebos through their use in studies by pharmaceutical companies testing new drugs. A placebo is defined as "a treatment or aspect of a treatment that does not have a specific action on a patient's symptom or disease; an inactive substance, a procedure with no therapeutic value."[16] In other words, placebos are considered to be *useless* substances or procedures. What is amazing is that in study after study, across a broad range of medical conditions, 25 to 35 percent of patients consistently experience satisfactory relief when placebos are used instead of regular medicines or procedures. This means that 25 to 35 percent of patients consistently experience satisfactory relief when these *useless procedures and substances* are used to treat a broad range of medical problems! In fact, drug companies will not even consider marketing new drugs unless they outperform this "placebo effect."

Perhaps even more amazingly, research has shown that when many of these procedures, surgeries, or drugs are first introduced the placebo rates are often much higher, up to 70 or 80 percent! A good example of this is work that was done by Herbert Benson, author of a groundbreaking book on the placebo effect, *Timeless Healing: The Power of Biology and Belief.*[11] He compared the results of five different treatments for angina pectoris, commonly referred to as chest pain, including a couple of surgeries, some medications, and some vitamins that were commonly used in the 1920s and 1930s. The effectiveness of these treatments was measured by improvements in exercise performance, decreased need for medication and so on. Initial studies showed these treatments to be 70 to 90 percent effective. Later studies showed these treatments to be only 25 to 30 percent effective, in other words, no better than a placebo.[17] It is hypothesized that the fact that the patients and physicians believed these treatments would help is what made their initial effectiveness so great. All of these treatments are now considered useless. There are many similar examples in the literature going back more than one hundred years. In fact, the French physician Armand Trousseau commented on the phenomenon in the nineteenth century, saying: "You should treat as many patients as possible with the new drugs while they still have the power to heal."[17]

A more recent example of the same phenomenon came from the *Journal of the American Medical Association* in 1994. It involved a review of pain treatments over the previous twenty years, including both medications and surgery. The researchers found that placebo response rates varied greatly and were frequently much higher than the expected 25 to 35 percent. Their powerful conclusion was that:

> The quality of the interaction between the patient and the physician can be extremely influential in patient outcomes and in some, perhaps many cases, patient and provider expectations and interactions may be more important than the specific treatments.[18]

Remember that this was published in the *Journal of the American Medical Association,* not some "New Age" periodical. It is powerful support for the existence of a connection between thoughts, beliefs, and physical outcomes. There are numerous other examples of the power of the placebo effect. Placebo treatments (remember these are "useless" substances and procedures) have been shown to do the following.

Increase hair growth in balding men.[19] Men told that they were receiving a drug that would increase hair growth indeed experienced such growth even when the substance given was a placebo.

Increase lung capacity in children with asthma.[19] Children with asthma who were given a drug and told it would improve their breathing experienced increased lung capacity, even though the drug was a placebo.

Provide pain relief equal to that of real knee surgery.[19] Adults undergoing surgery for knee pain experienced the same relief when they were told they had received the surgery, although in fact only a "sham" surgery was done.

Cure nausea and vomiting.[20] Pregnant women were cured of their nausea and vomiting when given a substance they were told would cure these conditions.

This last example is all the more powerful because the substance that was used as the placebo to stop nausea and vomiting in pregnant women wasn't a "useless" substance but rather Ipecac, which under most circumstances is known to cause vomiting!

The Nocebo Effect

If our thoughts and beliefs can affect us in positive ways it makes sense that they might also affect us in negative ways. In fact, the "nocebo" effect has been described as "The causation of sickness or death by expectations of sickness and death and by associated emotional states."[21] People commonly equate the nocebo effect with the concept of voodoo. There is, however, substantial scientific evidence that our thoughts can negatively affect our health. Research shows, for instance, that:

- Women who are fearful of dying from a heart attack are more likely to do so than women who do not express this fear.[22]

- When individuals with asthma are told they are taking a drug that will make their breathing more difficult, the drug will indeed increase their airway resistance, even though it is composed simply of saline solution.[23]

- Individuals who are susceptible to poison ivy will develop rashes if they are given a harmless look-alike plant and told it is the real thing.[19]

- Cancer patients will experience hair loss when given a completely benign substance and told it is a powerful anticancer medicine that causes hair loss![24]

Negative feelings, beliefs, and expectations on the part of health care professionals can also translate into potentially dangerous and even life-threatening consequences for the people we are trying to help. In *The Placebo Response,* Dr. Howard Brody says that anytime a patient "feels less listened to, without a good explanation, uncared for, and less in control, then we'd predict that a nocebo effect is possible." He goes on to say that: "in our complex and often too impersonal health care system, nocebo effects must be rather common."[25]

In fact, the literature is replete with stories of individuals who appear to have suffered serious untoward consequences as a result of nocebo effects or what Andrew Weil refers to as medical "hexing." In *Spontaneous Healing,* Dr. Weil relates the story of a woman in her early forties who came to see him from Finland after being diagnosed with multiple sclerosis. Although the symptoms to that point were very mild and limited to muscle weakness in one leg, she behaved as if she were extremely ill. She was also depressed and related her story almost without emotion, as if it was happening to someone else. It turns out that, as can be the case with this type of disease, the initial diagnosis had taken a long time to make and involved many tests. After finally sitting her down in his office and delivering the bad news, her neurologist excused himself and left the room, only to return a moment later with a wheelchair, which he invited her to sit in to "practice" for the time when she would be totally disabled.[2]

Research, perhaps a little less spectacularly but no less powerfully, supports the power that these kinds of interactions can have. In one such study at Massachusetts General Hospital, patients about to undergo surgery were randomly assigned to control and experimental groups that were matched for age, gender, underlying disease, severity of disease, and type of operation. Those in the control group were addressed by anesthesiologists in a cursory manner. The anesthesiologist gave them his name, told them that he would be administering the anesthesia the next day, and assured them that everything would be fine. The same anesthesiologists spoke warmly and sympathetically to the experimental group, sitting on the bed, holding the patients hand, and discussing exactly what he or she should expect in the way of pain and suffering. The operations were performed the next day by surgeons and nurses who were not aware of which patient belonged to which group. The patients who experienced that simple five-minute act of compassion needed only half the painkilling medication and were released from the hospital 2.6 days sooner than those in the other group![27]

Contrary to the traditional dogma of the separation of the mind and body, as espoused by Descartes, the literature on placebo and nocebo effects clearly demonstrates that our thoughts, beliefs, and emotions can powerfully affect our physical health.

Perceived Health

Numerous studies have shown that how we feel about our health is a powerful predictor of how healthy we actually are and how long we are going to live. For example, in a study done with seniors in Canada 3,500 participants were asked "for your age would you say in general your health is excellent, good, fair, poor or bad?" The seniors were also examined by physicians and followed for seven years.[28] The researchers controlled for risk factors and prior illness, so it wasn't that people who thought they were sicker knew that because they had high cholesterol or high blood pressure. It turns out that those individuals who believed they were in poor health were three times more likely to die than those who believed they were in good health. Even more interesting, their answer to this single question was a better predictor of mortality than all the physician's tests and exams! Imagine the savings on health risk assessments! Furthermore, the increased risk for premature death associated with this negative health perception was at least equal to the risk created by traditional factors such as high blood pressure or cholesterol.

In fact, in similar studies the increased risk associated with having a negative perception of one's health has been as high as five or six times.[29,30]

Health Risk Appraisals and Perceived Health

Do health risk appraisals create poor perceived health and an expectation of illness? When individuals complete a health risk appraisal, they answer pages of standard biomedical health-related questions and are then given an estimated "risk age," which is compared to their biological age. For example, a forty-year-old person who is currently experiencing no health problems and feels fine may be told that he or she has the heart attack or cancer risk of an older person because of a sedentary lifestyle or a high-fat diet. This process literally tells the person that he or she should expect to get ill. Given what the literature suggests about the power of "perceived health" to affect future physical health, we need to think twice about these types of interventions.

Optimism and Pessimism

People have different ways of viewing positive and negative life events. This is often referred to as a person's "explanatory style." People seem to lean toward one of two explanatory styles—optimistic or pessimistic—although it is certainly most accurate to represent these styles on a continuum for any one individual. The components of the extremes of these two styles may be summarized as follows.

Optimistic Explanatory Style. These people generally

- View success as due to their own efforts and skill
- View failure as due to other people or bad luck
- View crisis as a temporary challenge to be overcome
- Feel a sense of control over their lives

Pessimistic Explanatory Style. These people generally

- View success as due to others or circumstances
- View failure as due to personal faults
- View crisis as an overwhelming obstacle
- Feel a lack of control over their lives

Perhaps the most common understanding of these differences comes from the well-known phrase that some people see the same glass of water as either "half full or half empty." By assessing people's answers to certain questions researchers can get an idea about the their explanatory styles—whether they tend to be more optimistic or pessimistic. By following these individuals for extended periods of time they can see how these styles relate to death and illness. Research in this area clearly shows that people who are optimistic enjoy better health and more rapid healing, including such things as less illness, fewer doctor visits, improved survival following heart attacks, and increased survival time with breast cancer.[3,4,31,32]

Summary

The information about psychoneuroimmunology presented in this chapter provides a scientific and medical basis for understanding the new beliefs, values, and underlying philosophy of holistic health. At this point in time, we know that the function of the immune system and our ability to be healthy are powerfully affected by our attitudes, beliefs, and emotions. What we don't know is the extent to which these variables must be modified in order to make a difference. How many movies of Mother Teresa do we have to watch or how many times a day do we need to laugh to reduce the threat of the common cold? How much relaxation or meditation is needed to reduce the chances of developing cancer or hypertension? How much of our explanatory style is subject to change, and how much do we have to change it in order to enhance immune function? As research in PNI becomes more sophisticated, we may be able to tap into this new wisdom to the potentially tremendous benefit of all of humanity.

Before we begin to explore the ramifications of this new information for health promotion, we want to turn to one of the best-researched areas in the study of the mind/body health connection: the power of relationships. In the next chapter we examine how social connectedness, love and spirituality contribute to health.

References

We wish to especially give credit to the work of Dr. Candace Pert for helping us to better understand the tremendous implications of psychoneuroimmunology for the health professions. Her wonderful book, *The Molecules of Emotion,* is both a marvelous textbook for learning about this newly emerging science and an insightful exposé of the far-reaching power of the patriarchy.

1.   Pert, Candace B. *Molecules of Emotion: Why You Feel the Way You Feel.* New York: Scribner, 1997.

2.   Harmon, W. *Global Mind Change: The Promise of the Twenty-first Century*. San Francisco: Berrett-Koehler, 1998.

3.   Peterson, C. "Explanatory Style as a Risk Factor for Illness." *Cognitive Therapy and Research* 12, no. 2 (1988): 119–32.

4.   Peterson, C., G. Vaillant, and M. Seligman. "Pessimistic Explanatory Style Is a Risk Factor for Physical Illness: A Thirty-Five-Year Longitudinal Study. *Journal of Personality and Social Psychology* 55, no. 1 (1988): 23–27.

5.   Cohen, S., D. Tyrrell, and A. Smith. "Psychological Stress and Susceptibility to the Common Cold." *New England Journal of Medicine* 325 (1991): 606–12.

6.   Kiecolt-Glaser, J., et al. "Slowing of Wound Healing by Psychological Stress." *Lancet* 346 (1995): 1194–96.

7.   McClelland, D., and C. Kirshnit. "The Effect of Motivational Arousal Films on Salivary Immunoglobulin A." *Psychology and Health* 2 (1988): 31–52.

8.   Olness K, T. Culbert, and D. Uden. "Self-Regulation of Salivary Immunoglobulin A by Children." *Pediatrics* 83, no. 1 (1989): 66–71.

9.   Hewson-Bower B., and P. Drummond. "Secretory Immunoglobulin A Increases during Relaxation in Children with and without Recurrent Upper Respiratory Tract Infections." *Developmental and Behavioral Pediatrics* 17, no. 5 (1996): 311–16.

10.   Lefcourt H., K. Davidson-Katz, and K. Kueneman. "Humor and Immune-System Functioning." *Humor* 3, no. 3 (1990): 305–21.

11.   Benson, H. *Timeless Healing: The Power and Biology of Belief.* New York: Scribner, 1996.

12.   Kabat-Zinn J., A. Massion, J. Kristeller, L. Peterson, K. Fletcher, L. Pbert, W. Lenderking, and S. Santorelli. "Effectiveness of a Meditation-Based Stress Reduction Program in the Treatment of Anxiety Disorders." *American Journal of Psychiatry* 149, no. 7 (1992): 936–43.

13.   Kiecolt-Glaser J., R. Glaser, D. Williger, J. Stout, G. Messick, S. Sheppard, D. Ricker, S. Romisher, W. Briner, G. Bonnell, and R. Donnerberg. "Psychosocial Enhancement of Immunocompetence in a Geriatric Population." *Health Psychology* 4, no. 1 (1985): 25–41.

14.   Amparo C.R., et. al. "Effects of Stress Reduction on Carotid Atherosclerosis in Hypertensive African Americans." *Stroke* 31 (2000): 568–73.

15. Miller R.S. *"As Above, So Below: Paths to a Spiritual Renewal in Daily Life.* New York: Putnam's, 1992.

16. *Dorlands Pocket Medical Dictionary.* 23d ed. Philadelphia: W. B. Saunders, 1982.

17. Benson, H., and D. McCallie. "Angina Pectoris and the Placebo Effect." *New England Journal of Medicine* 300, no. 25 (1979): 1424–29.

18. Turner, J., et al. "The Importance of Placebo Effects in Pain Treatment and Research." *Journal of the American Medical Association* 271, no. 20 (1994): 1609–14.

19. Blakeslee, S. "Placebos Prove So Powerful Even Experts Are Surprised: New Studies Explore the Brain's Triumph over Reality." *New York Times,* October 13, 1998.

20. Wolf, S. "Effects of Suggestion and Conditioning on the Action of Chemical Agents in Human Studies: The Pharmacology of Placebos." *Journal of Clinical Investigation* 29 (1950): 100–109.

21. Hahn, R. "The Nocebo Phenomenon: Concept, Evidence, and Implications for Public Health." *Preventive Medicine* 26 (1997): 607–11.

22. Eaker, E., J. Pinsky, and W. Castelli. "Myocardial Infarction and Coronary Death Among Women: Psychosocial Predictors from a Twenty-Year Follow-Up of Women in the Framingham Study." *American Journal of Epidemiology* 135 (1992): 854–64.

23. Luparello T. J., H. A. Lyons, E. R. Bleecker, and E. R. McFadden. "Influences of Suggestion on Airway Reactivity in Asthmatic Subjects." *Psychosomatic Medicine* 30 (1968): 819–25.

24.   Fielding, J. W. L. "An Interim Report of a Prospective, Ran-
       domized, Controlled Study of Adjuvant Chemotherapy in Op-
       erable Gastric Cancer: British Stomach Cancer Group." *World
       Journal of Surgery* 7 (1983): 390–99.

25.   Brody H. *The Placebo Response: How You Can Release the
       Body's Inner Pharmacy for Better Health.* New York: Cliff
       Street Books, 2000.

26.   Weil, A. *Spontaneous Healing.* New York: Knopf, 1995.

27.   Egbert, L., et al. "Reduction of Postoperative Pain by Encour-
       agement and Instruction of Patients." *New England Journal of
       Medicine* 270, no. 16 (1964): 825–27.

28.   Mossey, J., and E. Shapiro. "Self-Rated Health: A Predictor of
       Mortality among the Elderly." *American Journal of Public
       Health* 72 (1982): 800–807.

29.   Idler, E., and S. Kasl. "Health Perceptions and Survival: Do
       Global Evaluations of Health Status Really Predict Mortal-
       ity?" *Journal of Gerontology* 46, no. 2 (1991): 555–65.

30.   Kaplan, G. A., and T. Camacho. "Perceived Health and Mor-
       tality: A Nine-Year Follow-Up of the Human Population
       Laboratory Cohort." *American Journal of Epidemiology* 117,
       no. 3 (1983): 292–304.

31.   Maruta T., R. Colligan, M. Malinchoc, and K. Offord. "Opti-
       mists vs. Pessimists: Survival Rate among Medical Students
       over a Thirty-Year Period." *Mayo Clinic Proceedings* 57
       (2000): 140–43.

32.   Segerstrom S., S. Taylor, M. Kemeny, and J. Fahey. "Opti-
       mism Is Associated with Mood, Coping, and Immune Change
       in Response to Stress." *Journal of Personality and Social Psy-
       chology* 74, no. 6 (1998): 1646–55.

Chapter 8

RELATIONSHIPS

How Human Connection Creates Health

No one has shown that quitting smoking, exercising or changing the diet can double the length of survival in women with metastatic breast cancer, whereas the enhanced love and intimacy provided by weekly group support sessions has been shown to do just that.

Dean Ornish
Love and Survival

We know from quantum physics that physical reality in our universe is determined not so much by the existence of things as by the relationships between things. It is therefore not surprising that human relationships have a powerful impact on our health and our ability to heal ourselves, even though they fall into that other "difficult to measure" universe. In this chapter we review some of the highlights of the research that supports the critical contribution of relationships to human health.

Social Connectedness

It is well known that people with the fewest social ties have at least two to three times and sometimes much higher mortality rates independent of the traditional biomedical risk factors, socioeconomic level, life satisfaction, and so on. So many studies have supported this powerful link that it has been given a name—the Rosetto effect. The name comes from a study conducted in the little town of Rosetto, Pennsylvania, between the years of 1935 and 1985.[1] The researchers discovered that the incidence of coronary heart disease in Rosetto at the beginning of this period was about half that of two neighboring towns despite the fact that the traditional risk factors were the same in all three locations. They were intrigued by this and spent the next fifty years studying every detail of life in these three cities in order to try to determine the root cause of this paradox.

They discovered that Rosetto was settled by a tightly knit group of religious immigrants from southern Italy. During the first thirty years of the study Rosetto was characterized by a high level of social homogeneity: extensive intermarriage, strong family ties, and a supportive, nurturing community environment. The researchers theorized that this social connectedness might act as a buffer protecting the inhabitants against heart disease and premature death. And sure enough, in the 1960s and 1970s as the cohesiveness of the community began to weaken, heart disease rates in Rosetto climbed to the same levels as those in the surrounding communities. In their book *The Power of Clan,* the researchers concluded that:

> Those with the conventional risk factors are more likely to develop myocardial infarction than those without the risk factors, but an even larger proportion of the population may have the risk factors and not succumb to myocardial infarction over a period of nearly three decades.[2]

The researchers believed that this protection from coronary heart disease was provided by the strong sense of connection and community in Rosetto. Since this study there has been a veritable avalanche of research supporting the critical importance of social connectedness to health. Here is a summary of the highlights of some of the best-known of these.

Alameda County Study
(7,000 men and women studied for nine years)[3]

Community and social ties were more powerful predictors of health and longevity than age, race, gender, socioeconomic status, smoking, alcoholic beverage consumption, overeating, physical activity, and use of preventive health services. Individuals with close social ties and unhealthful lifestyles lived longer than those with poor social ties and more healthful behaviors.

Tecumseh Community Health Study
(2,754 men and women followed for nine to twelve years)[4]

People who were the most socially involved and had the strongest social ties had the best health after controlling for age, occupation, and initial health status. People who were more socially isolated had four times the mortality rate of those who were more socially active.

Swedish Studies
(More than 17,000 men and women followed for six years)[5,6]

The most isolated and lonely had four times the risk of dying during that period after controlling for age, education, occupation, smoking, exercise, and preexisting disease. In another prospective study of elderly men, those who lived alone or had minimal social support had two times the mortality rate after controlling for similar potential confounding variables.

Beta-Blocker Heart Attack Trial
(2,300 men who had survived a heart attack)[7]

Men who were socially isolated and stressed had four times the risk of dying after controlling for genetics, exercise, diet, weight, smoking, alcohol, and so on. Psychosocial factors had a much stronger relationship to mortality than did the drug being tested in the study, even though they are often ignored by physicians prescribing such drugs.

The Finland Study
(more than 13,000 people followed for five to nine years)[8]

Men who were socially isolated had 2 to 3 times higher mortality than those who were the most socially connected. This graded relationship remained even after extensive controlling for traditional biomedical, cardiovascular disease risk factors.

The Evans County Study
(more than 2,000 people followed for nine to thirteen years)[9,10]

Marriage, contacts with extended family and friends, church membership, and group affiliations were associated with decreased mortality in men even after controlling for other variables (mortality in women over the period was too small to demonstrate statistically significant findings). Reductions in social connections over the period were prospectively associated with increased mortality.

Coronary Angiography Study
(1,400 men and women who had at least one severely blocked coronary artery followed for five years)[11]

Unmarried men and women without someone to talk to on a regular basis were more than three times more likely to die after controlling for confounding factors. Married people without a confidant lived longer than unmarried people who did have a confidant.

The Power of Love:

Treating the "Broken" Heart

The information on social connectedness and health is in fact now being utilized successfully in clinical situations. Perhaps the best-known example is Dr. Dean Ornish's intervention for reversing heart disease. Over the past twenty years Dr. Ornish has shown that making lifestyle modifications can cause the regression of blockages in the coronary arteries, something no surgical or medical treatment has been able to accomplish. When most people think of this program they tend to think of the low-fat, exercise, and meditation components. But if you ask Dr. Ornish to comment on what he believes is the most important part of his program his answer may surprise you. He believes that the critical component has to do with "transcending that isolation that I think really is the root cause of so many of the self-destructive behaviors and emotional stress which in turn are such major contributors to so many of the illnesses of which so many people suffer."[12]

In another work, Dr. Ornish writes about this critical component.

> I am not aware of any other factor in medicine—not diet, not smoking, not exercise, not stress, not genetics, not drugs, not surgery—that has a greater impact on our quality of life, incidence of illness, and premature death from all causes."[13]

The factor he is referring to is love! His book *Love and Survival: The Scientific Basis for the Healing Power of Intimacy* describes in detail the abundant research in this area and is an excellent resource for all of us in the health care field.

Love and Cancer

The power of love and social connection is also being utilized in the treatment of cancer. One classic study involved women with metastatic breast cancer. In addition to the regular oncology treatments half of the women participated in a weekly ninety-minute support group where they were able to discuss their concerns and fears and participate in relaxation exercises. At the end of six months the women in the support group experienced half as much pain and suffering and felt decreased anxiety, depression, fatigue, and confusion. The patients not involved in the support group experienced increased depression and anxiety. The authors stated that, for the women in the support group, "Even a confrontation with death in the form of a terminal illness could be a period of growth and enlightened enhancement rather than emotional decline."[14]

The most interesting part of this study, however, occurred later, when some of the researchers theorized that the women in the support group might live longer as a result of the intervention. The lead researcher, Dr. D. Spiegel, was skeptical. But he agreed to follow the participants for five years to *disprove* the hypothesis that the psychosocial intervention could make a difference in longevity. Contrary to the hypothesis, the women who participated in the support group lived, on average, twice as long as those who had not! After five years, only women who had been in the intervention group were still alive.[15]

In a similar study, a group of patients with malignant melanoma participated in a six-week, ninety-minute, weekly support group focused on education, relaxation, problem solving, and social support. Six years later this group had a 60 percent reduction in death rate, compared to a control group, and about half as many recurrences of the disease.[16] Excitingly, research suggests similar findings involving people with breast, lung, and colorectal cancer.[17]

It is extremely important not to oversimplify the powerful processes that may be at work regarding the effect of social connectedness on health. It is certainly likely that individuals who have more connection and love in their lives may lead healthier lives by eating better, being more active, avoiding harmful habits, and having a better relationship with their health care providers. Yet, just as the new information emerging from PNI suggests a powerful, direct effect of our thoughts and emotions on our health, so, too, does it suggest that our relationships may directly influence our health by altering immune function. Studies have now linked social connectedness with enhancement of immune function and loneliness and social isolation with immunosuppression.[18,19]

Loving Touch

Touch is perhaps the ultimate expression of social connectedness. There is a substantial body of research in both animals and humans documenting the fact that loving touch is necessary for proper growth and successful healing. For example, monkeys deprived of touch when they are young grow up with a variety of emotional abnormalities that lead them to be aggressive and incapable of exhibiting warmth and affection toward their offspring.[20]

Touch, Rabbits, and Heart Disease

Loving touch also appears to be able to ameliorate the effects of disease-promoting behavior in animals. Rabbits have often been used to study heart disease because they develop clogged arteries when fed a high-fat diet. In one study rabbits were fed a high-fat, high-cholesterol diet and then autopsied. As expected, there was considerable blockage in the coronary arteries. Rather surprisingly, however, half of the rabbits had 60 percent less plaque in their arteries than the other half: same strain of rabbit, same diet, same exercise regimen, same cholesterol levels, but 60 percent less plaque. The researchers went over the experiment thoroughly to try and find some factor that might have caused this difference. The only thing they could come up with was that in the lab the rabbits were kept on either a low shelf or a high shelf. During the day, the lab technician would come through and pet the rabbits on the lower shelf.

Could the mere touch of the lab technician be protecting some of the rabbits from heart disease? Even though this seemed somewhat incredulous and definitely outside of the prevailing paradigm, the researchers didn't dismiss the possibility. They repeated the experiment exactly as before, this time directing the lab technician to regularly play with one-half of the rabbits. Lo and behold, they got the same results—60 percent less plaque in the rabbits that were touched![21]

What about the power of touch in human beings? The conventional wisdom with preterm babies is to minimize touching them because their immune systems are so underdeveloped and there is much risk of infection. In one study, researchers wanted to test the possibility that touch might have some beneficial effects. Therefore, an experimental group of premature babies received three fifteen-minute sessions of baby massage for ten days, for a total of 450 minutes of touching. The result? The babies who were touched:

- Experienced 47 percent greater weight gain per day
- Were more active, alert, and mature
- Required six fewer days in the hospital

The result of this inexpensive intervention was an average savings of $3,000 per infant![22] How many other potentially life- and cost-saving interventions are we missing by not looking at the power of mind/body/spirit interventions?

Spirituality and Prayer

A large body of research supports the contention that spirituality and religious involvement are associated with improved health and healing. We suggest the recently published book, *The Link Between Religion and Health,* edited by Harold Koenig and Harvey Cohen, for people who wish to investigate further this fascinating area of study. For the purposes of this chapter we want to talk particularly about the research related to prayer.

Clearly, many people have an intuitive belief that prayer is an effective means of speeding the healing process. Recently, however, researchers have attempted to study this question scientifically. The most famous published study involved a group of some four hundred patients on a cardiac care ward in a hospital.[23] Patients in the experimental group had three to seven people outside the hospital assigned to pray for them during the course of the next ten months. They were instructed to pray for the patients' quick recovery and for the minimization of pain and suffering. The study was "double blind," meaning that neither the patients nor the doctors involved knew who was being prayed for. At the end of ten months patients in the group that was prayed for:

- Were five times less likely to need antibiotics
- Had three times less pulmonary edema
- Needed fewer diuretics and had less coronary heart failure, pneumonia, and cardiac arrest
- Needed no mechanical ventilation (during the ten-month period)

How can we understand what is happening here? Clearly, there is no adequate traditional scientific explanation. Could these results have been attained by chance? Just as with any experimental study, that is a possibility. However, the results of this research have been replicated in a small study with AIDS patients and in a very recent study involving women undergoing in vitro fertilization-embryo transfer.[24, 25] In addition, a much larger study is now being conducted at the Harvard Medical School. It is interesting to speculate on the potential ramifications if these outcomes are replicated. If it turns out that prayer is shown to be an effective intervention for speeding the healing process, would *not* praying for patients be considered malpractice?

Everyone in Relationship with Everyone

Certainly, if future studies do confirm that prayer can affect the healing process this will require a complete rethinking of our understanding of health and healing, not to mention the universe and our place in it. In *Reinventing Medicine,* Larry Dossey suggests that this emerging information will move us beyond mind/body medicine to a new era of health care based on the concept of *nonlocal mind*; the ability of the mind to affect other people and things at a distance.[26] He suggests that each of us is involved in relationships at some level with everyone else through a universal mind or collective consciousness.

While the concept of nonlocal mind is certainly outside the realm of traditional scientific understanding, we have seen that the latest scientific findings support the possibility of such a phenomenon.

Quantum physics tells us that at the most basic level of existence it is the relationship between things and other things that really matters. Chaos theory tells us that complex systems are characterized not by simple "cause and effect" but by the notion that "everything affects everything else." Quantum physics has also shown us that our universe is decidedly nonlocal, that the subatomic particles of which it is composed retain some type of instantaneous connectedness that persists regardless of the distance between them.

As mentioned earlier, literally thousands of studies document the ability of the human mind to cause effects at a distance.[27] Although we do not understand the mechanisms of this nonlocal mind, Dossey uses an analogy to Newton's discovery of gravity to argue that this inability should not blind us to the apparent fact of its existence. As he explains, Newton's concept of universal gravity was so outrageous in the 1600s that his colleagues accused him of selling out to mysticism.

> Newton . . . had no explanation for how this invisible force worked, and he could not clarify how solid objects could obey the dictates of invisible gravity even if they wanted. . . . Newton's colleagues eventually got over their intellectual indigestion about gravity, and today gravity passes for common sense. But this is not because we understand it. We *still* don't know how gravity works; we have merely gotten use to it.

Dossey continues:

> So it is with nonlocal mind. We are required to propose its existence because of scientific data and our own experience. Skeptics may moan, bellow, howl and whine as they did against gravity, but nonlocal mind is an idea whose time has come. And years hence, when the smoke of controversy clears, we shall regard nonlocal mind as obvious, natural and *right*—as gravity.[26]

Summary

In the last two chapters, we have sought to whet your appetite with the powerful new research that has been emerging from the field of PNI. It is critically important that those of us engaged in the health professions become familiar and conversant with this research. This is true not only for researchers but also for health professionals in the field. While many of us have seen the power of these concepts in practice, we have also met with the resistance that comes from the "paradigm paralysis" of others. Fortunately, the latest research in mind/body medicine can help those who still cling to the outdated, biomedical paradigm grasp the tremendous implications this new information holds for our profession.

References

1. Egolf, B., J. Lasker, S. Wolf, and L. Potvin. "The Rosetto Effect: A Fifty-Year Comparison of Mortality Rates." *American Journal of Public Health* 82, no. 8 (1992): 1089–92.

2. Wolf, S., and J. Bruhn. *The Power of Clan: The Influence of Human Relationships on Heart Disease.* New Brunswick, NJ: Transaction, 1993.

3. Berkman, L., and S. Syme. "Social Networks, Host Resistance, and Mortality: A Nine-Year Follow-Up Study of Alameda County Residents." *American Journal of Epidemiology* 109 (1979): 186–204.

4. House, J., C. Robbins, and H. Metzner. "The Association of Social Relationships and Activities with Mortality: Prospective Evidence from the Tecumseh Community Health Study." *American Journal of Epidemiology* 116 (1982): 123–40.

5. Orth-Gomer, K., and J. V. Johnson. "Social Network Interaction and Mortality: A Six-Year Follow-Up Study of a Random Sample of the Swedish Population." *Journal of Chronic Diseases* 40, no. 10 (1987): 949–57.

6. Hanson, B. S., S. O. Isacsson, L. Janzon, and W. E. Lindell. "Social Network and Social Support Influence Mortality in Elderly Men: The Prospective Population Study of Men Born in 1914." *American Journal of Epidemiology* 130, no. 1 (1989): 100–111.

7. Ruberman, W. E., J. Weinblatt, D. Goldberg, and B. S. Chaudhary. "Psychosocial Influences on Mortality after Myocardial Infarction." *New England Journal of Medicine* 311, no. 9 (1984): 552–59.

8. Kaplan, G. A., et al. "Social Connections and Mortality from All Causes and from Cardiovascular Disease: Prospective Evidence from Eastern Finland." *American Journal of Epidemiology* 128, no. 2 (1988): 370–80.

9. Schoenbach V. J., B. H. Kaplan, L. Fredman, and D. G. Kleinbaum. "Social Ties and Mortality in Evans County, Georgia." *American Journal of Epidemiology* 123, no. 4 (1986): 577–91.

10. Kaplan, G. A. "Social Contacts and Ischemic Heart Disease." *Annals of Clinical Research* 20, nos. 1–2 (1988): 131–36.

11. Williams, R. B., et al. "Prognostic Importance of Social and Economic Resources among Medically Treated Patients with Angiographically Documented Coronary Artery Disease." *Journal of the American Medical Association* 267, no. 4 (1992): 520–24.

12. Ornish, D. "Healing the Heart, Reversing the Disease." *Alternative Therapies* 1, no. 5 (1995): 84–91. Interview.

13. Ornish D. *Love and Survival: The Scientific Basis for the Healing Power of Intimacy.* New York: HarperCollins, 1998.

14. Spiegel, D., H. Kraemer, J. Bloom, and E. Gottheil. "Effect of Psychosocial Treatment on Survival of Patients with Metastatic Breast Cancer." *Lancet* 2 (1989): 888–91.

15. Spiegel, D. "Psychosocial Intervention in Cancer." *Journal of the National Cancer Institute* 85, no. 15 (1993): 1198–1205.

16. Fawzy, I. "Malignant Melanoma: Effects of an Early Structured Psychiatric Intervention, Coping, and Affective State of Recurrence and Survival Six Years Later." *Archives of General Psychiatry* 50 (1993): 681–89.

17. Ell, K. O., J. E. Mantell, M. B. Hamovitch, and R. H. Nishimoto. "Social Support, Sense of Control, and Coping among Patients with Breast, Lung, or Colorectal Cancer." N.s., 7, no. 3 (1989): 63–89.

18. Kennedy S., J. Kiecolt-Glasier, and R. Glaser. "Immunological Consequences of Acute and Chronic Stressors: Mediating Role of Interpersonal Relationships." *British Journal of Medical Psychology* 61 (1988): 77–85.

19. Justice B. *Who Gets Sick: Thinking and Health.* Houston: Peak Press, 1987.

20. Huebner A. "The Pleasure Principle." *East/West*, May 14–19, 1989.

21. Nerem, R., M. Levesque, and J. Cornhill. "Social Environment as a Factor in Diet-Induced Atherosclerosis." *Science* 208 (1980): 1474–76.

22. Field, T., et al. "Tactile/Kinesthetic Stimulation Effects on Pre-term Neonates." *Pediatrics* 77, no. 5 (1986): 654–58.

23.   Byrd, R. "Positive Therapeutic Effects of Intercessory Prayer in a Coronary Care Unit Population." *Southern Medical Journal* 81, 7 (1988): 826–29.

24.   Sicher, F., E. Targ, D. Moore II, and H. S. Smith. "A Randomized Double-Blind Study of the Effect of Distant Healing in a Population with Advanced AIDS: Report of a Small-Scale Study." *Western Journal of Medicine* 169, no. 6 (1998): 356–63.

25.   Lobo, R. A. "Intercessory Christian Prayer Improves IVF Outcome." *Journal of Reproductive Medicine* 46 (2001): 781–87.

26.   Dossey, L. *Reinventing Medicine: Beyond Mind-Body to a New Era of Healing.* San Francisco: HarperSanFrancisco, 1999.

27.   Radin, D. *The Conscious Universe: The Scientific Truth of Psychic Phenomena.* New York: HarperEdge, 1997.

Part Three

"GETTING" PEOPLE TO CHANGE

Chapter 9

SURVIVING "RISK FACTOR FRENZY"

The Perils of Applying Epidemiological Research

Although we would all like to believe that changes in diet or lifestyle can greatly improve our health, the likelihood is that, with few
exceptions such as smoking cessation, many if not most such
changes will produce only small effects. And the effects may not be
consistent. A diet that is harmful to one person may be consumed
with impunity by another.

Marcia Angell and Jerome Kassirer
New England Journal of Medicine

Health educators teach people how to adopt a "healthy lifestyle" by
changing behavior: learning how to eat right, exercise correctly, lose
weight, stop smoking, and manage stress. But on what are traditional
behavior change guidelines based? Behavior change guidelines and
healthy lifestyle recommendations come primarily from epidemiological research that focuses on biomedical risk factors for various
diseases. Unfortunately, there are many limitations inherent in this
type of research, and attempting to translate research findings on
populations into specific health recommendations for individuals
creates problems that are not well understood by many health professionals.

Heart disease provides an excellent example of the problem. As
was discussed in chapter 4, measuring cardiovascular risk factors in a
group of people doesn't tell us which individuals in the group will
have a heart attack. It turns out that in the case of heart disease and
most other noninfectious diseases as well, biomedical risk factor research provides only minimal value in predicting who will get sick
and who will stay healthy. Furthermore, we believe that our society's

119

almost obsessive focus on epidemiology and these risk factors may actually be interfering with truly helping people to heal. It is very important that health professionals begin to have a more thorough understanding of how to read, interpret, and apply this type of health-related research. Therefore, in this chapter we will:

1. Discuss the most commonly encountered limitations inherent in epidemiological research
2. Explore the problems and potential negative consequences of incorrectly applying epidemiological research in health promotion
3. Make recommendations to help health professionals more skillfully interpret and incorporate this research into their work

We wish to acknowledge the fact that many health professionals have had only limited exposure to statistical techniques used in evaluation and research. For this reason we have written this chapter using a minimum of statistical terminology and jargon. This has necessarily required omission of some issues and oversimplification of others. We believe, however, that health professionals have much to gain from an understanding of the general concepts presented here. We have also included a number of references for those who wish to delve more deeply into the complexities of these issues.

The Nature of Epidemiological Research

Epidemiology is defined as "the study of the relationship of various factors determining the frequency and distribution of diseases in the human community."[1] Epidemiologists draw conclusions about the most important causes of a disease by studying large populations over time and examining the relationship between a variety of lifestyle and environmental factors and the occurrence of that disease. Epidemiological research is called observational because, unlike experimental research, usually there is no intervention attempted. There are two major types of epidemiological research studies: case control and cohort. Both types are described below.

Case Control Studies

Researchers select a group composed of individuals who already have the disease in which they are interested. They identify another group that is similar in as many ways as possible (age, gender, etc.) but whose members do not have the disease. This is the control or comparison group. The research process involves comparing lifestyle and environmental factors in the two groups prior to the onset of the disease. Because the most important information comes from the past this type of epidemiological research is called retrospective. As an example, researchers might compare past birth control use in women with and without breast cancer in an attempt to determine if using these medicines might affect the risk of developing the disease.

Cohort Studies

In this case, researchers closely examine the lifestyle habits and environment of a large population that is presently free of the disease of interest. Over the course of many years they continue to monitor the population by comparing and contrasting the lifestyle and environmental factors of those who do and do not get the disease. By doing this they hope to uncover the potential causes of the disease. Because this research begins in the present and goes into the future it is called prospective. Perhaps the best-known example of this type of research is the ongoing Framingham Heart Study, which has focused on a long-term examination of cardiovascular disease risk factors in a Massachusetts population.

From both of these types of research, scientists determine which lifestyle and environmental factors seem to appear more often in those individuals who have the disease than in those who don't. In this way we have learned, for instance, that people with high blood pressure are more likely to have a heart attack. We say, therefore, that high blood pressure is a risk factor for heart disease. The same can be said for high cholesterol, smoking, diabetes, and so on. In fact, there are currently over 350 risk factors for heart disease!

Correlation versus Cause

The most serious problem with epidemiological research comes from a lack of understanding about the difference between a correlation and a cause. A correlation (or association) describes the strength of the relationship between two factors (often referred to as variables). This association can either be positive or negative. With a positive association, as the value of one variable increases so does the value of the other. For example, we say that there is a positive association (correlation) between age and mortality. This means that in a group of older people more individuals are likely to die in a specified period of time than in a group of younger people. With a negative association, as the value of one variable increases the value of the other variable decreases. We say that there is a negative association between eating fruits and vegetables and certain types of cancer because epidemiological studies have shown that populations of people who eat lots of fruits and vegetables have a lower occurrence of these diseases.

Although there is much we can learn from examining these types of relationships, it is important to understand that associations or correlations are not the same as causes. For example, baldness in men is one of the 350 known risk factors for heart disease. We have learned from epidemiological research that there is a positive association, or correlation, between these two variables; in other words bald men are more likely to have heart disease than are men with a full head of hair.[2] This does not suggest, however, that we can lower a bald man's risk by giving him a toupee! This is because the baldness itself is not a cause of heart disease but only a factor that seems to appear more often in men who have heart attacks. In fact, bald men have an elevated level of testosterone, which leads to baldness and also promotes the development of heart disease. Baldness is therefore a risk factor for heart disease, but it is certainly not a cause!

Similarly, in the example on the previous page, just because people who eat more fruits and vegetables have a lower occurrence of certain types of cancer does not necessarily mean that this is a result of their diet. It could be that people who eat more of these foods also happen to have better access to preventive screenings, are more physically active, or have a different ethnic background. These "confounding factors" may be what make the difference between those who do and do not get cancer.

Confounding Factors

The existence of confounding factors is perhaps the major source of confusion about the distinction between association and causation. A confounding factor is a variable on which study and control groups differ that affects the outcome measure of a study. As an example, let us say we want to study whether heavy coffee drinking is related to the likelihood of developing lung cancer. We identify a group of five hundred heavy coffee drinkers and five hundred nondrinkers and follow them for ten years. After ten years our data indicate that the risk of lung cancer is ten times higher in the coffee drinkers. We then conclude that heavy coffee drinking is a risk factor for lung cancer. What is the problem? The problem is that heavy coffee drinkers also are very likely to be heavy smokers, and we know that smoking is strongly associated with an increased risk for lung cancer! So smoking is a confounding factor that must be dealt with or the research will suffer from "selection bias," which will render the data from the study inconclusive at best.

To be sure that this is clear, let us take one more example. To determine the relative danger to the heart of pipe versus cigarette smoking, we follow ten thousand pipe smokers and ten thousand cigarette smokers for ten years and see how many in each group have heart attacks. We discover that the respective rates of heart attack for the two groups are seven out of a hundred for the pipe smokers and four out of a hundred for the cigarette smokers. On the basis of this information we conclude that pipe smoking is considerably more dangerous than cigarette smoking. Unfortunately, we have forgotten to take into account the fact that cigarette smokers are both men and women whereas pipe smokers are mostly men. Since men have a much higher risk of having a heart attack than women, we cannot compare pipe smoking to cigarette smoking without first controlling for gender. Otherwise gender in this case will become a confounding factor that invalidates our conclusions.

Perhaps the major limitation of epidemiological research is that it is difficult and in many cases impossible to account for all the potential confounding variables. This is true particularly with regard to the kind of risk factor studies that form the foundation for so much of health promotion, Therefore, with few exceptions, risk factors are most accurately understood as "markers for" (variables that are associated with) rather than "causes of" disease. Unfortunately, as James McCormick writes in "The Multifactorial Aetiology of Coronary Heart Disease: A Dangerous Delusion":

> Not everyone makes a clear distinction between associations and causal relationships, and it is easy to find doctors and others talking about risk factors as if causal relationships had been established. Such an assumption leads almost inevitably to the belief that modification of risk factors will lead to a reduction of disease incidence. It is this faulty logic which is responsible for the dangerous delusion.[3]

Risk Factor "Mania"

Unfortunately, the distinction between cause and association is often blurred by scientists and health professionals and misunderstood and misreported by the media. Let us see how this might happen. A new, large epidemiological study suggests that some disease is positively associated with eating some type of food. This means that people who ate this food in this particular study were more likely to develop the disease than people who didn't eat the food. It is then often reported in the media that eating this food may increase the risk of getting this disease. If the report garners enough attention health professionals may begin to make recommendations for changes in people's eating habits based on the reported findings.

The problem is, of course, that the identification of this particular food as a risk factor in this study may or may not indicate any causal link to the disease. In fact, it is very likely that subsequent studies will not find an association between this food and the disease in question and may even find the opposite; that eating this food is associated with a decreased likelihood of getting the disease. It is therefore possible that the recommendations may not be beneficial, and it is even possible that they may be harmful. The recent frenzy over the supposed health benefits of beta-carotene is an excellent illustration of the significance of this problem.

The Rise and Fall of Beta-Carotene

By the early 1980s there was a substantial amount of epidemiological literature associating high intakes of fruits and vegetables, primarily those containing the antioxidant beta-carotene, with low incidences of cancer, particularly of the lungs. When these findings reached the public, food supplements containing beta-carotene and beta-carotene-enriched foods flooded the market and were routinely recommended by health professionals. As a result, the National Cancer Institute launched a number of large-scale human experimental trials in the mid-1980s to test the cancer-preventing properties of beta-carotene. To make a long story short, the two largest, best-controlled national trials not only showed no beneficial effect of beta-carotene but in fact needed to be halted due to the discovery of "major adverse effects—more lung cancers, more cardiovascular deaths, and higher overall mortality"— in the groups receiving supplementation. These findings "forced scientists, regulators and health educators to re-examine our scientific knowledge about the effects of beta-carotene and to rethink our recommendations for diet and for supplements."[4] The results were so disturbing that there was even some talk of regulating beta-carotene as a potential carcinogen!

More Confusion and Anxiety

This eye-opening example is by no means an isolated one. If we look back over just the last few years we can see many examples of conflicting and confusing recommendations coming out of "the latest" epidemiological research.

Fiber and Colon Cancer:
New England Journal of Medicine *(NEJM)*

As far back as the 1950s researchers observed that countries where fiber intake was high had relatively low rates of colon cancer. It was therefore an easy decision to recommend increased fiber intake to prevent the disease. Unfortunately, recent studies have not found a cause and effect relationship between these two variables, and a large prospective study of some 88,000 women "found no association between the intake of dietary fiber and the risk of colorectal cancer."[5] As one of the main authors of the study summarized the impact of the new information, "There has been such an abundant enthusiasm for this hypothesis, so the important message here is that fiber, overall, has no protective effect."[5]

Eggs and Cholesterol:
Journal of the American Medical Association *(JAMA)*

For years we have been warned of the dangers of the dreaded cholesterol-containing egg. It was suggested that eating even a few eggs a week could increase the risk of developing premature atherosclerosis and heart attack. Then, in 1999, two large prospective studies reached basically the opposite conclusion: "After adjustment for age, smoking and other potential CHD factors, we found no evidence of an overall significant association between egg consumption and risk of CHD in men or women."[6]

Cholesterol and Heart Disease:
Website—The Cholesterol Myths

On a related note, although almost all the major health organizations in this country support the relationship between blood cholesterol levels and coronary heart disease, many noted scientists around the world believe that the cholesterol–heart disease hypothesis has been, at the very least, exaggerated. As one leading expert put it:

> The level of one's blood cholesterol is, at best, nothing more than an extremely rough indicator. . . . At worst, it can be more the cause of stress and the diseases that stress brings on.[7]

Dietary Fat, Breast Cancer, and Heart Disease:
NEJM, JAMA

Due to large-scale public health campaigns women most likely fear breast cancer more than any other disease, although heart disease kills more women. Although it has been commonly recommended that women reduce the fat in their diet as a way of preventing both diseases, the latest prospective research concludes the following.

> Total fat intake was not significantly related to the risk of coronary heart disease.[8]

> No evidence that lower total intake of fat or specific major types of fat was associated with a decreased risk of breast cancer.[9]

Salt and Hypertension:
NEJM, Science

Although many major health organizations have been recommending that all Americans reduce their salt intake to lower blood pressure for over four decades, many respected researchers in the field believe that this recommendation is not supported by the data. The debate continues to rage, with experts often disagreeing about the results of the research even when they are looking at the same data; some say lowering salt is beneficial, some say it has little impact, and some say it may be dangerous, as the following quotations indicate.

> Although diet can strongly influence blood pressure, salt may not be a player.[10]

> Low salt diets may increase mortality—People just rely on statements that salt reduction can't really do any harm. . . . It may or may not be true.[11]

In 2001 the government announced data from a new study that it said put to rest all dissent by proving the beneficial role of salt reduction, yet many experts remain unconvinced, and there is little research to suggest that lowering salt intake leads to improvements in health.[12]

Fatness, Fitness, and Health:
International Journal of Obesity

For decades we have been told that fatness and fitness were mutually exclusive, with fatness being positively associated with premature mortality. Once again, this conclusion was based largely on data from observational studies that failed to take into consideration a large number of potentially confounding variables. Recent experimental data on both men and women tell quite a different story. Using physiological measures of fitness, Dr. Steven Blair, a senior researcher at the Cooper Clinic in Dallas, Texas, has shown that for both women and men it is fitness, not fatness, that has the stronger association with mortality. Blair concludes from his research that:

> If you're fit, being 25 or even 75 pounds overweight is perfectly healthy. And if you aren't fit, being slim gives you no protection whatsoever. I am convinced you can be fat and fit.[13]

Hormone Replacement Therapy:
JAMA

For years, millions of healthy women have been prescribed hormone replacement therapy (HRT) to prevent heart disease. The justification for this recommendation came from a large body of observational data suggesting a 40 to 50 percent reduction in this disease for women using HRT. Just as occurred with beta-carotene, however, a large, randomized, experimental study of this hypothesis was recently halted by the National Heart, Lung and Blood Institute because those assigned to take the HRT experienced a significant *increase* in coronary heart disease as well as increases in invasive breast cancer, stroke, and pulmonary embolism.[14]

Damned If You Do . . . Damned If You Don't

No wonder people are confused and anxious about the relationship between their lifestyle behaviors and their health! We are constantly being told that something we are doing or not doing is likely to lead to premature disease or death. This creates an ongoing state of anxiety and a feeling of helplessness. As we discussed in a previous chapter, this may have deleterious effects on our health via emotions that impact our immune system. In their landmark book *Healthy Pleasures,* doctors Sobel and Ornstein refer to this continual assault on our sensibilities as "medical terrorism," saying:

> The important point is that worrying too much about anything—be it calories, salt, cancer, or cholesterol—is bad for you, and that living optimistically, with pleasure, zest and commitment, is good. Medical terrorism shouldn't attack life's pleasures.[15]

To make matters worse, as we have seen in the above examples, the things that are labeled as healthy or unhealthy are constantly changing. So not only are people worried, but they are not sure what is or is not on the danger list from day to day. This contributes to a loss of credibility for us as health professionals. We are viewed as health fanatics who cannot make up our minds and are often just as anxious and confused as the people we are trying to help! Interestingly, epidemiologists themselves are aware of the significance of the problem, as is clearly demonstrated in this recent comment on his profession by a leading epidemiologist at Harvard.

> We are fast becoming a nuisance to society. . . . People don't take us seriously anymore, and when they do take us seriously, we may unintentionally do more harm than good.[16]

The Role of the Media

If researchers and health professionals have difficulty interpreting epidemiologic findings, it is not surprising that the media does as well. Reports in newspapers and magazines and on radio, television, and the Internet continually refer to cause and effect when the research is only suggesting associations. The media also have the added interest of selling their product, so studies that have a positive outcome, however small, are more likely to be reported to consumers. This has led to what epidemiologists refer to as an "unholy alliance" among epidemiology, the scientific journals, and the lay press. As Brian MacMahon, professor emeritus of epidemiology at Harvard, wrote in 1994:

> However cautiously the investigator may report his conclusions and stress the need for further evaluation, much of the press will pay little heed to such cautions. . . . By the time the information reaches the public mind, via print or screen, the tentative suggestion is likely to be interpreted as fact.[16]

Often the next step involves health professionals reading about these findings and recommending changes in lifestyle behaviors based on them. The unfortunate result is the atmosphere of anxiety referred to above.

Putting Epidemiology in Perspective

Health professionals must understand the difference between epidemiological (observational) and experimental (intervention-based)
research. They must also be clear about the distinction between correlation and cause. When interpreting epidemiologic studies, unless
consistent results are overwhelming and repeatedly demonstrated, we
should refrain from inferring causality. For example, cigarette smoking has been shown repeatedly to be associated with an increased
risk of lung cancer, sometimes by as much as 3,000 percent. All
types of studies have reached similar conclusions over the course of
many years and experimental research has established cigarette
smoke as containing potent carcinogens. Therefore, although there
will never be a randomized double-blind trial, it is appropriate to talk
about cigarettes as a cause of lung cancer.

The vast majority of epidemiological research is not nearly as
conclusive however. Most studies indicate increased risks in the
range of two or three times normal or even less. These should be
viewed with skepticism until they are replicated and supported by
experimental research. This is particularly true when other studies
don't support or, as we have seen, contradict the original findings.

Given the potential consequences of our actions, we must also
take great care in translating this research into recommendations for
lifestyle change. As the respected epidemiologist Gilbert Omenn
suggests in a recent article in the *Annual Review of Public Health:*

> We should be fastidious in referring strictly to "associations"
> when the studies have generated associations; we should reserve
> the terms *effects, reductions, decreases* and *protects* to studies
> that actually alter incidences of endpoints, preferably in a ran-
> domized, double-masked design.[4]

Many of the pitfalls discussed in this chapter could be avoided by
heeding Dr. Omenn's advice. In this context, it is certainly accurate
to say, for instance, that there appears to be an association (correlation or relationship) between fruit and vegetable intake and the inci-

dence of certain types of cancer—in this case a negative association because populations with a higher fruit intake have a lower incidence. However, until such time as we have experimental studies that provide evidence of causality it is not accurate to say that fruit decreases the incidence of or protects against these types of cancers. Perhaps even more importantly it is not appropriate to speak of some component of fruit (such as antioxidants) being responsible for the association and it is even less accurate to claim a causal relationship between the component and the incidence of disease.

As you read the journals in your respective fields and explore all the different health media, we believe you will see these mistakes being made on a daily basis. For the reasons discussed in this chapter, we believe it is critical for health professionals to avoid becoming entangled in these types of problems. Table 9.1 summarizes recommendations for more appropriate use of epidemiological research in health promotion.

Summary

We would like to emphasize that this chapter is not meant as an indictment of the field of epidemiology or of epidemiologists themselves. Epidemiological research has made tremendous contributions to public health in such areas as infectious diseases, environmental and workplace health concerns, the health impact of smoking, and so on. Epidemiologists are keenly aware of the difficulties in their field. In fact, much of the material for the discussions presented in this chapter originates in the recent epidemiological literature, where such concerns have been recognized and discussed by some of the leading researchers in the country. As health promotion professionals, we will be better able to help and less likely to do harm if we become more aware of the issues surrounding the use of epidemiological research.

TABLE 9.1. Evaluating Epidemiological Research

Major Issue	Recommendation
Study design	Distinguish between studies designed to generate hypotheses (observational) and studies designed to test or confirm them (experimental)
Correlation vs. Causation	A statistically significant correlation may or may not indicate that one variable causes another. It may be the case that both variables are related to a third variable that influences both. Or it may be a random coincidence in the numerical arrangement of the data.
Risk factors for disease	Do not confuse risk factors with causes of disease. They are not good predictors of who will and will not acquire a particular disease. An individual's disease is not necessarily a result of their risk factors and will not necessarily be prevented by their elimination.
Confounding Variables	Consider other plausible explanations for apparent associations. Did investigators consider, measure, and/or address these?
Statistical vs. practical significance	Statistical significance does not mean important, meaningful, or useful. It means only that the observed association is different from a zero correlation. Determine whether there is an important (meaningful) difference or change.
Risk ratios (RR)	Studies yielding RR (increased risk of disease associated with a particular variable) of 3 or less should be viewed with skepticism. The practical significance of such RRs can vary tremendously, depending on a variety of factors.
Study replication	Be wary of making recommendations for change on the basis of results from one or two studies. Evidence suggestive of causality requires replication of high-quality studies with many different samples.
Size of study and number and type of subjects	Beware if, for instance, results from a small study looking at diet and cholesterol in fifteen elderly black men are used to generate guidelines for an entire population of both men and women of all ages and races.
Review articles	Current review articles that have been well researched and summarized can provide a more balanced and reasoned view of current thinking and recommendations regarding particular risk associations.
Stakeholders	Check to see what the relationships are between the researchers and organizations that might have a vested interest in the outcome of the research.
Populations vs. Individuals	Results of population-based research are not meant to be directly applied to evaluation of or intervention with individuals.
Information vs. Meaning	People are meaning generating beings, not information-processing machines. Help people understand that, no matter what any study says, they must decide for themselves what a living "healthy life" means.

References

1.   *Dorland's Pocket Medical Dictionary,* Philadelphia: W. B. Saunders, 1982.

2.   Lotutu P. A., C. U. Chae, V. A. Ajani, C. H. Hennekens, and J. E. Manson. "Male Pattern Baldness and Coronary Heart Disease." *Archives of Internal Medicine* 160 (2000): 165–71.

3.   McCormick, J. "The Multifactorial Aetiology of Coronary Artery Disease: A Dangerous Delusion." *Perspectives in Biology and Medicine* 32, no. 1 (1988): 103–8.

4.   Omenn, G. S. "Chemoprevention of Lung Cancer: The Rise and Demise of Beta-Carotene." *Annual Review of Public Health* 19 (1998): 73–99.

5.   Fuchs, C. S., et al. "Dietary Fiber and the Risk of Colorectal Cancer and Adenoma in Women." *New England Journal of Medicine* 340, no. 3 (1999): 169–76.

6.   Hu, F. B., et al. "A Prospective Study of Egg Consumption and Risk of Cardiovascular Disease in Men and Women." *Journal of the American Medical Association* 281, no. 15 (1999): 1387–94.

7.   Pinckney, E. R., and C. Pickney. *The Cholesterol Controversy.* Los Angeles: Sherbourne, 1973.

8.   Hu, F. B., et al. "Dietary Fat Intake and the Risk of Coronary Heart Disease in Women." *New England Journal of Medicine* 337, no. 21 (1997): 1491–99.

9.   Holmes, M. D., et al. "Association of Dietary Intake of Fat and Fatty Acids with Risk of Breast Cancer." *Journal of the American Medical Association* 281, no. 10 (1999): 914–20.

10.   Appel, L. J., et al. "A Clinical Trial of the Effects of Dietary Patterns on Blood Pressure." *New England Journal of Medicine* 336, no. 16 (1997): 1117–24.

11.   Taubes, G. "The (Political) Science of Salt." *Science* 281 (1998): 898–907.

12.   Taubes, G. "Hypertension: A DASH of Data in the Salt Debate." *Science* 288 (2001): 1319–21.

13.   Barlow, C. E., H. W. Kohl, L. W. Gibbons, and S. N. Blair. "Physical Fitness, Mortality, and Obesity." *International Journal of Obesity* 19 (supp.4) (1995): S41–44.

14.   Writing Group for the Women's Health Initiative Investigators. "Risks and Benefits of Estrogen plus Progestin in Healthy Postmenopausal Women." *Journal of the American Medical Association* 288 (2002): 321–33.

15.   Ornstein, R., and D. Sobel. *Healthy Pleasures*. Reading, MA: Addison-Wesley, 1994.

16.   Taubes G. "Epidemiology Faces Its Limits." *Science* 269 (1995): 164–69.

Chapter 10

TO REWARD OR NOT TO REWARD

Questioning the Use of Behavior Modification

There's a time to admire the grace and persuasive power of an influential idea and there's a time to fear its hold over us. The time to worry
is when the idea is so widely shared that we no longer even notice
it. When objections are not even raised we are not in control. We do
not have the idea . . . it has us.

Alfie Kohn
Punished by Rewards

Criticizing the use of behavior modification in health promotion can
stir up a great deal of controversy. Yet few approaches traditionally
used in health promotion have such a high failure rate and are so bla-
tantly out of sync with the philosophy and thinking that underlie holistic health. Therefore, we want to be very clear in this chapter regarding two things.

1. Research and experience suggest that behavior modification
    techniques are successful in creating short-term change. How-
    ever, these techniques fail when it comes to long-term change,
    and they often lead to unintended and undesirable outcomes.

2. Behavior modification is inconsistent with the holistic views
    of health, illness, and healing discussed in this book. The use
    of behavior modification is more likely to interfere with rather
    than support the healing process.

This chapter will explore the origins of behavior modification techniques, what research and experience tell us about their use, and why

it is so important for health promotion to find alternatives to the traditional "b-mod" focus on behavioral control.[1]

A Widely Accepted Approach

Positive reinforcement through the use of rewards and incentives is widely accepted as an effective technique for promoting behavior change. It would, in fact, be difficult to overstate the extent to which this theory of human motivation has saturated our culture. From enticing children to behave by offering them extra TV time, desserts and toys to inducing students to learn with stickers, gold stars, and grades to rewarding employees with parking places, bonuses, and vacations, the "carrot and stick" approach to motivation is rarely questioned. Ironically, there is little research that supports the notion that rewarding people in this manner results in lasting behavior change and significant evidence that it may make things worse.

Nevertheless, health promotion programs, from smoking cessation classes to exercise and weight-loss competitions and work site initiatives for lowering blood pressure and cholesterol, have incorporated the use of rewards and incentives to help promote behavior change. It is therefore essential for health professionals to examine the use of this approach in terms of both effectiveness and its potential to cause harm.

Behavior Modification:

The Legacy of Skinner

B. F. Skinner developed his theory of human behavior, most accurately described as behavior modification or behaviorism, in the 1950s. At that time, Freudian psychology, which depicts all human problems as emanating from deep, unconscious urges, was the dominant theory of human behavior. Skinner developed a much simpler view. He believed that all human actions could be explained through the principle of "reinforcement." This is closely akin to what we commonly think of as reward. Skinner's theory states most basically that behaviors that are followed by rewards (positive consequences) are likely to be repeated. So, for instance, when the phone rings, we pick it up. The reason we pick it up is because we know someone will be there to talk with us. If every time the phone rings we pick it up and nobody is there, we will eventually stop picking up the phone. Thus, the behavior of answering the phone is reinforced by the consequence of human contact on the other end.

Skinner believed that *all human actions* were the result of this process. His theory states that human beings have essentially no free will. All of our actions are mindless "repertoires of behavior" that can be fully explained by the environmental consequences that followed them. It is not difficult to see the link between this theory of human behavior and the Cartesian worldview we spoke of earlier in the book. Skinner was perhaps the "ultimate Cartesian," for he took the concept of mind/body separation one step further, believing that "there is no place in the scientific analysis of behavior for a mind or self."[2]

Skinner was so confident in this theory of human behavior that he felt it explained even the most complicated human experiences. He described the evolution of love between two people as follows.

> One of them is nice to the other and predisposes the other to be nice to him and that makes him even more likely to be nice. It goes back and forth and it may reach the point at which they are very highly disposed to do nice things to the other and not to hurt and I suppose this is what would be called being in love.[3]

Hardly something you might choose to say to a loved one over a candlelight dinner! Another example is what Skinner had to say about the genius of Beethoven.

> Beethoven was someone who, when he was very young acquired all the available music at the time and then because of things that happened to him personally as accidents and variations, he introduced new things which paid off beautifully. So he went on doing them. He wrote because he was highly reinforced for writing.[3]

Skinnerian Behaviorism:
A Theory of *Human* Motivation?

It is important to note that Skinner did all of his experimental work on animals—rats, mice, and pigeons—and then extrapolated the results to humans. This was not a problem for Skinner and other behaviorists. In true Cartesian fashion, they believed that humans were just more sophisticated machines. And so from Skinner's animal studies we have inherited one of the most widely accepted theories of *human* motivation.

The bottom line for behaviorism in terms of explaining human motivation can be summed up as "do this and you'll get that." Take a minute and think about all of the different areas of our culture this has infiltrated. In our schools—do this work and you'll get a good grade (don't do this work and you'll get a bad grade). At home with our children—if you clean up your room five days this week you can go to the zoo on Saturday or if you eat your broccoli you can have some ice cream. At the workplace—if you produce this you'll get paid that. What does the research say about the effectiveness of this approach?

Research on Behavior Modification:

Does It Work?

Given the widespread use of this approach, it is perhaps surprising that there is so little evidence of its effectiveness for promoting long-term, positive behavior change. In fact, scores of studies show that the use of rewards and incentives often has the opposite of the intended effect with both children and adults. In his groundbreaking book *Punished by Rewards,* Alfie Kohn explores this research in detail.[4] We strongly recommend that all health professionals read this material, as we will touch on just a few representative studies here.

- Children who are rewarded for tasks such as drawing lose interest in these tasks over time compared to children who are not rewarded.[5] These children also do more poorly on the tasks even when they are able to pick rewards they like.[6] They are also less likely to find certain foods appealing over time if they are paid to eat or drink them.[7]

- Adults performing tasks for reward, especially tasks in which there is creativity involved, such as storytelling or collage making, may produce more, but it is always less creative.[8] Adults offered rewards for performing boring tasks have more negative evaluations of the tasks.[9]

- Sixth-grade girls who were promised free movie tickets for tutoring younger girls in how to play a new game got frustrated more easily, took longer to get the job done, and ended up with pupils who understood the game more poorly than those who were taught by tutors who were not promised anything.[10]

- Children who love to draw with felt-tip markers and pastel crayons show diminished enjoyment of both if doing one is made a prerequisite for doing the other.[11] They are also less likely to choose a snack food previously given to them as a reward for finishing another snack food, even though the two foods were rated as equally appealing before the experiment.[12]

Reflecting on this information, it is interesting to think about the common practice of cajoling our children to finish their broccoli (or other vegetables) by offering ice cream (or other sweets) as a reward. The research suggests that this practice will most likely lead to a decreased preference for broccoli and an increased preference for ice cream!

As we will discuss later in the book, children have an innate ability to choose and eat a variety of foods without being pressured to do so. The bigger issue is, however, that attempting to externally control human behaviors usually ends up being unsuccessful and often creates additional problems.

Pizza for Reading: Who's Fooling Whom?

In recent years, children around the country have been involved in school programs that use pizza as a reward for reading books. As might be expected, children who are going to be rewarded do read more books. However, on closer inspection the books they read tend to be easier and shorter than those read by children not rewarded for reading. This should not come as a surprise. If you were rewarded for the number of books you read, your first choice would probably not be *War and Peace!* What is even more disturbing about this practice, however, is that the rewarded children also remember less about what they read. The reward, not the enjoyment of reading and learning, becomes the central purpose of the activity.

Behavioral techniques such as rewards and incentives do produce results. The critical question is what kinds of results do they produce? In *Punished by Rewards,* Kohn summarizes the answer succinctly and powerfully.

> If your objective is to get people to obey an order, show up on time and do what they are told, then bribing or threatening them may be sensible strategies. But if your objective is to get long-term quality in the work place, to help students become more careful thinkers and self-directed learners, or to support children in developing good values, then rewards like punishments are absolutely useless.[4]

As Kohn's research indicates, it is likely that these approaches are more than useless. There is substantial evidence that rewarding people in this manner retards learning, suppresses creativity, inhibits productivity, and reduces intrinsic motivation. Yet, the Skinnerian approach to motivation is rarely questioned. Now, let's see how this applies to health promotion.

Behavior Modification in Health Promotion:

Assessing the Damage

Due to widespread cultural acceptance of behaviorism it is not surprising that health promotion has fully embraced the use of behavior modification strategies. Very often these approaches may be called something different. Health professionals may refer to social cognitive theory, relapse prevention, stages of change theory, and so on. There is an old saying that goes "if it walks like a duck and quacks like a duck, it is probably a duck." The reality is that most of these theoretical models include behavioral techniques as an important component of their change strategies. Interventions incorporating these theories therefore often rely heavily on Skinnerian motivational techniques to achieve the desired ends. As an example, social cognitive theory, perhaps the most widely used theory in health promotion, teaches that "the frequency and durability of a given behavior depends on how the prevailing contingencies of reinforcement are structured."[13]

The use of behavior modification techniques in health promotion is ubiquitous. In fact, a recent national benchmarking study of work site health promotion programs revealed that most "use some sort of incentive program, especially for joining (81%) or successfully completing a behavior change (62%)."[15] As a leader in the field recently wrote:

> Incentives are one of the ten major strategies for maximizing program participation. They are likely to be a permanent fixture in the technology of health promotion.[16]

No matter what they are called, these are all forms of behaviorism. What are the specific problems associated with the use of these strategies in health promotion?

What about Stages of Change?

Many health professionals tell us they agree that behavior modification creates its own problems and is generally ineffective in the long run. They then go on to say that they use stages of change instead. Unfortunately, this is really just an elaborate application of behavior modification. In the transtheoretical model (stages of change) individuals in the action and maintenance stages use contingency management, stimulus control, contracting, and so on as the primary tools for effecting change.[14] These tools are all drawn directly from behavior modification as envisioned by Skinner. For all of the reasons already detailed in this chapter, stages of change is just as incompatible with a holistic approach.

Outcomes versus Behaviors

Health professionals frequently use positive reinforcement in a manner in which even Skinner would have disapproved. In doing so, not only have we failed to help people achieve desired behavior changes, but we have often creating additional problems as well. In health promotion, the most frequent example of this occurs when we reward outcomes rather than behaviors.

Weight loss programs are a prime example. Rewarding people for losing weight does result in short-term weight loss for many individuals. How will people lose weight in these programs? The best answer is *any way they can*. In fact, the methods participants will use are likely to be those that are least desired, such as restricting eating, skipping meals, taking laxatives, and exercising excessively.[17] As health professionals we certainly do not want to reinforce these types of behaviors and yet that is precisely what happens when we reinforce outcomes rather than behaviors. A person's weight is an outcome, not a behavior, and is determined by a complicated interaction among behavior, genetics, and other factors. Therefore, we believe that weight loss programs, that are by nature always behaviorally based are inappropriate for everyone. (This is an issue we will discuss at great length in chapters 15–17.)

Rewarding employees for lowering their blood pressure or cholesterol as part of a worksite competition or risk-rated insurance plan is another example of the same mistake. As with weight loss, these changes are outcomes, not behaviors. Unless you are an accomplished yogi it is unlikely that you can go to the corner and lower your blood pressure. Because such outcomes are the result of a complicated interaction among many variables over time, individuals will have different responses to similar interventions. (Remember that 90 percent of high blood pressure is *essential*—meaning that we have no explanation for why it exists. Regarding cholesterol, many people can drastically change their diet and still see no reduction in their blood values.) For employees who fail to reduce their blood pressure or cholesterol with a particular intervention, the result is likely to be anger, resentment, and shame, contributing to a *less* healthy workplace.

Health outcomes such as weight, blood pressure, and cholesterol are often strongly influenced by genetic, social, cultural and environmental conditions not directly controllable by the individual. In such instances, the use of rewards and risk-rating techniques often results in "systematized lifestyle discrimination . . . under the guise of incentives that encourage health improvement and individual responsibility."[18] In fact, The Health Insurance Portability and Accountability Act passed by Congress in 1996 puts rather strict limitations on the use of incentives for changing health-status-related factors such as cholesterol, blood pressure, and weight. Although many health professionals are unaware of this, all health promotion programs were required to be in compliance with these new regulations by April of 2003.[19]

Initial Change versus Maintenance

Behaviorally oriented health promotion programs do help some people initially to lower their cholesterol, start exercising, or stop smoking. However, even when behavioral principles are used as intended by Skinner, the evidence that these programs result in long-term change is sparse. Thus, a recent benchmarking review of the best three hundred work site health promotion programs concluded that "While short term gains in attitudes and behavior are common, there is little evidence that these changes last after programs end."[20] Skinner was well aware of this phenomenon, which he called extinction.

145

As he described it, "removal of a reinforcer results in the disappearance of the behavior that was originally reinforced."

Once again we would like to emphasize our message. Initial compliance to new health behaviors will almost certainly increase with the implementation of behavior modification approaches. However, once the reinforcements are removed the frequency of these new behaviors will diminish. It works this way with mice, rats, pigeons, and, not surprisingly, humans.

Internal versus External Motivation

It is commonly argued by health promoters that, while not a good long-term fix, the use of rewards and incentives (often called external motivation) is advantageous for buying time until the development of more internal motivations can occur. Thus, the use of rewards and incentives in health promotion programs is said to lead to increased participation and adherence, which in turn lead to improvements in health, fitness, and self-esteem and then contribute to increased internal motivation to continue the desired behavior. This argument is often portrayed as a proven scientific fact in the health promotion literature. According to one study, "people take four to six weeks to get over the initial discomfort both physical and psychological and begin to see positive changes in their stamina, waistline and mental outlook. Incentives bridge the gap between starting a program and feeling good."[21]

Ironically, the lack of success of these types of interventions is well documented: generally a six-month dropout rate of 50 percent in exercise programs and a long-term failure rate of greater than 95 percent in weight loss programs. Despite the fact that some people do lose weight or increase their activity initially, most do not maintain these new lifestyle changes in the long term.

While these high failure rates may seem curious on first inspection, they are not surprising given the literature on external and internal motivation that we have mentioned. Contrary to the prevailing wisdom in health promotion and elsewhere, numerous studies with both adults and children have clearly demonstrated that the use of external motivation does not lead to increased internal motivation.[32] In fact, the research demonstrates that:

People's interest in what they are doing typically declines when they are rewarded for doing it. Rewards actually undermine the intrinsic motivation that promotes optimal performance.[4]

Thus, it appears that external motivators may be detrimental because "intrinsic motivation occurs without external prods, controls, rewards, and in fact, is often undermined by their presence."[23] This may help to explain the limited effectiveness of behavior change programs in health promotion. It also brings up an additional intriguing and potentially unsettling possibility. Could the high dropout and recidivism rates seen in many health promotion programs actually be related to decreased internal motivation as a result of the use of the interventions based on external motivation techniques? Although more research is needed to answer this question, results from a recent large smoking cessation intervention give us a glimpse of the possible answer. In this study, individuals who were offered prizes for turning in weekly progress reports were twice as likely to turn in the first week's report. However, after three months they were more likely to have relapsed than were those who were not rewarded, and saliva samples showed that they were also twice as likely to have lied about quitting.[24]

Behavior Modification Interferes with Healing

Applying rewards and incentives is a simple way to "get people" to behave differently for a little while. These behavioral approaches, however, fail to help a person understand and explore how addictive, compulsive behaviors (smoking, drinking, and emotional eating, for example) are symptoms of underlying emotional and spiritual struggle. In order to work with people holistically, it is important to consider the following.

- "Unhealthy behaviors" are not the enemy. Like illness, they often manifest themselves due to underlying emotional or spiritual disturbances. These addictive, compulsive behaviors are very compelling and difficult to change because they so effectively sooth or distract us from more significant and often unbearably painful life struggles.

- When we teach people to place all their focus on "control" of their symptomatic behaviors, we rob them of the opportunity to learn from these behaviors. Every ounce of their consciousness goes into staying in control: avoiding certain foods, staying away from cigarettes, sticking to a regimented exercise program. This process of avoidance and rigidity leaves a person with no energy to explore the underlying causes of their behavior.

- Our most beneficial role as health professionals is to compassionately help people to unlock the information embedded in a behavioral struggle. When did this behavior become a problem? What thoughts, feelings, or events precede the need to pick up a cigarette, emotional eating, or spending money compulsively? How does this behavior serve us? Does it keep us company when we are lonely, soothe us when we are angry about our marriage, distract us when we feel unhappy at work? What would have to change in our lives for us to no longer need this behavior in this way?

- Everyone reaches out to addictive behaviors at some point in their lives. We have all used one (and often more than one) behavior at some time to cope with the distresses and emotional hurts we have picked up over the course of our lives. For each of us, there is always opportunity in understanding and "dancing with" these behaviors when they appear. Working *with* these behaviors instead of suppressing or controlling them, or shaming ourselves for them, helps each of us figure out what we need to be happy. When we are happy, the need for addictive, "unhealthy" behaviors diminishes of its own accord.

It is extremely important to understand that many behaviors in a person's life can be addictive or compulsive. Some, such as emotional eating, smoking, drinking excessively, drug use, raging, and even being chronically sedentary, are discouraged by our society. Other addictive behaviors, on the other hand, are accepted or even encouraged. People are rarely chastised for dieting obsessively, exercising rigidly, working endlessly, or spending too much money. However, any behavior that becomes driven and rigid in a person's life can become a serious problem.

What about Twelve-Step Programs?

Twelve-step programs have saved many lives, especially those of people with severe drug or alcohol addictions. There are, however, some problems that arise when using the twelve-step approach in conjunction with Holistic Health Promotion. Our concerns include the following.

1. Abstinence Isn't Always Possible. Twelve-step programs are based on an abstinence philosophy. Participants in twelve-step groups (such as Alcoholics Anonymous) have access to a mentor, group support/meetings, and specific strategies to help them avoid addictive substances or behaviors that are causing their lives to spin out of control. While abstinence can make sense in the case of drinking and alcohol, it does not make sense in relation to food and eating. Drinking alcohol is not needed for a healthy life. Therefore, abstaining completely from ingesting alcohol is possible for many alcoholics. Abstinence in relation to food, however, is clearly a problem. We obviously need food to live, and a relaxed, normalized relationship with food is important for health (see chapters 15 through 17). We cannot nourish ourselves and develop this type of healthy eating through abstinence. For this reason we feel it is very important to explore alternatives to twelve-step-based eating programs such as Overeaters Anonymous and any other programs that promote dietary restriction or abstinence from certain foods.

2. ***People with Addictions Are Not "Flawed."*** There is a subtle in-
ference in twelve-step programs that people with addictions are
somehow flawed and must rely on a higher power, "one day at a
time," to overcome their problems. While we acknowledge that
all people are imperfect, the Holistic Health Promotion philosophy, as detailed earlier in the book, assumes that we are all basically good and inherently whole, and that we naturally seek
health. Each of us has the most critical of resources *within us* to
create a successful path for our own healing. This holistic assumption is potentially in contrast to the message of twelve-step
programs.

3. ***People Can Get Addicted to Twelve-Step Programs!*** Many
twelve-step program participants successfully stop using alcohol
or drugs. Some, however, may become overly reliant on the program and its people and meetings. This type of rigid participation
allows the person to successfully avoid alcohol, but it also enables them to avoid addressing the pain and issues that lie beneath the addiction. Remember that any addiction, whether it is
seen positively or negatively by society, distracts a person from
the most significant issues of his or her life and therefore diminishes healing. Being addicted to a twelve-step program is certainly better than being addicted to alcohol, but people need encouragement and resources to heal even this addiction.

We feel that twelve-step programs can be life-saving for people who
struggle with behaviors that are not naturally part of daily healthy
life such as taking drugs or drinking alcohol. These programs can
promote wisdom and growth when practiced in an authentic, conscious manner. However, just like anything else – therapy, religion,
etc – when used as dogma, they can become simplistic, rigid, and
interfere with true healing.

For further exploration of this and other issues surrounding addiction we suggest reading *The Truth about Addiction and Recovery,*
by Peele and Brodsky.[25]

Summary

A substantial body of literature documents the failure of behavioral interventions in a wide variety of areas. While there is no question that rewards and incentives increase initial compliance with new health behaviors, the overwhelming evidence tells us that these approaches invariably fail in the long term. More disturbing is the way behavioral strategies in health promotion distract us from knowing and addressing the underlying life struggles that lie beneath our "unhealthy" behaviors. For all of the reasons we have discussed in this chapter, we believe that it is best to find other ways of helping people to change their lives for the better, for the healthier.

We do, however, want to acknowledge the difficulty involved in considering the possibility of eliminating behavior modification approaches in a culture in which they are so widely accepted. We need to remember that it is not surprising, given the seventeenth-century legacy that we have inherited, that health promotion would choose as its major form of motivation an approach based on the need to control human "nature." We will discuss alternatives to this approach in detail in the last section of the book. For those who do not feel ready to eliminate traditional behavioral approaches altogether, we will also include suggestions on how to modify existing programs so as to minimize the potential for damage

References

We would like to give special thanks to Alfie Kohn for spending his life helping people to understand the ineffectiveness and dangers of Skinnerian behaviorism in all its forms. Our work in this chapter is based largely on his book *Punished by Rewards* and *No Contest,* which we strongly recommend to all health professionals (and parents as well).

1.   Robison, J. I. "Questioning the Wisdom of Using External Reinforcement in Health Promotion Programs." *American Journal of Health Promotion* 13, no. 1 (1998): 1–3.

2.   Skinner, B. F. "Can Psychology Be a Science of Mind?" *American Psychologist* 45 (1990): 1209.

3.   Skinner, B. F. *Walden Two.* New York: Macmillan, 1948.

4.   Kohn, A. *Punished by Rewards: The Trouble with Gold Stars, Incentive Plans, A's, Praise, and Other Bribes.* Boston: Houghton Mifflin, 1993.

5.   Lepper, M. R., D. Greene, and R. E. Nisbett. "Undermining Children's Intrinsic Interest with Extrinsic Reward: A Test of the Overjustification Hypothesis." *Journal of Personality and Social Psychology* 28, no. 1 (1973): 129–37.

6.   McCullers, J. C., and Martin J. A. Gardiner. "A Reexamination of the Role of Incentive in Children's Discriminative Learning." *Child Development* 42 (1971): 827–37.

7.   Birch, L.L., D.W. Marlin and J. Rotter. "Eating as the 'Means' Activity in a Contingency: Effect on Young Children's Food Preference." *Child Development* 55 (1984): 431–39.

8.   Amabile T. M., B. A. Hennessey, and B. S. Grossman. "Social Influences on Creativity: The Effects of Contracted-for Reward." *Journal of Personality and Social Psychology* 50, no. 1 (1986): 14–22.

9.   Freedman, J. L. "Attitudinal Effects of Inadequate Justification." *Journal of Personality* 31 (1963): 371–85.

10.   Garbarino, J. "The Impacy of Anticipated Reward upon Cross-Age Tutoring." *Journal of Personality and Social Psychology* 32 (1975): 421–28.

11.   Lepper, M. R., G. Sagotsky, J. L. Dafoe, and D. Greene. "Consequences of Superfluous Social Constraints: Effects on Young Children's Subsequent Intrinsic Interest." *Journal of Personality and Social Psychology* 42 (1982): 51–65.

12.   Newman J., and A. Taylor. "Effect of a Means-End Contingency on Young Children's Food Preferences." *Journal of Experimental Child Psychology* 64 (1992): 200–216.

13.   Bandura A. *Social Learning Theory.* Englewood Cliffs, NJ: Prentice-Hall, 1977.

14.   Prochaska, J.O., and W. F. Velicer. "The Transtheoretical Model of Behavior Change." *American Journal of Health Promotion* 12, no. 1 (1997): 38–48.

15.   O'Donnell, M. P., C. A. Bishop, and K. L. Kaplan. "Benchmarking Best Practices in Workplace Health Promotion." *American Journal of Health Promotion: The Art of Health Promotion* 1, no. 1 (1997): 1–8.

16.   Chapman, L. S. "What Newer Forms of Health Management Technology Can Be Used in Programming?" *American Journal of Health Promotion: The Art of Health Promotion* 1, no. 4 (1997): 1–6.

17.   O'Banion, D. R., and D. L. Whaley. *Behavior Contracting: Arranging Contingencies of Reinforcement.* New York: Springer, 1981.

18.   Terry P. "Health Promotion, Demand Management and Social Justice: Three Ships Passing or a Powerful Flotilla?" *Association for Worksite Health Promotion's Worksite Health* (fall 1996): 8–15.

19.   Chapman L., and J. McKneight. "Impact of HIPAA on Health Promotion." *The Art of Health Promotion* 6, no. 2 (2002): 1–10.

20.   O'Donnell, M. P. "Health Impact of Workplace Health Promotion Programs and Methodologic Quality of the Research Literature." *American Journal of Health Promotion: The Art of Health Promotion* 1, no. 3 (1997): 5.

21.   Witherspoon, D. "What I've Learned about Using Incentives in Worksite Health Promotion Programs." *The Art of Health Promotion: The Role of Incentives in Health Promotion* 2, no. 3 (1998): 7.

22.   Deci, D. L., and R. M. Ryan. *Intrinsic Motivation and Self-Determination in Human Behavior.* New York: Plenum, 1985.

23.   Ryan, R. M., and J. Stiller. "The Social Contexts of Internalization: Parent and Teacher Influence on Autonomy, Motivation, and Learning." *Advances in Motivation and Achievement* 7 (1991): 120.

24.   Curry, S. J., and E. H. Wagner. "Evaluation of Intrinsic and Extrinsic Motivation Interventions with a Self-Help Smoking Cessation Program." *Journal of Consulting and Clinical Psychology* 59, no. 2 (1991): 318–24.

25.   Peele, S., and A. Brodsky. *The Truth about Addiction and Recovery.* New York: Simon and Schuster, 1991.

Chapter 11

TRADITIONAL HEALTH PROMOTION
Disease Focus, Fear, and External Control

How can people who are able to be controlled by other people be
called healthy? By definition, these controlled people are, in fact,
unhealthy. . .. They are likely to be conformists and easily swayed
by others towards unhealthy behaviors, just as they are easily
swayed by health educators towards healthy behaviors.

Jerrold Greenberg
Health Education

Worldview
Mechanistic
(nature as machine)

↓

Science
Reductionist
(whole equals the sum
of its parts)

↓

Culture
Dominator
(patriarchal)

↓

Medicine
Biomedical
(fix the machine)

↓

**Traditional Health
Promotion**

The Traditional Approach

The mechanistic worldview and reductionist
science of the seventeenth century formed the
foundation for the biomedical model of medicine. The biomedical model then led directly
to the fields of psychiatry and psychology,
and more recently to the field of health promotion. Traditionally, health promotion professionals have prided themselves on being
more progressive and prevention focused than
workers in these other fields (medicine, psychiatry, and psychology are considered very
crisis and treatment oriented). In reality,
however, health promotion mirrors all the
same values, beliefs and definitions that trick-
led down from the Scientific Revolution to
these other health-related professions.

155

In this chapter we will take an in-depth look at the traditional model of health promotion, its goals, its underlying assumptions and the role of professionals working from this still very biomedically based approach. While the traditional model for health promotion is based on thinking that is almost four hundred years old, it is still the dominant model found in the majority of today's corporate, hospital, community, and academic programs.

Figure 11.1 outlines the underlying assumptions and primary components of the traditional, biomedically-oriented model of health promotion. The information therein is discussed in more detail in the remaining portions of this chapter.

Focus

Disease. Main objective is to identify and eliminate biomedical risk factors for physical disease.

Emphasis

"Unhealthy" Behaviors. Poor individual lifestyle choices are considered the primary determinants of sickness and disease.

Motivation

Fear. Reason for change is primarily to prevent disease and premature death.

Primary Assumption

"Bad" Human Nature. Left to their own devices people will naturally gravitate towards "unhealthy" behaviors.

Professional Role

Expert. Primary job is to uncover unhealthy behaviors and recommend alternative, healthier behaviors.

Change Process

Controlling Behavior. Behavior change techniques are used to suppress or eliminate targeted behaviors.

Figure 11.1. Traditional health promotion

Focus: Disease

It makes perfect sense that the emphasis in health promotion, evolving out of disease-focused, biomedical science has been primarily on disease and not on health. Take a typical traditional "health fair" for example. We check for high blood pressure, elevated cholesterol, diabetes, and so on. It would probably be more accurate to call these "disease fairs!" Similarly, our traditional "health risk" assessments more accurately fall into the category of "disease risk" assessments. Most of what we do in health promotion is concerned with discovering and/or preventing physical disease. People's issues and struggles tend to be viewed as medical problems—a conceptualization referred to as "medicalization."

Medicalization is a process by which nonmedical problems, often involving things that we don't understand or like, become defined and treated as medical problems, usually in terms of diseases and disorders.[2] A good recent example of this is the labeling of obesity as a chronic disease. According to present guidelines 55 percent of the U.S. population now has the chronic disease of obesity. By the year 2030, according to a leading obesity expert, 100 percent of us will have this disease![3] In chapter 15 we will discuss in detail the tremendous harm being caused by the medicalization of obesity.

As another example, the state of Michigan recently had a year-long focus on women's health. As part of this event, the following public service announcement was read over the radio by the wife of the governor.

> We salute our heroes. Our mothers, grandmothers, sisters and daughters, every woman who has ever overcome heart disease, cancer, osteoporosis, menopause, and depression. Survivors remind us to take care of ourselves and make lifestyle choices that can protect us from disease.[4]

As the old saying goes, "What is wrong with this picture?" Since when did menopause become a disease from which women must be saved? In addition to the problem of medicalization this is another example of an Epoch II, patriarchal science attempting to overcome and control a feminine nature. By now this repeated scenario probably doesn't come as a surprise to anyone. It is also important to take notice of the terminology used in traditional, biomedical health promotion. It is no coincidence that terms like *aggression, war, overcoming, killing,* and *destroying* are most often used to describe our relationship with illness. Disease is believed to be an enemy that must be controlled and destroyed.

Emphasis: "Unhealthy" Behaviors

In traditional health promotion, disease or illness is seen primarily as a result of individual lifestyle choices. Heart disease happens because we don't exercise and we eat too much fat. Cancer is a result of not eating our fruits and vegetables. Determining the "health" of individuals and intervening to improve that health are accomplished largely by identifying and attempting to eliminate the "risk factors" and "risk-related behaviors" that lead to disease. Below is a list of the major targets of most traditional "health promotion" interventions.

blood pressure	cholesterol	HDL, LDL
cholesterol ratio	blood glucose	triglycerides
smoking, drinking	abdominal strength	cardiovascular fitness
upper body strength	flexibility	back care
body weight	waist/hip ratio	percentage of body fat
fat, salt, sugar, fiber		

The majority of these are physical risk factors for disease that can be easily measured and quantified. Given our understanding of the origins of our field, this should not come as a surprise. These are all things that exist in the "measurable" universe. We have already discussed in detail, however, the limitations and pitfalls of epidemiological research and the inability of risk factors to be predictive of who will and will not get a particular disease. We also have explored the negative consequences of applying this type of research to individuals when it really pertains to populations.

Additionally this reductionist approach fails to account for the social, ecological context of the individual. Yet an abundance of solid research over many years tells us that "social forces such as housing, employment, income and education are the most telling predictors of poor health."[6] Interestingly, this reductionist focus on the unhealthy behavior of the individual as the "cause" of his or her health or lack of health is not limited to biomedical approaches. So-called alternative and complementary approaches to health often fall into this trap as well. While biomedical approaches may suggest that people get a disease because they don't exercise or eat right, alternative/complementary approaches may give the message that people contract their illnesses because they don't think positively or meditate enough. As we explore newer understandings of the nature of health and illness, we will see that this type of approach is neither helpful nor scientifically defensible.

Motivation: Fear

Once we have identified the risk factors, the next step in traditional health promotion is to attempt to "motivate" people to change. As we see in the public service announcement in the box on the next page, the way we usually try to accomplish this is by scaring people about their current habits. "If you don't *stop doing this* you are going to get this disease and die. If you don't *start doing this* you are going to get this disease and die." Thus, the primary motivation for change is fear of disease and death. Unfortunately, there is little evidence that fear is a good long-term motivator for health behavior change. As Dr. Judd Allen has commented:

> It has been common practice to describe the disease which might result from a health risk behavior in order to frighten the client into changing his or her behavior. Unfortunately, this method has not led to the intended result and it has been linked to actual increases in the health risk behavior which was the target of the effort.[6]

Our collective experience certainly reinforces the finding that fear is a poor motivator for health behavior change. After all, if fear was a good motivator, everybody in this country would be eating healthy and exercising and nobody would be smoking!

When fear does not work, well-meaning health promotion efforts have often resorted to shame and guilt. "You still smoke? What's the matter with you? Haven't you heard how bad it is for your health?" or "You don't exercise? Didn't you see the Surgeon General's Report? Don't you know how good it is for your health?"

Interestingly, we have also discussed how attempts by health professionals to motivate people to change using rewards, incentives, contests, and so on, not only appear to be mostly unsuccessful but also can lead to unwanted consequences. Both experience and a good deal of research suggest that successful motivation comes mostly from the inside and not from the outside through fear, guilt, shame, or reward.

Helping People to Be Healthier . . . by Scaring Them to Death?

The following public service announcement from the National Heart, Lung and Blood Institute (although it truly could be from almost any of the major health organizations in this country) serves as an excellent example of traditional health promotion approaches.

Public Service Announcement:
Working Together to Lower High Blood Pressure
It'll be a warm sunny afternoon at the stadium; the skies are just screaming blue. The beer man is flying up and down the stairs, the crowd is wild 'cause everybody's favorite guy is up to bat, up to knocking his umpteenth career homer. The pitch comes, you hear a big loud smack as the ball sails away over that silly embarrassed pitcher, way over left field, high into the sky section, and look, it's headed right to your seat. You heard me, your seat. But you know what, you quit treating your blood pressure so you had a stroke and you're dead. And somebody else is in your seat screaming and jumping and waving their glove and guess what, that bozo got your ball. Don't lose a minute of life. Exercise, eat right, cut the salt, treat your high blood pressure. For more information, call . . .

As we read this announcement to groups of health professionals around the country we usually get a twofold response. The first is some gentle laughing, as the silliness of the story tickles some of their "funny bones." At the same time, however, we almost always feel and very often see people wincing or cringing as they read below the humor to the focus of the message. When we ask people to comment on the message, they generally say that they don't believe it is a particularly effective communication. In addition, usually at least a few say they are offended by the overt effort to force people to do something by scaring them in this fashion.

Primary Assumption: "Bad" Human Nature

In traditional health promotion, the primary assumption about human nature is that left to their own devices people will naturally gravitate toward "unhealthy" behaviors. The belief is that without a myriad of rules and guidelines and ongoing expert supervision people are likely to come home from work and do nothing but drink, smoke, eat junk food, and lay around watching TV. It is believed that our naturally self-destructive human nature thus needs to be controlled from the outside. As an example, here is a call to action for exercise professionals regarding the "war on obesity" from the recent cover of a widely distributed business magazine for health clubs.

> Conservative estimates claim that one in five Americans is obese. What are you going to do about it?[7]

A similar sentiment is echoed in this quotation from a leading expert in the field regarding the proper use of incentives in the behavior change process.

> Incentives can jar the attention of someone in precontemplation and force them to at least think about improving their health.[8]

The purpose of these examples is not to pass judgment on anyone or to question their helpful intentions. If we remember the statement from seventeenth-century worldview architect Sir Francis Bacon about the purpose of science being to control nature (so it can be squeezed and molded), we can begin to understand why these types of approaches are so widely accepted and deeply entrenched in the health professions.

Professional Role: Expert

In traditional health promotion the client is seen basically as a passive recipient of guidelines and information. Just as with physicians under the biomedical model, our role is to "fix" our clients before they contract a disease and die prematurely. As health educators and promoters we arrive in the nick of time to police "unhealthy" behaviors and prescribe changes to save people from themselves.

This is not to say that all health professionals adhere strictly to this type of approach. Many, through years of experience with people, have moved away from this type of relationship. However, despite the well-meaning intentions of most health professionals, by and large this philosophy and strategic approach remain at the heart of health promotion.

One of the reasons why the traditional health promotion approach is so problematic is that interventions on both the individual and population levels often end up being driven more by what "expert" professionals think rather than what clients believe is important. For example, as part of a survey in the state of Michigan some years ago researchers asked people what they thought were the most significant factors contributing to poor health in their community. They presented participants with a list of factors and asked them to rate how big a risk each was. The results from the survey are given below. (The percentages indicate the number of people who thought that each factor was one of the top three contributors to poor health in their community.)

Community Health Concerns

Drug abuse	47%
Alcohol abuse	34%
Violence	31%
Drinking and driving	28%
Poor parenting	23%
No health insurance	21%
Poverty	19%
Tobacco use	13%
Teenage pregnancy	12%
Homelessness	9%
Poor diet/lack activity	7%
Emotional problems	5%
Serious mental illness	4%

As you can see, drug and alcohol abuse, violence, drunk driving and poor parenting were among the top concerns in most people's minds. Traditional risk factors such as poor diet and lack of physical activity were much farther down the list—only 7 percent of those interviewed saw them as among the most pressing problems. Community members seemed to be sending a clear and powerful message about their major health concerns. Unfortunately, the health professionals conducting the survey already had their "expert" opinions about what the health risks were. This can be clearly seen in their evaluation of the data.

> Personal health issues such as diet and exercise and smoking are not connected to community health in many people's minds suggesting to health professionals a need for education about the implications to the community.[9]

So the experts asked for the participants' input and then proceeded to disregard it in favor of what they already "knew" to be true. Instead of following up on the real concerns of those questioned, interventions would likely fall back on the old standbys: another billboard telling people how good exercise is for them or another brochure telling them how they can prevent cancer by eating five fruits and vegetables a day.

Change Process: Controlling Behavior

Once we've scared people enough to get their attention we are ready to implement behavioral control so that we can "get them to change" their "unhealthy" behaviors. As previously described in detail in chapter 10, however, there are significant negative consequences associated with this approach.

Remember that the behavior modification approach to change follows naturally from the mechanistic, control-oriented worldview and as such is deeply embedded in all aspects of our culture. With relation to health promotion, this concept is well illustrated by Glanz, Lewis, and Rimer in their widely acclaimed textbook *Health Behavior and Health Education: Theory, Research and Practice* when they write that:

As science and technology advance, the least conquered force of nature remains the human being and his actions and human experiences.[10]

Just as modern medicine has developed treatments to control and conquer infectious disease, it has become the major thrust of health promotion to develop strategies to control and conquer human behavior. We use exercise "prescriptions," stress management "plans," and nutrition "guidelines" to externally direct people's behavior. This teaches people to look outside rather than inside to find out what being healthy really means to them.

Also following the seventeenth-century worldview, lifestyle change and behavioral control are viewed as linear processes. Like a line of dominoes in which each one knocks down the next, the human experience is simplified into something that happens, that causes something else to happen, that causes something else to happen. It is thought that unhealthy behaviors lead to risk factors that lead to disease, and that changing these behaviors reduces risk factors and prevents disease. Furthermore, according to traditional health promotion, all of these "somethings" must be measurable because otherwise they would be of little consequence.

Summary

It should come as no surprise to learn that traditional health promotion efforts do not serve society's needs as we move into Epoch III humanity. These programs are based on Epoch II dominator values and thinking that comes from seventeenth-century reductionist, mechanistic science. In fact, all of the traditional model's assumptions run directly parallel to the outdated ideas that continue to dominate traditional biomedical approaches to health and the process of change.

The failures of the traditional health promotion model are in no way due to a lack of desire, effort or compassion on the part of health promotion professionals. We have merely been doing what we were trained to do—and it is hard to give up something that has been in place for four hundred years!

Let us now turn our attention to an exciting alternative to traditional health promotion. In the next chapter we will introduce this approach, which we call Holistic Health Promotion.

References

1. Robison J. I., and K. Carrier. "Reinventing Health Promotion: Moving from Biomedical, Risk-Factor Control to Holistic Health and Healing." *Wellness Management: Newsletter of the National Wellness Association* (spring 1998): 1, 8–9.

2. Sobal, J. "The Medicalization and Demedicalization of Obesity." In Donna Mauer and Jeffery Sobal, eds., *Eating Agendas: Food and Nutrition as Social Problems.* Hawthorne, NY: Aldine de Gruyter, 1995.

3. Foreyt, J. "An Etiologic Approach to Obesity." *Hospital Practice,* August 15, 1997, 123–48.

4. Michigan Department of Community Health. *"Michigan's Year of Women's Health."* Introduction by Michelle Engler. 1997. Radio script.

5. Terry P. "Health Promotion, Demand Management, and Social Justice: Three Ships Passing or a Powerful Flotilla?" *AWHP'S Worksite Health* (fall 1996): 8–15.

6. Allen, J., and R. F. Allen. "From Short-Term Compliance to Long-Term Freedom: Culture-Based Health Promotion by Health Professionals." *American Journal of Health Promotion* (fall 1986): 39–47.

7. *Club Industry: The Business Magazine for Health and Fitness Facility Management,* January 2000. Cover story.

8.   O'Donnell, M. P. "Characteristics of the Best Workplace Health Promotion Programs." *Wellness Management: Newsletter of the National Wellness Association* (summer 1997).

9.   "Community Perceptions of Health and Health Care in the Capital Area Community." Barry-Eaton District Health Department, Clinton-Eaton-Ingham Community Mental Health, Ingham County Health Department, Mid-Michigan District Health Department. January 1997.

10.   Glanz K., F. Lewis, and B. Rimer. *Health Behavior and Health Education: Theory, Research, and Practice.* 2d ed. San Francisco: Jossey-Bass, 1997.

Part Four

MORE THAN EXERCISE, NUTRITION, AND INCENTIVES

Chapter 12

HOLISTIC HEALTH PROMOTION
Joy, Meaning, and Internal Trust

The field of health promotion needs to revive and reorient its practices toward bringing people together as citizens and community members to decide for themselves the kinds of lives they think are most worth living.

David Buchanan
An Ethic for Health Promotion

Worldview
Organic
(living, spiritual)

Science
Holistic
(whole is greater than the sum of its parts)

Culture
Partnership
(egalitarian)

Medicine
Bio-psycho-social-spiritual

Holistic Health Promotion

The Holistic Approach

The twenty-first century's emerging worldview provides a radical new way to think about health promotion. Remember that this new worldview supports the existence of an organic, spiritual universe rather than a mechanical one and a "holistic" rather than a reductionist science. Further, the latest research in psycho-neuroimmunology, quantum physics, chaos theory, and so on, which forms the foundation for this holistic science, is anything but touchy-feely, New Age, or unscientific. It is in fact the most up-to-date scientific understanding of the universe in which we live. This holistic science informs a bio-psycho-social-spiritual model of health and medicine that honors the critical importance of examining human health in the context of the web of life in which it is embedded. From this model, then, naturally flows what we call Holistic Health Promotion.

Figure 12.1 outlines the underlying assumptions and primary components of the Holistic Health Promotion model. The information in this figure is then discussed in more detail in the remaining portion of the chapter.

Focus	*Health.* The main objective is to address the interconnected web of genetic, social, emotional, spiritual, lifestyle and environmental factors that contribute to health.
Emphasis	*Meaning and Support.* Meaning in life, relationships and work along with supportive human systems are considered the primary determinants of health.
Motivation	*Happiness.* The reason for change is primarily to enhance a sense of purpose and enjoyment of life.
Primary Assumption	*"Good" Human Nature.* People have a natural desire and ability to seek out healthy behaviors.
Professional Role	*Ally.* The primary job is to facilitate people's reconnection with their own internal wisdom about their bodies and lives.
Change Process	*Creating Consciousness.* People are assisted in understanding and healing the life issues that underlie illness and behavioral struggles.

Figure 12.1. Holistic Health Promotion

Focus: Health

Despite being called *health* promotion, our profession has remained largely rooted in the biomedical "disease-focused" paradigm. Holistic Health Promotion encourages movement away from this orientation. World-renowned physician Andrew Weil suggests the same thing for medicine when he says that "Rather than wage war on disease agents in the hope, in vain I suspect, of eliminating them, we ought to worry more about strengthening resistance and learning to live more in balance with them."[1] In Holistic Health Promotion the shift in focus emanates from a new conceptualization of health. We learned from quantum physics that it is the relationship between subatomic particles that gives meaning to their existence. Similarly, in Holistic Health Promotion we emphasize that it is the relationships among the spiritual, biological, psychological, social and environmental dimensions of the human experience that are critical to a true understanding of health and healing. Therefore, rather than defining health in terms of the absence of disease or the accumulation of some ideal list of "healthy" behaviors, we believe that:

> Health can be redefined as the manner in which we live well despite our inescapable illnesses, disabilities, and trauma.[2]

Traditionally, even when health is defined as more than just the absence or opposite of disease it is still most often described as some optimal state of well-being that can be achieved if we just try hard enough. The World Health Organization, for example, defines *health* as "a state of complete physical, mental and social well-being." A trip to the local bookstore will reveal a seemingly endless supply of books by health experts that claim to provide the steps needed to reach this proposed state of "optimal health." The problem is, of course, that as human beings we all live with varying amounts of physical, psychological, and spiritual "baggage." How many people have ever experienced or ever known anyone in optimal health? What does that mean? As medical writer David B. Morris suggests in his insightful book *Illness and Culture in the Postmodern Age:*

> Complete well-being is a fantasy. Health, whatever else it might be is something that happens not so much in the absence of illness as in its presence.[2]

It is more than likely that we will all struggle with emotional, spiritual, and physical issues during our lifetimes, and it is inevitable that we will die. Understanding and living skillfully and compassionately with these struggles, rather that perpetually searching for the latest "holy grail" of "optimal health" may come closer to what it truly means to be healthy.

The critical point in understanding health from a truly holistic perspective is that health really has to do with the manner in which we deal with what we are given in life. The concept of health therefore becomes much less black and white (just as the principle of complementarity teaches us both/and rather than either/or), a complex and dynamic "dance" that must be looked at in a systems context. As we will see, this shift in our conceptualization has tremendous ramifications for health promotion and our roles as health professionals. Can a person be sedentary and still be healthy? Can a person smoke cigarettes and still be healthy? Can a person be in a wheelchair and still be healthy? Can a person have cancer and still be healthy? Can a person eat high-fat food and still be healthy?

Emphasis: Meaning and Support

In Holistic Health Promotion, the emphasis in both assessment and intervention shifts from "risk factors for disease" to what we have termed "supportive factors for health." These factors (listed below) strengthen us and help us to cope more skillfully with the inevitable struggles and life difficulties that come our way.

purpose in life	spiritual connections	social support
work satisfaction	emotional health	optimism
perceived happiness	perceived health	altruism
intellectual stimulation	restful sleep	time alone
pleasure and play	financial resources	movement
laughter/humor	normal eating	contact with nature

This emphasis on supportive factors is underscored by the belief that meaning in life, relationships, and the supportive quality of human systems, rather than poor individual lifestyle choices are the primary determinants of true health status. However, most of our efforts in health promotion traditionally are spent on the "tip of the iceberg," addressing the "unhealthy behaviors" that people are using to survive their emotional pain. Rarely do we go below the "water line" to address the suffering that spawns these "unhealthy" behaviors. Yet, without addressing the part of the iceberg that is under the water, we find that the ship still runs aground (see fig. 12.2).

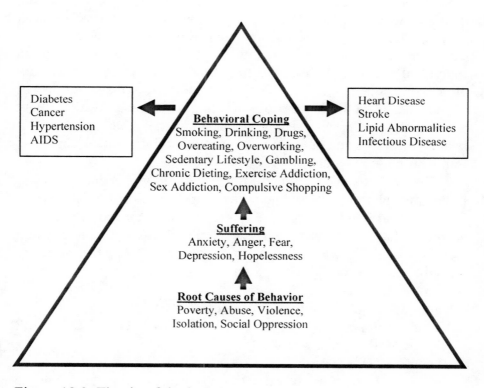

Figure 12.2. The tip of the iceberg

The change in emphasis with the holistic view of health does not mean disregarding traditional biomedical risk factors for disease but rather putting them into a new and broader perspective. We certainly would not suggest ignoring the dangers of elevated blood pressure or high cholesterol. However, we understand that these problems are often symptomatic of underlying emotional and/or spiritual distress and that true healing can best be facilitated by addressing traditional risk factors within the larger context of people's lives. We will discuss in detail the tremendous implications of this understanding for the role of the health professional in the next chapter.

Health and the Web of Life. Holistic Health Promotion views the world from a systems perspective, acknowledging the complex web of life in which we exist. From chaos theory we have learned that it is impossible to know all the interconnections in complex systems. Therefore it is impossible to know everything about the causes of an individual's health or disease. This allows us to work compassionately with people on an individual human level. Yet it also teaches us to understand the limitations of working this way because "Without concomitant attempts to redress social inequities, the probability of health promotion and demand management having a salient impact is remote if not non-existent."[3]

This is a crucial departure from the traditional reductionist approach, which fails to place the proper importance on the relationship between health issues and the larger cultural context. In today's world, perhaps more than ever, we cannot afford to separate health from economic, social, and political issues, a point powerfully brought home by the following statistics.

- The wealth of the top 1 percent of Americans is greater than the combined wealth of the bottom 95 percent (*Source:* U.S. Federal Reserve research).

- The assets of the world's 358 billionaires are greater than the combined incomes of countries with 45 percent of the world's population (*Source:* United Nations Human Development Report, 1996).

- Almost 39 million Americans have no health insurance including more than 8 million children (*Source:* U.S. Census Bureau, September 2001).

- Almost half of low-income, full-time workers were uninsured in 2000 (*Source:* Employee Benefits Research Institute).

Consider the potential impact that changes in these areas could make on people's health!

Where Is the Money Going?

It is estimated that 40 to 50 billion dollars are spent every year on weight loss interventions that even people in the industry admit don't work and that, according to a growing body of literature, have all kinds of decidedly unhealthy side effects. How much is 40 billion dollars? Let's just say for discussion's sake that starting today and for the next year every person in this country stops participating in this unproductive enterprise. The 40 billion dollars that would be saved could build 2.5 Habitat for Humanity homes for every one of the 2.5 million homeless people in the United States.[4] What effect might that have on the health of our nation?

The next time somebody tells you that we don't have enough money for the homeless understand that that is not the case. We have plenty of money to do what we need to do. The problem is that we are doing other things with the money. If in health promotion we don't take the social, political, and economic context into consideration, we are going to continue to miss the forest for the trees. Holistic Health Promotion demands that we shift our focus to the things that really matter the most—it helps us to figure out our real priorities.

Motivation: Happiness

In the holistic approach to health promotion, the primary reason for change shifts from fear of death and disease to enhancing a sense of purpose and enjoyment in life. The use of fear, guilt, and shame as "motivators" is seen as unproductive and inhumane. People are not blamed for eating the wrong foods or not doing enough exercise. It is understood that who gets sick and who stays healthy is the result of an infinite number of interacting variables, many of which will never be known for any particular individual. From a holistic perspective, then, the reason for change has more to do with enhancing how people feel about themselves and the meaning of their lives than with reducing the statistical probability that they will prematurely contract this or that disease.

Perhaps at this point you are beginning to think that helping people in this way sounds a lot like a spiritual endeavor. We couldn't agree more! To a large degree health promotion is indeed about helping people find happiness, meaning, and purpose in life, about helping them to find their joy and explore their spirituality. The great humanistic psychologist Carl Jung understood this when he said that "Every crisis a person has over the age of thirty is a spiritual crisis. Spiritual crisis requires spiritual cures."[5]

We wholeheartedly agree with Jung but would suggest that it would be appropriate to lower the age at which the spiritual dimension becomes the critical factor. For people of all ages, the real issues are almost always below the symptoms for which they are ostensibly seeking help.

Carl Jung: Physics and Spirituality

Interestingly, Jung was well acquainted and fascinated with the new discoveries in physics of the early 1900s. He had a close personal and professional relationship with Wolfgang Pauli, one of the major architects of quantum mechanics, with whom he cocreated the concept of *synchronicity.* According to this concept, many unexplained happenings in nature often occur not as a result of causal relationships between events but due to an underlying connectedness in the universe. Jung and Pauli believed that "synchronicity made it possible to begin a dialogue between physics and psychology in such a way that the subjective would be introduced into physics and the objective into psychology." Rather than looking exclusively to physics or psychology for the solution to nature's secrets, a complementary approach was called for in which subjective and objective aspects would reveal different features of the same underlying reality.[6]

A Case Study: Primarily a Spiritual Endeavor

A man was referred to us by his physician, who wanted him to lose some weight. He was middle-aged and had some adipose tissue around his abdomen, much as do many men his age. We asked him to tell us what his concerns were, and he began by saying that he had done everything he was supposed to do all his life and had been pretty successful. He had done well in college, found a good job, had a nice family, built a house in the woods, and acquired lots of "toys." He had a pretty good marriage and a couple of teenagers who were driving him crazy but were basically good kids.

The only thing he had not been able to get a handle on was his weight. He had tried everything, lost some weight only to gain it (and a trifle more) back each time. He was very frustrated and didn't know what to do. After he had talked at some length about his success in life, he paused and asked us what we thought he should do. After a reflective pause, we asked: What do *you* think about all this? There was a longer pause. Then he looked up with a somber face and said: "I have no joy in my life." After the power of that statement settled, he went on to relate that, although he had accomplished everything he had set out to do in life, there was very little that brought him pleasure. We ended our discussion with an acknowledgment of

177

where his efforts toward improving his health would probably be best put. And it had nothing to do with the food pyramid or weight loss!

From a "behavioral" point of view using joy and pleasure rather than fear as a "motivator" also makes a great deal of practical sense. Think of something that you love to do. It could be almost anything from hiking to cooking, playing a sport, or knitting. Often when you are engaged in this activity, you are completely absorbed and time seems to stand still. This is a state of being scientists call "flow." It feels wonderful and is associated with healthful biochemical changes in the body.[7] When something is this enjoyable, it is easier to sustain over time. On the other hand, we have seen that when we "get people to change" initially by bribing or coercing them with pressure or rewards, once the external motivation is gone the new behaviors quickly disappear.

The "secret" from a holistic perspective is that people do not need *incentives* or *motivation* or *stages of change* to "make" them do something they love! In Holistic Health Promotion our job is to help people to find their joy—to find what it is that puts them into a state of flow and that helps them to feel that their lives have meaning. Once they find these things, they will not need our water bottles and T-shirts to ensure maintenance!

Primary Assumption: "Good" Human Nature

While traditional approaches assume that people naturally gravitate toward unhealthy behaviors, in Holistic Health Promotion we assume that people are currently doing the best they can given their particular circumstances. If they are behaving in ways that are unhealthful or hurtful for themselves or others, it is because they are experiencing distress, which makes it difficult for them to act in ways that make more sense.

His Holiness, the Dali Lama, says, "The number one goal of every human being is happiness."[8] The number one goal of every human being is not to sit on the couch, eat junk food, be sedentary, and drink beer. This is not what we naturally seek for ourselves. In Holistic Health Promotion, we believe that people do have a natural desire and ability, an internal wisdom if you will, to be healthy. As Sobel and Ornstein say in their landmark book *Healthy Pleasures:*

> We know what to do [to be healthy], eat sweet fruit, feel the wind in the trees, smell the scent of a lover, cuddle a child, pet a dog, feel the warm wet earth in our hands as we dig a garden. Feeling good benefits us twice in immediate enjoyment and in better health.[9]

Professional Role: Ally

In order to be an ally, the role of the health professional in Holistic Health Promotion must differ significantly from that described in traditional approaches. In this context, promoting health involves helping people to uncover the barriers that are preventing them from accessing their own internal wisdom about their bodies and their lives. Just like the scientist who can no longer claim to be a detached observer of his experiment, the health professional is no longer a detached expert but a powerful partner, a cofacilitator, to help people reconnect with their own internal wisdom. The purpose is not to "get people" to do something but rather to assist them in understanding and healing the life issues that underlie illness and behavioral struggles. Therefore, the most important tools shift from behavior change strategies to listening skills, compassion, and the ability to make a human connection.

This change in roles is profound and is often understandably scary for those of us who were trained under the traditional model. From medicine to disease prevention to health promotion, our traditional focus has been on developing strategies and techniques to secure compliance or adherence. Holistic Health Promotion suggests a profoundly different approach, echoed by Dr. James Gordon in his *Manifesto for a New Medicine,* when he writes that "It would be far better and healthier for everyone concerned if we abandon the very concepts of compliance and adherence and regarded the health professional patient relationship as a full collaboration, a genuine, healing partnership."[10] We will discuss in more detail the tremendous implications of this shift for professional practice in health promotion in the next chapter.

Change Process: Creating Consciousness

In Holistic Health Promotion, the change process is about raising consciousness rather than changing behavior. Behavior change is no longer the primary focus of intervention or the primary role of the health professional. Instead, the health professional seeks to support people as they seek to better understand and more skillfully cope with their life struggles. Rather than decide for people what they should or should not do, the object now is to help people view health behaviors in the larger context of their lives. In this way they will be free to decide what the healthy or good life means for them. While this is a radical departure from traditional health promotion, it is an approach that is understood in many other areas, as reflected by the well-known saying

> If you give people fish they can eat today.
> If you teach people to fish they can eat forever.
> (variant of a quotation from Kuan-Tzu, 720–645 B.C.)

In his groundbreaking textbook Jerrold Greenberg applies this concept to health promotion, noting that "Giving fish in health promotion—telling people how to behave—is not freeing people. Teaching them to fish for themselves . . . is."[11]

This shift in focus is critical because Holistic Health Promotion does not view people as information-processing machines but as meaning-generating beings. This does not mean that we do not provide people with information. But at the same time we understand that the meaning that people attach to information is something that should not and cannot be controlled from the outside. In the text just mentioned, Greenberg continues:

> To determine what is really healthy for someone requires that person to judge the worth of the behavior using his or her value system. . . . If we really can't tell others what is healthy for them (since we do not have the same values as they do) how can we conduct health education that has as its goal predefined healthy behaviors?

We can tell people that having elevated cholesterol increases the statistical probability of having a heart attack by a certain percentage, but we cannot make the judgment for them as to whether it is "worth it" to give up their usual patterns of eating in order to reduce the probability by that percentage. Furthermore, we have also learned that the reduction in the probability of having a heart attack refers to populations, not to individuals, so it is not possible to know whether such changes will have any effect at all on a given individual!

From Control to Compassion

Quantum physics and chaos theory have shown us that change in complex systems (like the weather, the stock market, and human beings) is in fact not a linear process that can be controlled. The old idea of accurately predicting or quantifying outcomes is an illusion. If we can let go of the need to explain the exact cause of a particular illness or produce a specific behavioral change we can focus on developing the compassionate connection that we in Holistic Health Promotion believe is our most powerful "strategy" for helping people. We can discard our illusions of predictability and control as we realize that, for the vast majority if not for all of our endeavors:

> We can never be sure how important our own individual contribution will be. Our action may be lost in the chaos that surrounds us, or it may join with one of those many loops that sustain an open, creative community. On rare occasions it may even be taken up and amplified until it transforms the entire community.[12]

Although this may feel a bit unnerving at first, we would suggest that it opens up new and powerfully beneficial ways of looking at our personal and professional lives. Chaos theory tells us that, regardless of our knowledge, skills, and intentions, "our interventions are limited and . . . their outcome is always to a certain crucial degree unpredictable."[12] The lesson that chaos theory teaches us about the interconnectedness of things has another perhaps more subtle, but equally powerful, implication for the helping relationship because

> If we can see ourselves as connected, yet ignorant of most of the connections, then we have little choice but to be compassionate.[13]

Here we have scientific validation for making the feminine value of compassion rather than the masculine value of control the guiding principle for health promotion.

Seeing a Person through Two Sets of Eyes

We hope that it is becoming clear how much the approach we are describing departs from the traditional health promotion model. To illustrate this further, we would like to give an applied example that shows how an actual client would be viewed differently in the traditional versus the holistic approach.

Below we describe the case of a woman who was referred to us by her private physician for counseling and participation in wellness programs. She was experiencing health problems, and the doctor thought participation in a wellness program might be beneficial. Let's look at the information we were given about her and the kind of health recommendations that would likely have resulted using a traditional biomedical approach. Then, in contrast, let's take a holistic view of her situation and see how it changes the way we would seek to support her.

Seeing Marsha through Biomedical Eyes

Medical History. "Marsha" is a thirty-nine-year-old African-heritage female. She initially went to her doctor because she was experiencing frequent headaches. After ruling out physical causes for the headaches, her physician suspected that they were stress related and suggested exercise, dietary changes, and stress management information. Additional biomedical information about Marsha provided by her physician included the following.

- She is 5 feet, 3 inches tall and weighs 243 pounds.
- Her only reported significant illness or surgery in recent years was a partial hysterectomy at age thirty seven due to severe fibroids.
- Her blood pressure is currently 165/92.
- She has a total cholesterol value of 235.

Weight and Exercise History. In the last year Marsha lost 120 pounds on a very strict diet/exercise plan. In the last three months she has been on and off of her diet and has regained one hundred pounds. When she started regaining weight she found that she was also no longer able to "stick" to her exercise regimen.

Intervention: Fixing the Machine. Given this information and working from within the traditional health promotion model, it is likely that Marsha would have been offered the following.

- A thorough cardiovascular screening
- A fitness evaluation
- An individualized exercise prescription based on the results of her physical testing
- A recommendation to join a fitness facility or community program for exercise
- A referral to a dietician for weight loss and for suggestions on how to lower her cholesterol and blood pressure
- Information on stress management classes

In summary, with the traditional biomedical approach we would have tested and measured the physical aspects of Marsha's health and given her an exercise plan, eating guidelines and stress management techniques to help her be physically healthier and less stressed.

Seeing Marsha through Holistic Eyes

Holistic health reminds us that we cannot look just at a person's physical symptoms and we cannot view people as individuals in isolation from the systems in which they live. It's important to see the *whole person* as well as the relationships and environments that surround them. Considering Marsha's life from a broader holistic perspective can help us learn whether she will have the time, ability, or desire to follow the health advice she is getting.

Eating, Weight, and Body Image History. Marsha has struggled with her weight for most of her life. She has repeatedly lost and regained weight since she started dieting as a teenager. After rebounding from her most recent diet and exercise plan, she feels she is now constantly preoccupied with thoughts about food and her weight. She reports hating her body at her current size and starving herself periodically (usually followed by bingeing). She has enjoyed group exercise classes in the past, but after gaining one hundred pounds she feels too embarrassed to be seen wearing exercise clothes.

Family History. Her parents live two hours away. Both are of African heritage, and they are still married. Her mother was recently hospitalized for three weeks due to agoraphobia. Her father has hypertension and diabetes. He was recently hospitalized with serious heart trouble and *given* two years to live. Marsha travels to and from her parent's house, 120 miles away, in order to help them with their health problems. She has one older sister, who lives near her, and one younger brother out of state. She is not on speaking terms with either sibling, although she was very close to her brother ten years ago. Neither her brother nor her sister assists in the care of her parents, who are steadily becoming more ill and less able to care for themselves.

Relationship History. Marsha is heterosexual and has been married twice, the first time at age twenty. This marriage ended in a traumatic, bitter divorce after five years due to her spouse being unfaithful. She is required to have ongoing contact with her first husband because of his visitation rights with their child. She experiences almost constant stress due to bitter ongoing struggles with her ex-husband around his failure to pay child support.

Marsha avoided intimate relationships for thirteen years after her divorce. She then became involved in another love relationship and married a second time at age thirty-four. This second marriage lasted three months. She has not been involved in an intimate relationship since the second divorce five years ago. Marsha has one child, a daughter who is sixteen years of age. She has primary custody of her daughter, who has always lived with her. The daughter spends very little time with her father, who lives out of state, moves frequently, and often remarries.

Education/Job. Marsha has a high school degree and has been in her current job for ten years as a support person in a large, conservative, white-male-dominated organization. She is part of a staff comprised of African- and Latino-heritage women. Her supervisor is a white male with an autocratic leadership style. Their work group has had staff reductions three times in the last four years. Her job includes daily, urgent deadlines and requires that she sit at her desk on the phone and/or at the computer most of the day. She works ten-hour days on the average and some weekends. The company medical department recently sent her home on valium after an anxiety attack at work.

Finances. As a single mother on a low support staff salary Marsha lives under continuous, extreme financial pressure. She gets by paycheck to paycheck, is trying to pay off credit card debt, and is worried about helping to pay for her daughter's college tuition in the future.

Social Environment. Marsha reports no social activity. She cannot remember the last time she did something that was "fun" and says she cannot afford to go out to eat or to the movies with others. She feels she is too depressing to be around, so she avoids her friends. She used to attend church regularly but says she has lost interest and is too tired to attend.

Intervention: Healing The Whole Person. When we look at this comprehensive view of Marsha the limitations of traditional bio-medical health assessments and recommendations begin to become more obvious. It is hard to imagine that exercise prescriptions, eating plans, and stress management guidelines are going to help this woman, who is physically, emotionally, and spiritually exhausted. She is dealing with overwhelming relationship, financial, and job stress, all made even more difficult by the fact that she has no significant social or spiritual support systems to help her. It is certainly not surprising that she is experiencing such physical and emotional manifestations of her stress as headaches, high blood pressure, high cholesterol, emotional overeating, anxiety, and depression.

It is clear that Marsha is unlikely to have the time, energy, or money to join a traditional exercise facility or take weight control and stress management classes. In addition, the behavioral techniques employed by these traditional interventions would merely teach her how to keep herself "under control," essentially distracting her from the deeper issues in her life that need healing. The behavioral changes accomplished through these types of programs are usually only temporary anyway. By pursuing this approach, Marsha would be setting herself up to relapse into her old coping behaviors just as she has done before.

Listed below are more holistic types of help Marsha might access in order to heal and move toward better health. Please note these ideas provide only a brief overview of some alternative ways of supporting people. A more in-depth discussion of holistic programming and counseling techniques will be presented later in this book.

- First and foremost, Marsha needs loving, compassionate human support. Providing her with a regular opportunity to tell her story and express her emotions would be very healing. This simple type of support could be effectively provided by a health educator, a therapist, clergy, or a very good friend. It would be a big first step toward helping her to break out of the extreme social isolation and hopelessness she is experiencing.

- Marsha could benefit from financial counseling to help her consolidate debt, simplify her finances, and plan for her retirement and the future health needs of her parents. Assistance with applying for scholarships or college loans for her daughter would also be helpful.

- Marsha could be connected to community agencies that provide low- or no-cost assistance and advice to people who are caring for elders. Setting up a network of support where her parents live would reduce the stress she is experiencing around shouldering the burden of their care alone.

- Marsha could be encouraged to access resources provided by her employer such as Human Resources Department counseling for career advancement or company-subsidized education programs to help her obtain a college degree. Also, the company employee assistance program might provide counseling and therapy to help her pursue healthier intimate relationships in the future and heal the estrangement with her siblings.

- Information and support regarding programs that address compulsive eating, chronic dieting, and body hatred would help her move to a less painful place with food and her body.

- A size-friendly exercise environment that includes special exercise classes designed for the needs of large people and taught by large instructors and a protected locker space with larger towels would be helpful.

- A support group for African-heritage women could help her understand and heal the life-limiting distresses she has acquired in relation to women's oppression and racism.

We cannot overemphasize how important it is to help people with the *source* of their distress. How can exercising and eating less salt and fat possibly "fix" Marsha's life? They cannot because they do not address the relationship, job, and financial stresses that lie beneath her "health problems." Whether it is fitness level, weight, smoking, blood pressure, cholesterol, or "stress," all of these issues can be more compassionately and effectively addressed using holistic approaches that respond to the whole person and the environment in which he or she lives.

How Many Marshas Are There?

Upon hearing about a person like Marsha many health professionals say "wow, her life is really painful and complicated. I can see why she would have health problems, and I can see that she needs a lot more than eating guidelines and an exercise plan." But they then go on to say "most people do not have such difficult lives, and if they do they are not going to share all of that information with me when they are just coming in for cholesterol guidelines!"

We couldn't disagree more! The vast majority of people that come to us for help have lives that are just as complicated as Marsha's; the details may be different, but the level of challenge is often just as high. And most of these people are dying (sometimes literally) to share the story of their lives with someone who will listen without advising or judging them. If you provide this service, they will come, and it will help!

Summary

We understand that moving in a holistic direction is not an easy transformation for many health professionals. For this reason, we have devoted the next chapter to providing ideas for making the personal and professional transition from biomedical to Holistic Health Promotion. Holistic Health Promotion provides a compassionate approach for helping people heal physical, emotional, social, ecological, and spiritual struggles as they seek a more meaningful life. And it is consistent with all of the values and perspectives now emerging as we move toward Epoch III humanity.

TRADITIONAL HEALTH PROMOTION

Focus

Disease. The main objective is to identify and eliminate biomedical risk factors for physical disease.

Emphasis

"Unhealthy" Behaviors. Poor individual lifestyle choices are considered the primary determinants of sickness and disease.

Motivation

Fear. The reason for change is primarily to prevent disease and premature death.

Primary Assumption

"Bad" Human Nature. Left to their own devices people will naturally gravitate towards "unhealthy" behaviors

Professional Role

Expert. The primary job is to uncover unhealthy behaviors and recommend alternative, healthier behaviors.

Change Process

Controlling Behavior. Behavior change techniques are used to suppress or eliminate targeted behaviors.

HOLISTIC HEALTH PROMOTION

Focus	*Health.* The main objective is to address the interconnected web of genetic, social, emotional, spiritual, lifestyle and environmental factors that contribute to health.
Emphasis	*Meaning and Support.* Meaning in life, relationships and work along with supportive human systems are considered the primary determinants of health.
Motivation	*Happiness.* The reason for change is primarily to enhance a sense of purpose and enjoyment of life.
Primary Assumption	*"Good" Human Nature.* People have a natural desire and ability to seek out healthy behaviors.
Professional Role	*Ally.* The primary job is to facilitate people's reconnection with their own internal wisdom about their bodies and lives.
Change Process	*Creating Consciousness.* People are assisted in understanding and healing the life issues that underlie illness and behavioral struggles.

References

1. Weil, A. *Spontaneous Healing.* New York: Knopf, 1995.

2. Morris, D. B. *Illness and Culture in the Postmodern Age.* Berkeley: University of California Press, 1998.

3. Terry, P. "Health Promotion, Demand Management, and Social Justice: Three Ships Passing or a Powerful Flotilla?" *AWHP'S Worksite Health* (fall 1996): 8–15.

4. Wann, M. *Fat! So? Because You Don't Have to Apologize for Your Size!* Berkeley: Ten Speed Press, 1998.

5. Freeman, J. Interview with Carl Jung. British Broadcasting Corporation, 1959. Film.

6. Peat, F. D. *Synchronicity: The Bridge between Mind and Matter.* New York: Bantam, 1987.

7. Csikszentmihalyi, M. *Flow: The Psychology of Optimal Experience.* New York: HarperCollins, 1991.

8. Dalai Lama and H. C. Cutler. *The Art of Happiness: A Handbook for Living.* New York: Putnam, 1998.

9. Ornstein, R., and D. Sobel. *Healthy Pleasures.* Reading, MA: Addison-Wesley, 1989.

10. Gordon, J. S. *Manifesto for a New Medicine.* Reading, MA: Addison-Wesley, 1996.

11. Greenberg, J. S. *Health Education: Learner-Centered Instructional Strategies.* 4th ed. Dubuque: William C. Brown, 1998.

12.   Briggs J., and D. Peat. *Seven Life Lessons of Chaos: Spiritual Wisdom from the Science of Change.* New York: Harper Perennial, 1999.

13.   Michael, D. "Competence and Compassion in an Age of Uncertainty." *World Future Society Bulletin* 17, no. 1 (1983): 1–6.

Chapter 13

FROM HEALTH PROMOTER TO HEALER
Holistic Counseling 101

The Heart is the place within each of us that we can count on
to tell us what's really going on.

Jacquelyn Small
Becoming Naturally Therapeutic

In the Beginning

Virtually all of us began our work in the field of health promotion
feeling enthusiastic about sharing wellness information with anyone
who would listen. But somewhere along the way many of us realized
that traditional biomedical recommendations and motivation from
"health experts" were not what people most wanted or needed in order to be healthy.

What most people *really* need to improve their health and move
forward in their lives are supportive environments with allies: people
who know how to authentically care and listen *without* giving tons of
information. More often than not, they don't need medication, advice, guidelines, and experts telling them what to do. Therefore, a
key to the holistic approach is transitioning from the limiting role of
motivational expert to the role of compassionate ally.[1]

Unfortunately, this transition is difficult for many of us. It is
probably the most challenging aspect of learning to work holistically.
Our traditional biomedical training has taught us to operate on the
periphery of our client's lives. We have learned to distance ourselves
emotionally from the people we are trying to help. We know how to
dispense nutrition guidelines, exercise prescriptions and stress man-

agement techniques while keeping our clients at arm's length emotionally. If there is mention of a marriage problem, financial struggles, or memories of sexual abuse, many health professionals feel anxious and unequipped to deal with it. Yet, given the prevalence and power of emotional life issues, health promotion that avoids discussion of these issues is not an option.

As mentioned throughout this book, it is critical to remember that isolation, social oppression, parenting difficulties, job dissatisfaction, financial problems, early life trauma, and lack of purpose in life lie beneath the surface of most of the illnesses and health-damaging behaviors we are trying to address. We *must* encourage people to talk about the issues closest to their hearts. It is the *only way* we can help create a process of meaningful healing.

A New Foundation for Helping

So let us now explore how Holistic Health Promotion invites us to change the way we think about helping people. Below we discuss key steps for making the transition from health promoter to healer.

Seek Alternatives to Fixing

Giving up trying to fix people is very difficult because we have been trained in the biomedical, Cartesian, "fix the clock" paradigm. And we really do want to help. For most of us it is not a coincidence that we ended up in a helping profession. It is not a coincidence that we are not automobile mechanics or mathematicians. We have a tremendous amount of compassion, and we want to help relieve people's suffering. But, as Ram Dass says in his inspiring book *How Can I Help?*

> Frequently our reactiveness to suffering takes the form of having instantly to do something, to do anything. It's the we gotta syndrome. We gotta fix this up right away. It's tricky because this impulse arises, I believe, from genuine empathy but the form of action is compulsive.[2]

We are so busy trying to figure out what to do to fix the machine that we often miss what is really going on. And this is only made worse by the systems in which we work, which, as we have seen, put extraordinary and unreasonable pressure on us to "get" people to change and to systematically measure and document outcomes.

Steer Clear of Reductionism

We have discussed in depth the limitations of the reductionist approach to health. We need to look beyond people's physical health and isolated risk factors for disease. Upon hearing us suggest this, health professionals often ask if this means that holistic counseling suggests ignoring high cholesterol or blood pressure readings. The answer is emphatically no! Of course, biomedical indicators are important. The difference is that they are now understood and addressed as part of the larger landscape of a person's life.

The issue is that people are more than their blood pressure, weight, and cholesterol. People are not "diabetics" but individuals who have the condition of diabetes. Human beings are complex, dynamic, living systems in which the whole is always greater than the sum of its parts. Furthermore, the human species exists as an integral part of the web of life and our physical health is inextricably interconnected with our social, economic, political and ecological environments. As helpers we must take this into account. If we deal only with symptoms, not underlying causes, our interventions will at best meet with only short-term, limited success.

It's Not Simple

We have previously discussed our lack of enthusiasm for stages of change approaches in health promotion because they are based on behavior modification strategies. Advocates claim that a major benefit of stage theories is that they can *simplify the job of health professionals*. Based on the answers to a few questions, individuals can quickly and simply be assigned to their current "stage of change" and prescribed the associated strategies to help them move to the next stage.

The problem is that simplification in this context is neither desirable nor helpful. As we learned from chaos theory, human beings are complex systems that cannot be understood using traditional, reductionist, analytic techniques. Although the practice of starting where the person is certainly makes sense (and has been around a lot longer than stage theories), what is needed to truly help people to grow and heal is not simplification but an understanding of the uniqueness, complexity, and chaos that are such critical components of the human experience. This is what is so often lost in the rush to identify, isolate, quantify, and alter human behavior.

Don't Blame the Victim

Exhaustive lists of "risk factors" for disease not withstanding, it is rarely possible to know exactly why someone gets a disease while someone else does not. Chaos theory shows us that there are so many interconnections and feedback loops in complicated systems such as human beings that there is no way we can possibly discover them all, and therefore at an individual level our attempts to predict who will get sick are at best an illusion. Traditional health promotion tends to "blame the victim" for getting a disease because he or she did not exercise enough or eat the right foods. Unfortunately, some alternative and complementary approaches fall into the same paradigm by blaming people's illnesses on a lack of positive thinking or the failure to meditate enough. It is critical to understand that, as Larry

Dossey says in *Healing Words,* "In nature the occurrence of disease is considered a part of the natural order, not a sign of ethical, moral or spiritual weakness."[3] All of the great spiritual masters (saints, gurus, etc.) down through the ages have died, many of them from cancer and other diseases, just like the rest of us. This is part of the human condition. Blaming people for their conditions is not only unscientific but inhumane, and it diminishes their ability to begin the process of healing. In *Why People Don't Heal and How They Can,* Carolyn Myss makes an important observation.

> A central misconception of today's holistic culture is the belief that all illness results from personal negativity, either from tragic past experiences, from negative attitudes that contaminate our minds and bodies or from bad past-life karma. Yet, negativity is not the only source of illness: It can also emerge as the answer to a prayer. It can physically guide us onto a path of insight and learning upon which we would otherwise never have set foot. It may be a catalyst for expanding personal consciousness as well as for understanding the greater meaning of life.

Set Aside Judgment

This is one of the most critical and difficult adjustments for health professionals to make. There is so much morality associated with health (healthism) in our culture today. People are particularly judgmental toward others (as well as toward themselves) in relation to smoking, exercise, food, and body shape. In this kind of atmosphere it is easy to be critical and ask, "How can this person smoke given all that we know about the dangers?" or "How can this person not exercise given all that we know about the benefits?" In a holistic approach, however, we recognize not only the barriers created by judgment but the healing power of nonjudgment. As Jack Kornfield says in *A Path With Heart,* "When we for so long have been judged by everyone we meet, just to look into the eyes of one who does not judge, can be extraordinarily healing."[4] This is, to be sure, a different approach to viewing health and health behaviors, but as we will see in a moment it is critical for helping people to begin the process of healing.

Be Aware of Our Own Issues

Many if not most of us, from doctors to dietitians, nurses, and health educators, came into our professions, at least in part, to help understand and heal our own struggles. This can help us serve as powerful allies or it can act as a significant barrier in our attempts to help others. What better person to help someone who is suffering than a person who has worked through (or is working through) a similar problem? At the same time, what a dangerous situation to have a health professional who is unaware of his or her issues attempting to help another human being with similar issues? As Ram Dass says, "we work on ourselves in order to help others, and we help others as a vehicle for working on ourselves."[2]

Again it becomes clear that our profession is truly a spiritual endeavor. This is certainly not meant to take away from the importance of professional training, but it serves to underscore the need to understand training in the context of the compassionate connection that leads to real healing. Once again, in the words of Ram Dass:

> Placing service in a spiritual perspective in no way diminishes what we have to offer through training, experience, individuality, special skills, or sense of humor. Quite the reverse. Our particular talents and unique qualities are likely to come forth more reliably when we have a richer and more spacious sense of who we are.[2]

A New Style of Interaction

At the core of a holistic healing relationship is the art of listening. Respectful listening is one of the greatest healing gifts we can offer another human being. It is a powerful tool because it contradicts the experiences many of us have all our lives. As young people we instinctively knew that we needed to talk and cry about distressing events, but our parents and other adults were often too busy to give us their undivided attention. As adults, we are never really listened to either. In many interactions with loved ones, coworkers, and friends the other person spends more time thinking about what they will say next rather than really listening to and understanding our reality as we are speaking.

Respectful listening is a relatively simple process. It allows us to immediately begin working with people holistically, and it is something that people from all types of professional backgrounds can learn to do. Below we discuss some specific ways in which you can begin to explore and practice relating to all the people in your life in this new way.[5]

Listen, Listen, Listen

Remind yourself that your primary role is simply to support the person. It is not your job to tell people what to do or to try to fix them! You are no longer expected to have all the answers or to know everything that a person may need. You are going to trust that, when people are given a safe space in which to tell their stories and a compassionate ally to listen to and honor those stories, they are capable of figuring out what they need to be healthy and happy in life.

Pay close attention, with lots of eye contact, and encourage people to express their experiences "as they see them," without advising or correcting them. (There should be significant periods during your interaction when you are mostly silent and the other person does all the talking). Listening supportively is more important for healing than providing all the right information and telling people what they should and shouldn't do.

In the box on the next page is an exercise designed to teach the process of "respectful listening." For anyone who wants to begin supporting people in a more holistic way, the repeated practice of this exercise may be one of the best places to start building new skills. This exercise can be done almost anytime and is useful with family, friends, and professional colleagues as well.

Respectful Listening Exercise:
Don't Just Do Something, Sit There

The respectful listening exercise is done with a partner; someone who will agree to confidentiality regarding the information shared. Follow the steps below to practice both giving and receiving the experience of respectful listening. You will need about fifteen minutes and a watch or clock to do this exercise.

1. Decide which person in the partnership is going to speak for the first half of the exercise (seven minutes). The person who is not speaking becomes the designated listener.

2. Notice the starting time so you can switch speaker and listener roles after seven minutes.

3. To begin, the person speaking takes the opportunity to talk about anything he or she wishes. It is best in this exercise for the speaker to take a risk and talk about something important, something close to his or her heart. The speaker may or may not choose to express strong emotions as part of this experience.

4. The person in the listening role is to give the speaking person the fullest possible attention. This includes good eye contact and body language that indicates interest in what the speaker is sharing. In addition, it very important that the listener:

    *   Resist the temptation to interrupt or make comments while his or her partner is speaking.

    *   Refrain from offering related stories, asking questions, or trying to guide the speaker in a specific direction. Simply listen!

    *   Resist the temptation to judge or interpret the speaker's comments in a way that frames them with your own reality. Try to stay open to hearing the speaker's view.

5. After seven minutes, switch roles. The person who was listening becomes the speaker, and the speaker becomes the listener. Follow the same process for another seven minutes, with the roles reversed.

6. Upon finishing the exercise, remind each other that what has been shared is confidential.

While this sounds like a simple exercise, most people find it very challenging. Listening to other people for seven minutes without advising them or trying to influence them is not an easy task. Witnessing strong emotions in others tends to bring up issues of our own, and the feeling of closeness that results when we do not "chatter" at people also feels strange at first.

The urge to fix and control, although it springs from a desire to help, represents a fallback to the outdated paradigm from which we are trying to evolve. It has been noted, for instance, that during an average office visit physicians wait eighteen to twenty-three seconds before they interrupt their patient.[6,7] If we can suspend our need to fix, we may open up new vistas of healing for those we serve. As Ram Dass suggests:

> Now we can begin perhaps for the first time to hear *them*. Less busy pushing away suffering, less frenzied having to do something about it, we're able to get a sense of what *they're* feeling, of what *they* feel they need. We may be startled to discover that what they've been asking for all along is entirely different from what we've been so busy offering.[2]

Nurture a Respectful Relationship

Use your counseling interaction to begin building a trusting relationship with each person. Everyone has the need to be accepted and respected no matter what his or her age, skin color, body size, sexual preference, gender, religion, or economic class. This is true regardless of the "unhealthy" behaviors in which he or she may be involved. When listening, it is critical to display an attitude of respect regarding all of these issues.

Encourage Emotions

If people express emotions (anger, fear, grief, embarrassment, etc.) while relaying their experiences, they may sob, cry, tremble, shake, cough, laugh, yawn, or talk compulsively. Try to stay open. Let them express their emotions without attempting to shut them down or gloss things over. The more they can express or "discharge" stored emotions and distress, the sooner they can think more clearly about their lives, reevaluate their behavior, and break out of old dysfunctional patterns.

Many of us were never allowed to express strong emotions when we were young. If we cried, got angry, or expressed disappointment, we were told to "straighten up and behave." If we continued to express our feelings, we were given a scornful look, spanked or put in time out. For this reason it can be very difficult to witness others having strong feelings; our first impulse is to shut them down, just as we were shut down earlier in our lives. It is very important to resist this pull toward minimizing emotional discharge in others. (Please note that during counseling it is best to keep the focus on the client's emotional issues. If strong emotions come up for us as counselors, it is best to wait and express these emotions at another time with our own supportive ally).

Unfortunately, because of the legacy of the mind/body separation, our health promotion training has all too often helped us learn to avoid and minimize the importance of dealing with emotional issues. A dietitian once confided in us after a presentation that that she had been taught that when clients brought up emotional issues such as memories of childhood trauma her job was to get them "back on track." She felt supported and liberated to hear us affirm the knowledge (which she intuitively had) that the trauma her client was disclosing was indeed "on track" and of the most critical importance for health and healing.

Acknowledge and Validate Pain and Suffering

Many health professionals tell us that they are often involved with people whose stories are so difficult that they can't begin to think of anything to *do* to help. They say that their instinct or their heart tells them to give their patient a hug, and say, "I can only imagine how hard that must have been." What should they do? We would answer, "go with your heart." As we have seen, people's illnesses and behavioral problems are almost always closely linked to underlying struggles in the form of social, emotional, and/or spiritual issues. Acknowledging these struggles and validating people's suffering can go a long way toward helping them begin the healing process.

Ask Permission Regarding Touch

Some people find it easier to express strong emotions if they are supported physically during the process. This can mean anything from simply moving closer, to holding their hand, to sitting side by side, to offering a hug. If your heart and intuition tell you a person is in need of some physical support, the appropriate thing to do is ask the client whether he or she would like this kind of support. The person we are supporting should always be the one to determine what type of support is desired, and the health professional should honor this by asking first.

Honor Confidentiality

Any information you gather about someone as you listen should be treated as confidential. This means that you do not discuss it with others or bring it up with the person again unless you have his or her permission. For example, you may have healing sessions in which clients reveal that they were sexually abused as a child. In a later session you may be discussing a different topic, which you want to relate back to the sexual abuse disclosure. It would be best to ask the person if it is OK in the current session to refer back to the sexual abuse issue before proceeding with the discussion. The person needs to be able to let you know if he or she is comfortable with discussing this painful issue again at this new time.

Share Information Carefully

We have emphasized the importance of minimizing expert advice and maximizing listening between health professionals and program participants. There are times, however, when your intuition will tell you that it would be useful to share information with a client. There are two key things to keep in mind regarding this process.

- *Help people explore pain, illness, or behavior struggles within the larger context of their lives.* If they can begin to link life issues to the onset of accidents or illness, they can move forward in healing. In this regard it can be useful to *obtain information* by asking the following types of questions.

  - When did this health problem begin?
  - What was going on in your life at the time?

- How can this pain, injury, or illness give you permission to begin doing something differently in your life?

- *Instead of providing tons of information, help people access mind/body/spirit resources.* It is usually not helpful to launch into long explanations unless you can keep clients actively involved in the conversation. Refer them to readings, programs, or videos and try to stay clear of suggesting they have been wrong while you have the "right information." (Remember, you are teaching them to fish, not buying them a fish dinner!)

Examples of Holistic Language

Here are three situations showing how health professionals can incorporate this new holistic language and information into interactions with a client.

1. I'm Such a Pig

Client: I can't believe how much weight I've gained. I really need to go on a diet. I've been such a pig over the holidays.

Professional: Wow . . . calling yourself a pig seems like such a harsh label. I do not see you that way at all. You know, you are not alone in feeling this way. Many of us get caught up in a repeated cycle of losing and regaining weight and feeling bad about eating and our bodies. It can become very frustrating. Did you know there is a new approach called Health at Every Size that helps people get out of this cycle? This approach can also help you understand this food and weight struggle in relation to other health issues or concerns you may have. Would you be interested in knowing more about this new approach? I can send you some things to read or you can attend our workshop on this topic next weekend.

2. Get Me Fit Fast!

Client: I need you to put me on an exercise program, and I need to get in shape fast.

Professional: As we start working together to determine what is going to work best for you, I want to emphasize that your own knowledge about yourself, your body, and your past experience with exercise is the best guide for determining what types of activities you want to get involved in now. And while you are currently most interested in short term results, if we do a good job of working together to figure out what types of activities you most enjoy, you will probably find yourself sustaining your activity over the long term as well.

3. I'm Broken, Please Fix Me

Client: I need some advice about this pulled ligament in my foot. I've taken time off work to rest it, I'm taking an anti-inflammatory, and I've been wearing a protective boot, but it doesn't seem to be getting better.

Professional: Any time we experience an illness or injury it is important to remember that many factors contribute to the problem. Our bodies are genetically predisposed to have weaknesses in certain areas and the physical and emotional stresses and strains in our daily environments can further stress our bodies in weakened areas. It is important to try to figure out if there is meaning in these things. You mentioned a moment ago that your foot injury was forcing you to miss work. Is there anything going on at work that is bothering you? If this injury is helping you to avoid something stressful at work, then it will be important to address the work issue as part of helping your foot heal.

Becoming a Healer

As health professionals we have been slow to include holistic counseling approaches in our programs. The predominant resistance or fear that many health professionals express regarding holistic counseling is: "I'm not a psychotherapist so I should not encourage people to express their feelings or talk about their problems. If a person brings up serious issues will I know what to do?" The answer is yes! *You will know what to do* if you begin to prepare yourself for this new way of working with people. Work from your heart, use your intuition, and expand your skills by considering the following suggestions.[5]

Network with Professionals in the Mental Health Industry

As you develop healing relationships with clients you may find that some individuals would benefit from connecting with a mental health professional. We always recommend that you network frequently with the psychotherapists, social workers, and chemical dependency and spiritual counselors in your area so that you will be comfortable making referrals and acting as part of a healing team that includes a therapist when necessary. The more you know about these professionals in your community, the more effectively you can recommend them. Seek out therapists who specialize in relationships, sexuality, work issues, parenting and family issues, chemical dependency, grief and loss, trauma, eating and body image difficulties, gambling, financial problems and body-based psychotherapy.

Just as we have outlined in relation to health promotion, there are two competing philosophies in the mental health field. There is the more traditional biomedical approach, which sees disturbed behavior as an illness and often suppresses symptomatic behavior with the use of drugs (such as Prozac for depression). However, there is a more holistic approach that views emotional and behavioral difficulties as metaphors for significant life struggles. Although the biomedical approach is sometimes effective, the more holistic approach emphasizes deep healing of underlying issues rather than just simple suppression of the problem behavior with medication. As you interact with mental health professionals to create your referral network keep in mind that the more holistic therapists are going to work best with your clients if you are introducing holistic concepts in your work.

Do Your Own Work

If you try to listen to and support others without actively working on your own issues, you are at risk for what Jacquelyn Small, author of *Becoming Naturally Therapeutic,* calls "toxic relating."[9] Small explains that:

> Toxic relating happens when a listener acts out of his or her own unmet needs and confuses them with those of the person seeking help. This lack of clarity will throw the "helper" into a role that can harm the very person seeking help. Those finding themselves in such a situation will usually resort to a role such as preacher, judge, teacher, or savior.

If you notice that you are feeling very urgent about "fixing and changing" a person, or if someone is very irritating to you, this usually means that your own issues are surfacing. Try to talk with someone who can respectfully support you with your difficulty in this area before you work further with this client.

Broaden Your Professional Training

If your ongoing professional training and certifications focus only on cardiovascular wellness and traditional behavioral control, you will not have the information and experiences you need to be comfortable with holistic counseling. You will need to actively seek out trainings, workshops, and conferences outside of traditional health promotion to obtain the necessary skills. Professional training experiences offered by the mental health industry, as well as less traditional mind/body/spirit health conferences can be a powerful place to get helpful information and networking opportunities. The alternative/complementary medicine community is also a rich resource. We highly recommend that you learn about and experience the healing modalities coming out of this exciting field, although it is important to remember that these types of therapies can also be used in a bio-medical way. Become familiar with the holistic approaches listed in figure 13.1 and the professionals in your area who provide them. They will help you to be a much more effective ally for your own clients and program participants.

	I have personally used this type of holistic therapy	I am professionally familiar with this type of holistic therapy
Acupuncture	( )	( )
Aromatherapy	( )	( )
Ayurvedic medicine	( )	( )
Biofeedback	( )	( )
Biological dentistry	( )	( )
Nondiet work	( )	( )
Chiropractic	( )	( )
Energy work	( )	( )
Homeopathy	( )	( )
Imagery	( )	( )
Massage/reflexology	( )	( )
Meditation	( )	( )
Midwifery	( )	( )
Music/art therapy	( )	( )
Naturopathy	( )	( )
Plant-based diets	( )	( )
Prayer	( )	( )
Psychotherapy	( )	( )
Psychotherapy (body based)	( )	( )
Size acceptance work	( )	( )
Support groups	( )	( )
Yoga/tai chi	( )	( )

Figure 13.1. Holistic healing approaches. Place a check mark in the indicated column if you personally or professionally are familiar with the therapies listed above.

Address Your Fears about Liability

When making the transition from traditional health promotion to holistic health and healing, fear of liability can become a paralyzing issue. Many health promotion professionals intuitively feel that they are ready to begin offering clients holistic counseling and support. They worry, however, that they might be seen as someone who is "posing" inappropriately as a licensed psychotherapist.

Here are some suggestions to follow regarding this concern.

- Be sure to represent yourself clearly and honestly. Do not call yourself a "psychotherapist" (unless you are one!) or put information in your brochures that implies that you do therapy. You are a holistic health educator who provides education and support that are designed to facilitate health and healing. Information about your services can, however, tell people that you support the mind/body/spirit connection and work holistically. This way potential clients are aware that you are interested in the newer views of health and well-being.

- Check the laws in your state. Some states do have laws that say formal counseling can only be offered by licensed individuals such as doctors, psychotherapists, and social workers. In some states, however, non-denominational ministers are exempt from this restriction. In order to counsel people without fear of restrictions, some healers take advantage of this exemption and become non-denominational ministers. Another option is to get certified as a Life Coach. This is a new field of professionals that helps clients reevaluate all areas of their existence in order to create a healthier, more meaningful life. (Keep in mind that in all fields you will encounter people who embrace a holistic philosophy, and people who have more traditional Epoch II values. This will be true among Life Coaching professionals and non-denominational ministers as well.) See the "Holistic Resources" section at the end of the book for more information on Life Coaching.

211

Overall, on the issue of liability, it can be helpful to keep the following in mind:

First, do not be intimidated by the concept of "licensing and credentialing." These regulatory systems have grown increasingly dysfunctional over the years. They often serve as a way to set up hierarchies for control and economic gain within professions. Yes, there are many traditionally licensed professionals who have provided excellent therapy for clients, but there are also traditionally licensed professionals who have behaved very inappropriately and provided bad therapy or treatments. Licensing is not necessarily a guarantee of good services.

Second, it is important to note that there are many holistic health professionals who are not licensed or credentialed in a traditional way. Yet these people are often doing some of the best thinking and best healing work in the world today. As we transition from Epoch II into Epoch III humanity, it is likely that we will see more of these types of nontraditional professionals emerging. There will be less emphasis on formal, structured systems like licensing and credentialing.

Summary

We want to emphasize that health promotion professionals can learn to use holistic counseling strategies that acknowledge feelings and life issues without inappropriately crossing into the realm of clinical psychotherapy or treatment. We may not all be licensed therapists, but we are all licensed human beings! All of us can provide a safe space and respectful listening, perhaps the two most powerful healing tools we can offer a client.

By encouraging people to tell their stories and express feelings, we are acting as a catalyst to help them begin their healing journey. This is supported by numerous studies that have found that many people, from grade schoolers to nursing home residents, medical students, and prisoners, feel happier and are healthier after disclosing deeply traumatic memories.[10] The bottom line is that we absolutely cannot separate life issues and personal emotions from the understanding of health or the treatment of pain and illness. They are inextricably linked and efforts to avoid addressing these aspects of a client's experience will substantially limit the effectiveness of our health promotion efforts.

This brings us to perhaps the most fundamental and important question concerning the role of health educators and promoters, a question whose answer illuminates one of the most basic and important distinctions between traditional and holistic approaches to health promotion. Is it *what we do* as health professionals or *who we are* as human beings that is the most critical component of helping people to grow and heal? Once again, Ram Dass explains that "We can of course help through all that we do but at the deepest level we help through who we are."[2]

In order to work effectively with the holistic approach, we *must* be aware of our own issues. In traditional health promotion approaches this is not necessary. We do not need to work on our own issues in order to write a behavioral contract, assign someone to a stage of change, or prescribe a diet or exercise regimen. But to listen, validate, exercise nonjudgment, and connect compassionately with a suffering human being is a different matter altogether—one that requires a much deeper level of self-awareness and growth.

Suggestions for Holistic Counseling:
A Path with Heart

Pause and relax
Listen, listen, listen
Nurture relationship
Encourage emotions
Acknowledge and validate pain and suffering
Ask permission regarding touch
Honor confidentiality
Share information carefully
Do your own work

References

Peter Breggin, a psychiatrist, has been a prominent voice in the mental health community calling for an end to the misuse of drugs and traditional treatments for emotional health problems. His books provide a compelling case for rethinking how we can help people explore physical, emotional, and spiritual well-being. We highly recommend his book *Toxic Psychiatry.*

1. Breggin, Peter. *Toxic Psychiatry.* New York: St. Martin's, 1991.

2. Dass R. *How Can I Help? Stories and Reflections on Service.* New York: Knopf, 1993.

3. Dossey L. *Healing Words: The Power of Prayer and the Practice of Medicine.* San Francisco: Harper, 1993.

4. Kornfield J. *A Path with Heart: A Guide through the Perils and Promises of Spiritual Life.* New York: Bantam, 1993.

5. Carrier K. "Guiding Clients in a New Direction: How You Can Help Empower Clients as They Move Forward on Their Journey to a Healthy Lifestyle." *IDEA Today,* April 1997, 62–66.

6. Beckman H.B., and R. M. Frankel. "The Effect of Physician Behavior on the Collection of Data." *Annals of Internal Medicine* 101 (1984): 692–96.

7. Marvel, M. K., R. M. Epstein, K. Flowers, and H. B. Beckman. "Soliciting the Patient's Agenda: Have We Improved?" *Journal of the American Medical Association* 281, no. 3 (1999): 283–87.

8. Myss, Caroline. *Why People Don't Heal and How They Can.* New York: Harmony, 1997.

9. Small, J. *Becoming Naturally Therapeutic: A Return to the True Essence of Helping.* New York: Bantam, 1990.

10. Pennebaker, J.W. *Opening Up: The Healing Power of Confiding in Others.* New York: Morrow, 1990.

Chapter 14

OUR STORIES

How the "New Paradigm" Found Us

Before you embark on any path ask the question:
Does this path have a heart?
If the answer is no, you will know it,
and then you must choose another path.

Carlos Castaneda
The Teachings of Don Juan

Karen' s Story:

No More Five-Pound Challenges!

Often after presentations at conferences people from the audience will ask me if my college degree is in psychology. They assume, after hearing about my work and my beliefs, that I must be a psychotherapist. In fact, my training and background are very traditional; an undergraduate degree in kinesiology and a master's degree in exercise science. My formal education was completely biomedical in orientation. In 1983, after completing my master's degree, I joined Conoco Inc. (an international oil and gas company known as ConocoPhillips today) and helped plan and launch their new health and fitness program and facilities.

We began Conoco's program from a very traditional, biomedical place. Early programming, from 1984 to 1987, included the usual fare. Everyone entering the program went through extensive cardiovascular testing and fitness evaluation. We had a state-of-the-art fitness center, exercise classes, and fitness competitions. All participants received elaborate exercise prescriptions.

In the areas of nutrition and weight, there were eight-week classes taught by a local dietitian. There was an "eating well" cafeteria program that featured "healthy" choices labeled with fat, calorie, and food exchange information. Participants were weighed, and body fat was tested upon entry into the program. Everyone was retested six months later. There were bulletin board and newsletter articles about eating less fat and about the importance of controlling body fat and weight. Locker rooms had scales and height-weight charts, and of course we featured periodic competitions and incentive programs to promote weight loss. Programs like the Five-Pound Challenge (employees were weighed weekly and given a mug and T-shirt if they lost five pounds or more by the end of the month), and Maintain Don't Gain (same concept but rewarding weight maintenance over holidays) were our most popular offerings.

After several years of this programming, I became increasingly distressed about what we were doing. I had always been personally uncomfortable with it. I did not realize it at the time, but my discomfort was due to the fact that I, like almost all other women, had struggled with eating and weight issues since I was about twelve. I became a full-blown compulsive eater while in college and was painfully obsessed with food and my body throughout my undergraduate years. I knew that the restrictive eating and weight loss focus we were teaching in our health promotion programs at Conoco had never helped me earlier in my life, and at an intuitive level I had a sense that it was the same for Conoco employees who were attending these offerings. I also knew that these programs could even be making things worse for some people—making them more obsessed about weight and preoccupied with food and possibly even driving weight fluctuations and long-term weight gain.

We tracked employees who participated in our weight loss competitions. As we anticipated, those who participated most, year after year, gained the most weight over time. Furthermore, rates of dropout and weight regain were consistently high among weight loss class participants, and many people in the employee population simply refused to sign up for any weight-related programs. So in 1988 we made a decision to discontinue *all* the weight- and nutrition-related programming in order to search for an approach that made more sense.

As Luke Seaward, friend and colleague often says, "the universe always provides." Early in my research for alternative approaches, I came across the work of Jane Hirschmann and Carol Munter. Jane and Carol are psychotherapists who pioneered the development of the Overcoming Overeating™ approach during the feminist movement in New York City in the 1970s. Their first book, *Overcoming Overeating: Living Free in a World of Food,* had just been published (see "Holistic Resources" at the end of the book). I read a review of the book, bought it, and read it. It profoundly changed my life. Their description of the food and eating problem, and their nondiet/size acceptance approach to healing it was the biggest paradigm change I had ever encountered.

Hirschmann's and Munter's work was also my first introduction to feminist issues relating to eating and weight. As radically different as their approach was, it immediately made perfect sense to me. I knew in my bones that it was powerfully true. And, as you will see upon reading further in this chapter, their work required me, as well as the rest of our staff, to rethink every single aspect of our health promotion efforts at Conoco. Even more significant, however, was the personal healing process each of us was able to begin as part of learning to use the Overcoming Overeating approach. To this day I feel this was one of the greatest gifts in my life, especially because I am the mother of two young women.

The rest is history, as they say. We brought the Overcoming Overeating approach into Conoco and redesigned every aspect of our eating programs (as described in detail in chapter 17). We also went on to eliminate all other areas of traditional health promotion programming and developed entirely new approaches that were consistent in message and process with our new eating programs. Much of what we learned in this process is detailed in the remaining chapters in this book.

This process has been a huge personal gift as well! Suffice it to say that every single aspect of my life was changed by this experience. Certainly, how I think about my health has changed but also how I parent, relate to my husband, and live my entire life has been revolutionized.

Jon's Story:

From Saving the World to Shifting the Paradigm

My initial interest in health grew out of experiences in my previous profession—playing rock and roll music six nights a week in a traveling band. I began doing this at the age of twenty-two when I graduated from college. While I loved the music, the lifestyle was a hard one and I knew many people who were traveling down a dangerous path living this lifestyle. After all, the bars were smoky and there was plenty of alcohol, drugs, and sexual partners available for the asking. Add to this the late nights and constant loud drone of the drums, electric guitars, and amplifiers and you have less than what would be considered by most experts to be a "healthy lifestyle."

As I progressed into my late twenties I began to wonder if this was really what I wanted to do as a full-time job for the rest of my life. At the same time I began to acquire an interest in physical activity and nutrition, perhaps as an antidote for the unhealthy atmosphere in which I regularly found myself. I became particularly fond of racquetball and then running and developed quite a passion for both, particularly because I had been so poor at sports in junior high and high school. Now I seemed to have acquired an aptitude for both of these activities.

I decided to go back to school to learn how to help other people enjoy the benefits of healthy living and initially pursued a master's degree in exercise physiology followed by another in human nutrition and eventually a doctorate in health education. I was enthralled by the focus on health promotion and disease prevention and became well versed in the traditional risk factor, behavior modification approaches we have talked so much about in this book. I designed courses for undergraduate and graduate students to help disseminate this knowledge more widely, helped to set up Michigan State University's Employee Health Promotion Program, and wrote my dissertation on a behavioral program I designed and implemented to motivate people to increase their exercise levels—a dissertation that landed me a full-page picture and story in *Health* magazine. I preached the virtues of my newfound information to everyone I met, including (often much to their dismay) the "boys in the band" and my parents. In my spare time I managed to adhere to a low fat diet and train for and participate in numerous road races and triathlons.

So there I was, graduating in 1992 with two master's degrees and a Ph.D. and ready to save the world from cholesterol, smoking, obesity, and sedentary lifestyles! I created the Michigan Center for Preventive Medicine and spent a number of years counseling people on the benefits and dangers of healthy and unhealthy living. I believed without a doubt that if people would just exercise and eat "healthy" (low fat, low cholesterol, low salt, high fiber, etc.) they could surely be thin and cured of whatever ailed them!

To make a long story short, I gradually became very frustrated because it seemed like so many of the people I was talking to were not doing what I was telling them to do. This was particularly true in the area of eating and weight loss, which soon became the main focus of the center and my primary area of interest. Furthermore, it began to dawn on me that the weight, eating, and exercise issues for which most people were ostensibly coming to see me were really symptoms of underlying conflicts and struggles.

As part of our program offerings we made available protein-modified fasts for people who wanted to lose quite a bit of weight. I worked individually with these people and also conducted group workshops while they were on the diet—talking about their relationships with food, exercise, and life. I began to realize that what we were doing was not helping. At the same time I met my wife (who is a psychotherapist), a local dietitian, and other health professionals around the country from whom I began to learn of a different way of approaching these difficult issues.

As I became aware of the pain and suffering that our clients experienced with the inevitable weight regain after participating in our programs, I grew more and more convinced that our traditional approaches to eating and weight were harming people in significant ways. I began to wonder why we continue to do these things in spite of the obvious failures when a good friend and colleague (my coauthor) introduced me to *The Turning Point* by Fritjof Capra—and the rest is history! Over the years I came to believe that traditional approaches to eating, weight, and health, as well as to other health-related issues, were an outgrowth of the cultural and scientific paradigm in which they developed—a paradigm that was limited, out-dated, and in desperate need of reevaluation. I became actively in-volved in the nondiet, size acceptance movement and began working to help people of all sizes be healthier by loving and caring for the bodies that they currently have.

An Invitation to Explore

Your Own Views on Weight and Health

For both of us, rethinking and dramatically altering our beliefs and work in the area of eating and weight was the main catalyst for initi-ating the search for alternative approaches in *all* areas of health pro-motion. Therefore, we have placed a special emphasis on these topics in this book. The next three chapters are designed to help you re-evaluate your personal and professional philosophies and feelings about eating and weight issues and to learn how to apply the holistic principles we have been discussing in these areas. The process of moving from the traditional "weight management paradigm" toward the holistic "nondiet/size acceptance/health at every size" paradigm involves several important steps.

> ***Step One***. Become well informed about the cultural, economic, and political issues tied to society's preoccupation with dieting and thinness.

> ***Step Two***. Become familiar with the research regarding weight and health issues and the failure of traditional approaches.

> ***Step Three***. Explore how eating, weight and body image issues are understood from a holistic perspective.

> ***Step Four***. Personally and professionally explore working with the nondiet/size acceptance approach for healing eating and body image difficulties.

The next three chapters will address these steps in detail. Please note that these chapters will be a bit different from the rest of the book. In them, we have provided more extensive referencing to enable readers to go to the original sources. We do this because the issues being discussed are very personal and emotionally charged, making investment in the status quo and resistance to change high. Many of the conclusions we will be drawing contradict what we as health professionals have learned from our education, health experts, and the culture as a whole. For this reason, we believe it is critically important for each person to be compassionate and gentle with themselves as they begin this journey.

Part Five

THE MOTHER OF ALL CHANGES

Chapter 15

WEIGHT, HEALTH, AND CULTURE
Exposing the Myths, Exploring the Realities

The data linking overweight and death,
as well as the data showing the beneficial effects of weight loss,
are limited, fragmentary and often ambiguous.

Jerome Kassirer and Marcia Angell
New England Journal of Medicine

There is no subject in health promotion more relevant to emerging
Epoch III humanity than eating and weight. That may sound very
strange! What do nutrition programming, weight loss classes, and
body fat testing have to do with the decline of dominator societies
and the arrival of a new human consciousness? They have *everything*
to do with it.

In earlier chapters of this book we outlined how reclaiming the
"feminine side of soul," as Bob Keck so beautifully describes it, is
pivotal to the process of crossing over to the Epoch III egalitarian,
peaceful societies of the future. The key ingredient to the reintegration of this lost feminine aspect is the full liberation of women from
the oppression imposed by thousands of years of Epoch II patriarchy.

Nothing has silenced the voices and energies of contemporary
women more than dieting and body hatred. The current culturally
induced obsession with thinness has led to, as Jean Kilbourne accurately describes in her video *Slim Hopes,* "an impoverishment of the
minds and souls of women" (see "Holistic Resources" at the end of
the book for more information on Slim Hopes). Women must be encouraged to live free of the emotional, spiritual and physical constraints of this obsession in order to assume a more powerful role in
shaping future societies.

Traditional weight management approaches, like all other aspects of Western health care, emanate from the biomedical, reductionist paradigm, which is rooted in patriarchy and the oppression of women. On the surface it may look as though efforts to control body weight are simply based on a desire to make people "healthier." On closer examination, however, the disparate societal emphasis on women regarding thinness, the emphasis on control over the body, and even the subtle messages that higher moral standing is obtained through starving and denial of pleasurable eating are all perspectives that run directly parallel to the values of Epoch II and the Scientific Revolution.

A Time for Change

Leading experts generally agree that diet programs are ineffective for the majority of participants. Yet research and intervention continue to focus on weight loss primarily through dietary restriction.[2] Ironically, with 50 billion dollars a year spent on weight loss efforts,[3] the American population continues to get heavier and we are faced with an epidemic of eating disorders.[4]

Please note that throughout this and the following chapter, when referring to an individual's weight, we will not use the terms *obesity, overweight,* or *overfat* except as part of a quotation. It is our opinion and the opinion of other professionals involved with nondiet/size acceptance approaches that these terms are scientifically ambiguous and culturally biased.[5] Although there is debate concerning the best terms with which to replace current terminology, *fat* or *large* will be the terms used in this book.

Body Mass Index

In the literature cited in this and the next chapter the most commonly used measure of an individual's weight is the body mass index (BMI). This measurement is determined by dividing the weight in kilograms by the square of the height in meters squared (kg/m^2). Federal guidelines identify overweight as a BMI of 25.0 to 29.9 and obesity as a BMI of 30.0 and above.[6] We will be discussing the problem with these standards in this and the next chapter.

This chapter is divided into two sections. The first is an in-depth look at the economic, social, and political issues that lie beneath our cultural obsession with weight control. The second details the broad range of research that calls into question most of today's firmly held assumptions about the relationship between weight, health, and mortality.

Weight and Culture:

Economic, Social, and Political Issues

An American Obsession

The current American obsession with dieting and slimness is a cultural aberration. Throughout history, most cultures have regarded fatness as a sign of success, health, and beauty.[7] Less than one hundred years ago Americans equated body fat with affluence and higher socioeconomic status. Excess fat was described as a "snug balance in the body bank and a comfortable reserve in the case of emergencies."[8] Victorian era women wore corsets to achieve the plump, hourglass figure deemed desirable for the leisure class. This style of dress was advocated by the medical establishment, although it often resulted in constricted lungs, squeezed livers and bladders, and dis-

229

located stomachs.[9-11] A 1908 article in *Harpers Bazaar* advised readers on "how to get plump," saying that "fat is force and stored up fat is stored up force."[12] Fashion models were advised to be "far from thin, with no suggestion of hollows in the face or the collarbones, for the camera seems to accentuate such defects."[13]

Anthropologists point out that the first strong cultural emphasis on weight loss appeared around the turn of the century. This coincided with women obtaining the right to vote and demanding a more visible and active role in shaping society. As women's power and status improved, the dictates of fashion began to change as well. Medical recommendations for women to lose weight also followed suit. For the next hundred years, medical science would promote a wide variety of potentially dangerous and sometimes lethal diets, drugs, and surgeries to help people reduce their weight in the name of health. A partial chronological list of these recommended treatments included the following.[14]

In the Name of Health

1893	Thyroid extract	1957	HCG
1920	Laxatives	1964	Total fasting
1933	Dinitrophenol	1969	Intestinal bypass
1937	Amphetamine	1974	Jaw wiring
1940	Atropine	1977	Gastric bypass
1940	Digitalis	1985	Gastric balloon
1946	"Rainbow pill"	1990s	Fen-Phen, Redux, Meridia, Xenical, etc.

The vast majority of those participating in and suffering from these "cures" would be women, despite the fact that women's fat confers only a fraction of the health risk of men's and may actually carry with it significant health benefits.[15-17] This legacy continues today, as young girls and women continue to divert significant proportions of their physical, emotional and financial resources to the pursuit of ideals of body shape and size that are, for the vast majority, neither achievable nor healthy.[2]

Keeping women occupied by continually striving toward an un-reachable ideal of perfection serves the purposes of a control-oriented, patriarchal society.[11,18] When women's energies are diverted by the pursuit of dieting and body improvement, they are kept from dealing effectively with the realities of existence in a man's world and from participating more fully in business, art, politics, literature, and life in general.

Much has been written concerning the historical association of female fat, particularly on the abdomen, buttocks, and breasts, with the "feminine" values of nurturance and compassion.[19-21] Throughout history, soft, rounded hips, thighs, and bellies have been considered ideal for women in the vast majority of cultures.[7] As long as women were content to stay at home and bear children, these associations remained relatively intact. It has been argued convincingly that the obsessive hatred of fat in this country began with the women's equality movement and that the more powerful women become the more pressure there is to alter the aspects of their bodies that distinguish them from their male counterparts.[20-23] For example, one of the things that women dislike most about their bodies is cellulite, a characteristic of the female body that is rarely found in men (cellulite is actually a made-up name referring to dimpled fat that some women accumulate as they age). The continuing trend toward an ever thinner, androgynous ideal for women would also seem to support this view.[24] Thus, "Taking on the accoutrements of the white male world may be experienced by many women themselves as a chance to embody qualities such as detachment, self-containment, self-mastery, and control which are highly valued in this culture."[22]

Since the 1960s, a preference for slenderness has taken hold in other Western, industrialized nations as well. However, due to a unique confluence of social, economic, and political developments favoring the desire for thinness, "no other culture suffers from the same wild anxieties about weight, dieting and exercise as we do."[13]

In fact, it is estimated that approximately 40 percent of adult women (versus 25 percent of adult men) are attempting to lose weight at any one time.[2] Research also suggests that 50 percent of young women are currently trying to lose weight, even though the majority is already at or below normal weight.[25] Even very young children are not spared. Research indicates that "fear of fat, restricted eating and binge eating are common among girls by age 10."[26]

The Body as Machine

Traditional treatment approaches to weight management strongly reflect the underlying assumptions of the seventeenth-century paradigm discussed in chapters 3 and 4. Thus, the human body is seen as a "finely calibrated combustion engine that should weigh a certain amount," and therefore scientists have issued "recommendations about exactly how many calories, calibrated to age, height, and activity levels are needed to achieve this goal."[20] Because body weight has been considered largely a mechanical matter of calories in (diet) and calories out (exercise), weight management is reduced to a measurable numeric equation and it is assumed that everyone can attain their weight goals by merely adjusting these variables. Furthermore, because scientists have now determined the exact amount of calories and nutrients needed for health and efficiency, food has increasingly become "an instrument of science, stripped down to a quantity of energy and deprived of all its sensual and emotional aspects."[20] The resulting reductionist view of weight- and eating-related issues "is typical of the medicalization of complex conditions, in which contextual factors are treated as single variables to be overcome."[18]

These premises continue to guide medical weight management efforts. Yet it is common knowledge that weight, like almost all other human characteristics, varies according to a "normal" distribution, meaning that a wide range of weights are considered to be normal. Furthermore, the existence of different body types (somatotypes in Western medicine, doshas in Ayurveda) is well documented, and it is likely that each has its own range of normally distributed weights and body fat percentages. Dr. William Sheldon, originator of the concept of the somatotype, commented in the 1930s on ideal weights such as those set forth by the height and weight tables, saying "this kind of foolishness gives some of our best people inferiority complexes."[24] Strong arguments have been made that these tables are flawed to the point of being relatively meaningless for the majority of people.[24,27] World renowned researcher Dr. Ancel Keys described them as:

> Arm-chair concoctions starting with questionable assumptions and ending with three sets of standards for 'body frames' which were never measured or even properly defined.[28]

The view of weight control as a simple mathematical relationship between caloric intake and expenditure has been shown to be inaccurate.[29,30] Furthermore, the reduction of food and eating to caloric input, devoid of other qualities, denies the reality of the complex interaction of emotional, psychological, and cultural variables that determines voluntary food intake.[31] The resulting diet mentality "reinforces the split between the dieter's mind and her body, and asks her to distrust her body, which is seen as the source of sabotage."[32] This separation of mind from body inhibits the development of internally regulated eating in children[33] and contributes to the current epidemic of adult eating disorders, disordered eating, and exercise addiction.[34,35]

We and others have discussed at length the power of paradigms to direct research and practice in science, even in the face of substantial conflicting information.[36–38] In his landmark book *Meaning and Medicine,* Dr. Larry Dossey writes that "our illusions regarding the body . . . that it behaves essentially like a machine . . . have paved the way for the loss of meaning in health and illness."[38] Our continued reliance on outdated interventions based on the "calorie in vs. calorie out" and "ideal weight" hypotheses may well be, at least in part, a result of this legacy.

The Food Industry and the Media

Food Advertising and Labeling. In keeping with the larger cultural agenda, today's media images constantly tell us that we should control our eating and our weight. We have become so accustomed to this phenomenon that we forget it is relatively new. Fifty years ago our grandparents did not walk down grocery store aisles surrounded by thousands of messages about food products being "low fat," "cholesterol free," "low sodium," or "high fiber." Concern about removing "undesirable" ingredients from our diet has led to product label-ing that categorizes foods as "good/healthy" versus "bad/unhealthy." Some health professionals have observed that this type of labeling by the food industry has contributed to the development of a food- and eating-based morality. The prestigious *Tufts University Diet and Nu-trition Letter* recently commented on the dangers of this trend, say-ing:

> Good nutrition is getting a bad name—one that smacks of rigid-ity, guilt-making and extremism . . . Worse still, some eight out of ten [Americans] think foods are inherently good or bad—that is, the decision to eat a particular item has nothing to do with its context in the diet as a whole, but every single bite they take represents an all-or-nothing choice either for or against good health. [For example,] two out of 10 Americans are even under the false belief that all fat should be eliminated from the diet.[39]

Because our culture encourages us to "think" constantly about our food choices, eating has become an intellectual activity that is in-creasingly disconnected from the physical body. We no longer know how to eat in response to hunger, fullness, and body cravings be-cause we are cognitively trying to sort out what we should eat, what we shouldn't eat, and how our choices will affect our weight and our health.

Images of Beauty. While advertising and cultural messages urge us to eliminate fat in foods, fat on our bodies is portrayed as even worse. The media bombard women with images of female fashion models who project an emaciated, adolescent, androgynous look as the aesthetic ideal. What most women do not realize is that the pub-lished images of these models have been airbrushed to remove any flaws (such as wrinkles or visible pores in the skin), photographi-cally elongated to maximize thinness, and in some cases generated entirely on a computer.

The content of many of the articles in women's magazines is also unhelpful. The main messages in most articles and ads are (1) your natural appearance, including your weight, is unacceptable, so buy something to disguise or fix it; and (2) "good" women nurture other people by preparing delicious recipes for loved ones, but they do not partake in these rich foods themselves.

Not surprisingly, the relentless pressure to conform to unrealistic body shapes and sizes is wreaking havoc with the body image and self-esteem of women of all sizes. A survey in *Psychology Today* questioned more than 3,400 women in their thirties and forties with an average weight of 140 pounds. Among the findings, 24 percent of the women said they would give up more than three years of their lives to lose weight, 35 percent considered pregnancy a major source of body hatred, and 50 percent reported that they smoked cigarettes in order to control their weight. The author of the article concluded that "the magnitude of self-hatred among women is astonishing. Despite being at a weight that most women would envy they are still plagued by feelings of inadequacy."[40] A substantial body of literature supports this extreme body dissatisfaction as a "normative discontent" in our culture, especially among young women.[21,41]

It is interesting to note that men's health and fitness magazines now routinely feature cover images of young, scantily clad, tan males with washboard abdominal muscles, broad chests, and full heads of hair. Not surprisingly, this new cultural interest in objectifying men has gone hand in hand with an increase in eating disorder rates in this population.[42]

The "Diet-Pharmaceutical-Industrial Complex"

The tremendous pressure to be thin is driven by the diet, fashion, cosmetics, fitness, insurance, and pharmaceutical industries, which reap tremendous financial rewards by promoting unattainable expectations, especially for women.[11] In addition, many obesity researchers have economic links to this so-called diet-pharmaceutical-industrial complex, creating powerful incentives for maintaining the status quo. For example, most members of the National Institutes of Health National Task Force on the Prevention and Treatment of Obesity serve as consultants to both commercial weight loss programs and pharmaceutical companies involved in the development of weight loss medications.[43] Furthermore,:

Obesity research is primarily funded by companies that make money by promoting short-term weight-loss methods, contributing, perhaps, to questionable objectivity in the reporting of research findings.[13]

Medical support for thinness is one of the important developments contributing to the growth of our current obsession. It is interesting to note that only a hundred years ago, American physicians were encouraging people to gain weight, believing that "a large number of fat cells was absolutely necessary to achieve a balanced personality."[44] As late as 1926, Dr. Woods Hutchinson, former president of the American Academy of Medicine, warned that "the longed-for slender and boyish figure is becoming a menace, not only for the present, but for future generations."[8] Today, fatness as chronic disease and weight reduction as cure stand as almost universally accepted medical dogma.

An extensive examination of the history of the development of the complex relationships between weight, health, and American culture is beyond the scope of this book, but can be found in the references listed at the end of the chapter.[20,24]

The Research

Continued reliance on weight loss programs as a solution to being "too fat" is based on and justified by the medical premises that (1) weights above recommended levels cause poor health and decreased longevity and (2) weight loss increases longevity and improves health. Although these premises are taken for granted by the medical establishment, they are, in fact, "not well supported by existing studies."[46] Below we present a summary of these conflicting data.[4,14,27]

Weight and Health

Weight and Mortality. Approximately 75 percent of all weight-mortality studies published since the 1950s "find weight to be irrelevant to health and mortality issues (except perhaps at the extremes of the Body Mass Index)."[27] The lack of support for a positive relationship between weight and mortality remains even after confounding factors such as smoking, preexisting illness, and length of follow-up are considered.[14] An in-depth meta-analysis of the literature concluded that weight levels currently considered moderately overweight were:

> Not associated with increased all-cause mortality . . . and body weight at or slightly below current recommendations was associated with increased risk of mortality. . . . This quantitative analysis of existing studies revealed increased mortality at moderately low BMI for white men compared to that observed at extreme overweight. . . . Attention to the health risks of underweight is needed, and body weight recommendations for optimum longevity need to be considered in light of these risks.[47]

While some studies do show increased mortality with increasing weight, most do not. A number of studies actually show an inverse relationship (decreased mortality with increasing weight) with mild to moderate fatness and in some cases even with extreme fatness. For example, data from the Norway Study, the largest epidemiological study of its kind, indicate that *maximum longevity is attained in women considerably overweight by medical standards* (BMI 26–28).[48] As BMIs ascend into the "very obese" range (34–36) mortality does begin to rise, but slowly. Even women considered to be medically "morbidity obese" (BMI greater than 44) have a better chance of surviving to age sixty-five than do women in the leanest group (BMI 18 or less). Similarly, in the Pooling Project data, representing results from the Framingham, Albany, Tecumseh, Chicago People's Gas, and Chicago Western Electric studies, the highest mortality for both men and women occurred in the underweight group. Mortality rates fluctuate considerably but appear to be optimal at levels currently considered 25 to 35 percent "overweight." And mortality rates in the fattest group are only slightly higher than in the "desirable weight" group.[49]

Weight and Morbidity. Upon thorough examination of the scientific literature, accepted notions about the relationship between atherosclerotic heart disease and weight also are questionable. Both angiographic and autopsy studies show no relationship between fatness and the degree or progression of atherosclerotic buildup in the coronary arteries.[49-53] Some research suggests that fatness may actually be associated with protection from the disease. For example, the largest angiographic investigation of the relationship between weight and coronary artery atherosclerosis concluded that for the 4,500 middle-aged and elderly men and women studied, every eleven-pound increase in body weight was associated with a 10 to 40 percent lower chance of having the disease.[54] Even with respect to extremely fat persons, weighing on the average well over three hundred pounds, studies fail to demonstrate an increase in atherosclerosis, seriously calling into question the link between fatness and this disease.[55] The relative unimportance of body weight in atherosclerosis is further supported by intervention studies demonstrating that disease progression can be halted or even reversed with dietary change without significant weight loss.[56,57]

It is well known that fatness is associated with an increased prevalence of health problems such as hypertension, blood lipid disorders, and type II diabetes, which are themselves risk factors for cardiovascular disease. However, such a statistically significant relationship between fatness and disease does not prove that fatness is the cause of these problems. In fact, *numerous studies have shown that these so-called weight-related health problems can be treated effectively with lifestyle interventions that do not result in weight loss.* For example, blood pressure, cholesterol, and glucose levels all improved in these studies even though individuals remain markedly "obese" by traditional medical standards.[58-63] This has led to the suggestion that for many people increased weight may be a relatively benign symptom that is related to but not necessarily the cause of insulin insensitivity, diabetes, hypertension, and atherosclerosis.[64-66]

What is extremely stunning and less well known is the fact that a significant body of research suggests that fatness is associated with a number of health *benefits*. Numerous studies have indicated an inverse relationship between fatness and cancer deaths.[67-71] With respect to lung cancer, the leading cause of all cancer deaths, "the overall consistency in the inverse association of body mass with lung cancer in reported studies is impressive. It is noteworthy that no study shows a significant contrary trend."[72] Fatness also has been shown to protect against osteoporosis, a major source of disability and death in older women, with thin women being twice as vulnerable to the disease as heavier women.[73,74] Additionally, being heavy has been shown to be an advantage in tuberculosis and respiratory diseases such as chronic obstructive lung disease, emphysema, and bronchitis, even when the effects of smoking are considered.[75,76] Finally, many studies suggest that fatness may actually be beneficial for older adults. One recent study of more than 7,000 men and women seventy years of age and over concluded that: "obesity may be protective compared to thinness or normal weight in older community-dwelling Americans."[77-79]

Weight Loss and Health

The widely accepted assumption that weight loss results in increased longevity and improved health also is not supported by the literature. In fact, "most epidemiologic studies suggest that weight loss is associated with increased mortality."[2] This consistent association holds for all-cause mortality and mortality from heart disease and stroke for both men and women. It emerges across studies of widely varying methodology and follow-up and remains unaffected after controlling for the potential effects of preexisting illness and smoking status.[27]

Due to the tremendous number of potentially confounding factors involved in epidemiological research, the reasons for these findings are not clear. Short-term weight loss is associated with reductions in risk factors for cardiovascular disease, including improvements in blood pressure, glycemic control, and lipid and lipoprotein profiles. However, "given the high likelihood that weight will be regained, it remains to be determined whether these time-limited improvements confer more permanent health benefits."[2]

Weight Cycling. The pattern of repeatedly losing and regaining weight experienced by most dieters may be one of the factors that contributes to the higher mortality rates found in people who have lost weight. Weight cycling has been shown to decrease metabolic rates at rest and during exercise, increase lipoprotein lipase activity (which makes the body more efficient at storing fat), and increase the proportion of fat to lean tissue in the body. With each weight loss/regain cycle, weight is increasingly redistributed from lower body subcutaneous fat—shown to have a protective effect against heart disease, diabetes, cancer and high cholesterol—to abdominal visceral fat, which does not confer these protective effects.[27] In addition, studies point to increased risk for heart disease, hypertension, and diabetes in individuals who are chronically losing and regaining weight.[80–85] Other studies have suggested links between weight cycling and gall bladder disease, low bone mineral density, and kidney cancer.[86,87,88] Most recently, research has suggested a potential relationship between weight cycling and breast cancer, with the authors concluding with a warning that "the mammary gland is adversely affected by chronic weight cycling" and "cyclic dieting attempts at weight loss should not be viewed as a benign behavior in women and may be an important risk factor for breast cancer."[89]

Negative Psychological Effects. Dieting is psychologically a very negative, shame-based experience.[90] In addition, the deprivation of dieting causes an increased preoccupation with food, overeating, and bingeing in response to the dietary restrictions. Increased body dissatisfaction also occurs with each repetition of the weight loss/regain cycle. Thus, what most people perceive as the "solution" to weight problems is actually one of their main causes. In fact, dieting behavior is the best predictor of bulimia. In studies conducted over the last twenty years, Polivy and Herman (1996) have shown that the more you teach a person to cognitively restrain eating through behavior modification techniques, the more subsequent bingeing behavior and weight fluctuations the person will experience.[91] Teaching people to diet actually sets them up for overeating in response to stressful situations, while many nondieters naturally reduce food intake when experiencing stress.

Animal Studies. Over the past forty years, there has been a great deal of research conducted on animal models of obesity, including dogs, swine, rats, and mice.[92–96] It is interesting to note that when these animals have their food intake restricted until they lose 20 percent of their weight and then are allowed to regain that weight ("weight cycled"), they develop abdominal obesity, hypertension, blood vessel damage, and heart disease, the same outcomes that have traditionally been blamed on obesity in humans. So, the hypertension and other cardiovascular pathologies seen in some fat humans may be the result of losing and gaining weight rather than of the weight itself.[97]

What Does It All Mean?

Clearly, there is a substantial body of research that contradicts many of the commonly held notions about the relationship between weight and health. Given the extremely complex and often contradictory nature of the available literature in this area, it has been suggested that:

> Definitive proof of any given hypothesis about the weight-health correlation is almost impossible at the present time . . . [and] in America today the real risks to health and longevity are more likely to come from dieting than from stable weights that are above those recommended by the height and weight tables.[27]

Summary

Our obsessive focus on weight control and thinness is, once again, a reflection of the larger cultural agenda. The simplistic, mechanistic theory of calories in versus calories out, the extreme emphasis on standardizing and controlling body size (especially for women), and the relentless pursuit of material and financial gain by the diet-pharmaceutical-industrial complex reflect and perpetuate the deepest values of Epoch II patriarchy. Perhaps nowhere is there a better example of *paradigm paralysis.* Years of data demonstrating that traditional approaches do not work and actually cause weight gain and eating disorders have not diminished enthusiasm for weight loss programs among medical and health promotion professionals.

As we close this chapter we would like to summarize what the research on weight and health actually tells us. The majority of studies find that

- Weight is irrelevant to health and mortality except at the most extreme levels of thinness and fatness.

- There is no relationship between fatness and the degree of atherosclerotic buildup in the arteries.

- Fatness is not a proven cause of hypertension, lipid disorders, or type II diabetes, and these conditions improve significantly with lifestyle changes that involve little or no weight loss.

- Fatness is associated with health benefits, including decreased death from some cancers, protection from osteoporosis, and improved recovery from respiratory diseases such as bronchitis and tuberculosis.

- Weight loss is associated with increased all-cause mortality and increased mortality from heart disease and stroke.

- Weight cycling is associated with increased risk for weight gain, heart disease, hypertension, diabetes, gall bladder disease, low bone density, kidney cancer, and breast cancer.

Ironically, the failure of traditional weight management approaches is as striking as is their almost universal appeal. As far back as 1958, pioneer obesity researcher Dr. Albert Stunkard summarized the ineffectiveness of these approaches, stating:

> Most obese persons will not stay in treatment for obesity. Of those who stay in treatment, most will not lose weight, and of those who do lose weight, most will regain it.[98]

Yet participation in these approaches continues to grow despite the fact that little has changed to alter the validity of this conclusion, and it is still true that "relatively few participants succeed in keeping off weight long term."[99,100]

It is essential for all of us as health professionals to open our eyes to the data and new perspectives on the controversial subject of weight and health. The next two chapters will explore how new perspectives have created an alternative paradigm for supporting people with eating and weight-related struggles.

References

For this chapter, we would like to acknowledge our special indebtedness to Dr. Glenn Gaesser for his tireless pursuit of the truth about the relationship between weight and health. His *Big Fat Lies: The Truth about Your Weight and Your Health* provides a beacon of light in an area of health promotion that is overwhelmingly darkened by ignorance, prejudice, and bigotry.

1. Kassirer, J. P., and M. Angell. "Losing Weight: An Ill-Fated New Year's Resolution." *New England Journal of Medicine* 338, no. 1 (1998): 52–54.

2. National Institutes of Health Technology Assessment Conference. "Methods for Voluntary Weight Loss and Control." *Annals of Internal Medicine* 116 (1992): 942–49.

3. Begley, C. E. "Government Should Strengthen Regulation in the Weight Loss Industry." *Journal of the American Dietary Association* 91 (1991): 1255–57.

4. Garner, D. M., and S. Wooley. "Confronting the Failure of Behavioral and Dietary Treatments for Obesity." *Clinical Psychology Review* 11 (1991): 729–80.

5.   Robison, J. I., and C. Erdman. "Needed: New Terminology for the New Paradigm." *Health Weight Journal* 12, no. 4. (1998): 58–59.

6.   "Clinical Guidelines on the Identification, Evaluation, and Treatment of Overweight and Obesity in Adults: The Evidence Report." Bethesda, National Heart, Lung, and Blood Institute, June 1998.

7.   Brown, P. J. "Cultural Perspectives on the Etiology and Treatment of Obesity." In A. J. Stunkard and T. A. Wadden, eds., *Obesity: Theory, and Therapy.* New York: Raven Press, 1993.

8.   Hutchinson, W. "Fat and Fashion." *Saturday Evening Post,* August 21, 1926.

9.   Bennett, W., and J. Gurin. *The Dieter's Dilemma: Eating Less and Weighing More.* New York: Basic Books, 1982.

10.   Brownmiller, S. *Femininity.* New York: Fawcett Columbine, 1984.

11.   Rothbloom, E. D. "I'll Die for the Revolution, but Don't Ask Me Not to Diet": Feminism and the Continuing Stigmatization of Obesity." In P. Fallon, M. Katzman, and S. Wooley, eds., *Feminist Perspectives on Eating Disorders.* New York: Guilford, 1994.

12.   "How to Stay Plump." *Harpers Bazaar,* August 1908.

13.   Fraser, L. *America's Obsession with Weight and the Industry That Feeds on It.* New York: Dutton, 1997.

14.   Ernsberger, P., and P. Haskew. "Re-thinking Obesity: An Alternative View of Its Health Implications." *Journal of Obesity and Weight Regulation* 6, no. 2 (1987): 1–81.

15. Schapira, D. V., N. B. Kumar, C. H. Lyman, D. Cavanagh, W. S. Robert, and J. La Polla. "Upper-Body Fat Distribution and Endometrial Cancer Risk." *Journal of the American Medical Association* 266 (1991): 1808–11.

16. Schapira, D. V., N. B. Kumar., C. H. Lyman, and C. E. Cox. "Abdominal Obesity and Breast Cancer." *Annals of Internal Medicine* 112 (1990): 182–86.

17. Terry, R. B., M. L. Stefanick, W. Haskell, and P. H. Wood. "Contributions of Regional Adipose Tissue Depots to Plasma Lipoprotein Concentrations in Overweight Men and Women: Possible Protective Effects of Thigh Fat." *Metabolism* 40 (1991): 733–40.

18. Allan, J. D. "A Biomedical and Feminist Perspective on Women's Experiences with Weight Management." *Western Journal of Nursing Research* 16, no. 5 (1994): 524–43.

19. Hutchinson, M. G. "Imagining Ourselves Whole: A Feminist Approach to Treating Body Image Disorders." In P. Fallon, M. Katzman, and S. Wooley, eds., *Feminist Perspectives on Eating Disorders.* New York: Guilford, 1994.

20. Seid, R. P. *Never Too Thin: Why Women Are at War with Their Bodies.* New York: Prentice Hall. 1989.

21. Wolf, N. *The Beauty Myth: How Images of Beauty Are Used against Women.* New York: Morrow, 1991.

22. Bordo, S. "Reading the Slender Body." In M. Jacobs, E. F. Keller, and S. Shuttleworth, eds., *Body/Politics, Women, and the Discourses of Science.* New York: Routledge, Chapman, and Hall, 1990.

23. Hirschmann, J. R., and C. H. Munter. *When Women Stop Hating Their Bodies: Freeing Yourself from Food and Weight Obsession.* New York: Ballantine, 1995.

24. Schroeder, C. R. *Fat Is Not a Four-Letter Word.* Minneapolis: Chronimed, 1992.

25. Rosen, J. C., B. Tacy, and D. Howell. "Life Stress, Psychological Symptoms, and Weight Reducing Behavior in Adolescent Girls: A Prospective Analysis." *International Journal of Eating Disorders* 9 (1990): 17–26.

26. Mellin, L. M., C. E. Irwin, and S. Scully. "Prevalence of Disordered Eating in Girls: A Survey of Middle-Class Children." *Journal of the American Dietetic Association* 92, no. 7 (1992): 851–53.

27. Gaesser, G. A. *Big Fat Lies: The Truth about Your Weight and Your Health.* Rev. ed. Carlsbad, California: Gurze Books, 2002.

28. Keys, A. "Overweight, Obesity, Coronary Heart Disease, and Mortality." *Nutrition Reviews* 38 (1980): 297–307.

29. Bjorntorp, P., and B. Brodoff. *Obesity.* New York: Lippincott, 1992.

30. Bouchard, C., A. Tremblay, J. P. Depres, A. Nadeau, P. J. Lupien, G. Theriault, J. Dussault, S. Moorjani, S. Pinault, and S. Fournier. "The Response to Long-Term Overfeeding in Identical Twins." *New England Journal of Medicine* 322 (1990): 1477–82.

31. Thomas, P. R., ed. *Determinants of Food Choice and Prospects for Modifying Attitudes and Behavior.* Washington, DC: National Academy Press, 1991.

32. Burgard, D., and P. Lyons. "Alternatives in Obesity Treatment: Focusing on Health for Fat Women." In P. Fallon, M. Katzman, and S. Wooley, eds., *Feminist Perspectives on Eating Disorders.* New York: Guilford. 1994.

33.   Satter, E. M. "Internal Regulation and the Evolution of Nor-
        mal Growth as the Basis for Prevention of Obesity in Chil-
        dren." *Journal of the American Dietetic Association* 96, no. 9
        (1996): 860–64.

34.   Kratina, K., N. King, and D. Hayes. *Moving Away from Diets:
        New Ways to Heal Eating Problems and Exercise Resistance.*
        Lake Dallas: Helms Seminars, 1996.

35.   Wiseman, C. V., J. J. Gray, J. E. Mosimann, and A. H.
        Ahrens. "Cultural Expectations of Thinness in Women: An
        Update." *International Journal of Eating Disorders* 11, no. 1
        (1992): 85–89.

36.   Dossey, L. *Meaning in Medicine.* New York: Bantam, 1991.

37.   Engel, G. L. "How Much Longer Must Medicine's Science be
        Bound by a Seventeenth-Century World View?" *Psycho-
        therapy and Psychosomatics* 57, nos. 1–2 (1992): 3–16.

38.   Gordon, J. S. *Manifesto for a New Medicine: Your Guide to
        Healing Partnership and the Wise Use of Alternative Thera-
        pies.* Reading, MA: Addison-Wesley, 1996.

39.   "Just What Is a Balanced Diet, Anyway?" *Tufts University
        Diet and Nutrition Letter* 9, no. 11 (1992): 3–6.

40.   Garner, D. M. "The 1997 Body Image Survey Results." *Psy-
        chology Today,* January–February 1997.

41.   Rodin, J., L. Silberstein, and R. Striegel-Moore. "Women and
        Weight: A Normative Discontent." In T. B. Sonderegger, ed.,
        *Nebraska Symposium on Motivation: Psychology, and Gen-
        der.* Lincoln: University of Nebraska Press, 1985.

42.   Woodside, B. "Eating Disorders in Men: An Overview."
        Healthy Weight Journal 16, no. 4 (2002): 52–55.

43. National Institutes of Health. "National Task Force on the Prevention and Treatment of Obesity: Long-Term Pharmacotherapy in the Management of Obesity." *Journal of the American Medical Association* 276 (1996): 1907–15.

44. Banner, L. W. *American Beauty.* Chicago: University of Chicago Press, 1983.

45. Nichter, M., and M. Nichter. "Hype and Weight." *Medical Anthropology* 13 (1991): 249–84.

46. Blair, S. N. Foreword to G. A. Gaesser, *Big Fat Lies: The Truth about Your Weight and Your Health.* New York: Fawcett Columbine, 1996.

47. Troiano, R. P., E. A. Frongillo, J. Sobal, and D. A. Levitsky. "The Relationship between Body Weight and Mortality: A Quantitative Analysis of Combined Information from Existing Studies." *International Journal of Obesity* 20 (1996): 63–75.

48. Waaler, H. T. "Height, Weight, and Mortality: The Norwegian Experience." *Acta Medica Scandinavia Supplement* 679 (1984): 1–56.

49a. McGee, D., and T. Gordon. "The Results of the Framingham Study Applied to Four Other U.S.-Based Epidemiological Studies of Cardiovascular Disease." In W. B. Kannel and T. Gordon, eds., *The Framingham Study: An Epidemiological Investigation of Cardiovascular Disease,* 1976. NIH Publication no. 76–1083, table 18.

49b. Barrett-Connor, E. L. "Obesity, Atherosclerosis, and Coronary Artery Disease." *Annals of Internal Medicine* 103 (1985): 1010–19.

50. Keys, A. "Obesity and Degenerative Heart Disease." *American Journal of Public Health* 44 (1954): 864–71.

51.   Kramer, J. R., Y. Matsuda, J. C. Mulligan, M. Aronow, and
       W. L. Proudfit." Progression of Coronary Atherosclerosis."
       Circulations 63 (1981): 519–26.

52.   McGill, H. C., et al. "General Findings of the International
       Atherosolerosis Project." *Laboratory Investigation* 18 (1968):
       498–502.

53.   Patel, Y. C., O. A. Eggen, and J. P. Strong. "Obesity, Smoking
       and Atherosclerosis: A Study of Interassociations." *Athero* 36
       (1980): 481–90.

54.   Applegate, W. B., J. P. Hughes, and R. V. Zwagg. "Case-
       Control Study of Coronary Heart Disease Risk Factors in the
       Elderly." *Journal of Clinical Epidemiology* 44 (1991): 409–
       15.

55.   Warnes, C. A., and W. C. Roberts. "The Heart in Massive
       (More Than 300 Pounds or 136 Kilograms) Obesity: Analysis
       of Twelve Patients Studied at Necropsy." *American Journal of
       Cardiology* 54 (1984): 1087–91.

56.   Arntzenius, A. C., D. Kromhoot, J. D. Barth, J. H. Reiber, A.
       V. Brurchke, B. Buis, C. M. van Gent, N. Kempen-Voogol, S.
       Strikwerda, and E. H. Vander Velde. "Diet, Lipoproteins, and
       the Progression of Coronary Atherosclerosis: The Leiden In-
       tervention Trial." *New England Journal of Medicine* 312
       (1985): 805–11.

57.   Blankenhorn, D. H., R. L. Johnson, W. J. Mack, H. A. El Zein,
       and L. I. Vailas. "The Influence of Diet on the Appearance of
       New Lesions in Human Coronary Arteries." *Journal of the
       American Medical Association* 263 (1990): 1646–52.

58.   Barnard, R. J. "Effects of Lifestyle Modification on Serum
       Lipids." *Archives of Internal Medicine* 151 (1991): 1309–94.

59. Barnard, R. J., T. Jung, and S. B. Inkeles. "Diet and Exercise in the Treatment of Non-Insulin-Dependant Diabetes." *Diabetes Care* 17 (1994): 1469–72.

60. Barnard, R. J., E. J. Ugianskis, D. A. Martin, and S. B. Inkeles. "Role of Diet and Exercise in the Management of Hyperinsulinemia and Associated Atherosclerotic Risk Factors." *American Journal of Cardiology* 69 (1992): 440–44.

61. Lamarche, B., J. P. Despres, M. C. Pouliot, S. Moorjani, P. J. Lupien, G. Theriault, A. Tremblay, A. Nadeau, and C. Bouchard. "Is Body Fat Loss a Determinant Factor in the Improvement of Carbohydrate and Lipid Metabolism Following Aerobic Exercise Training in Obese Women?" *Metabolism* 41 (1992): 1249–56.

62. Schieffer, B., D. Moore, E. Funke, S. Hogan, F. Alphin, M. Hamilton, and S. Heyden. "Reduction of Atherogenic Risk Factors by Short-Term Weight Reduction." *Klinische Wochenschrift* 69, no. 4 (1991): 163–67.

63. Tremblay, A., J. P. Despres, J. Maheux, M. C. Pouliot, A. Nadeau, S. Moorjani, P. J. Lupien, and C. Bouchard. "Normalization of the Metabolic Profile in Obese Women by Exercise and a Low Fat Diet." *Medicine and Science in Sport and Exercise* 23 (1991): 1326–31.

64. Ernsberger, P., and P. Haskew. "News about Obesity." *New England Journal of Medicine* 315 (1986): 130–31.

65. Iverius, P. H., and J. D Brunzell. "Obesity and Common Genetic Metabolic Disorders." *Annals of Internal Medicine* 103 (1985): 1050–51.

66. Kolata G. "Asking if Obesity Is a Disease or Just a Symptom." *New York Times,* April 16, 2002.

67.   Avons, P., P. Ducimetiere, and P. Rakoto. "Weight and Mortality." *Lancet* 1, no. 8333 (1983): 1104.

68.   Garn, S. M., V. M. Hawthorne, J. J. Pilkington, and S. D. Pesick. "Fatness and Mortality in the West of Scotland." *American Journal of Clinical Nutrition* 38 (1983): 313–19.

69.   Garcia-Palmieri, M. R., P. D. Sorlie, R. Costas, and R. J. Havlik. "An Apparent Inverse Relationship between Serum Cholesterol and Cancer Mortality in Puerto Rico." *American Journal of Epidemiology* 114, no. 1 (1981): 29–44.

70.   Keys, A., C. Arvanis, H. Blackburn, R. Buzina, A. S. Dontas, F. Fidanza, M. J. Karvonen, A. Menotti, S. Nedeljkovic, S. Punsar, and H. Toshima. "Serum Cholesterol and Cancer Mortality in the Seven Countries Study." *American Journal of Epidemiology* 121 (1985): 870–83.

71.   Wallace, R. B., C. Rost, L. F. Burmeister, and P. R. Pomrehn. "Cancer Incidence in Humans: Relationship to Plasma Lipids and Relative Weight." *Journal of the National Cancer Institute* 68 (1982): 915–18.

72.   Kabat, G. B., and E. L. Wynder. "Body Mass Index and Lung Cancer Risk." *American Journal of Epidemiology* 135 (1992): 769–74.

73.   Edelstein, S. L. and E. Barrett-Connor. "Relation between Body Size and Bone Mineral Density in Elderly Men and Women." *American Journal of Epidemiology* 138 (1993): 160–69.

74.   Felson, D. T., Y. Zhang, M.T. Hannan, and J. J. Anderson. "Effects of Weight and Body Mass Index on Bone Mineral Density in Men and Women: The Framingham Study." *Journal of Bone and Mineral Research* 8 (1993): 567–73.

75. Tverdal, A. "Body Mass Index and Incidence of Tuberculosis." *European Journal of Respiratory Disease* 69 (1986): 355–62.

76. Higgins, M. W., J. B. Keller, M. Becker, W. Howatt, J. R. Landis, H. Rotman, H. G. Wegmen, and I. Higgins. "An Index of Risk for Obstructive Airway Disease." *American Review of Respiratory Disease* 125 (1982): 144–51.

77. Grabowski, D.C., and J. E. Ellis. "High Body Mass Index Does Not Predict Mortality in Older People: Analysis of the Longitudinal Study of Aging." *Journal of the American Geriatric Society* 49 (2001): 968–79.

78. Diehr P., D. E. Bild, T. B. Harris, A. Duxbury, D. Siscovik, and M. Rossi. "Body Mass Index and Mortality in Nonsmoking Older Adults: The Cardiovascular Health Study." *American Journal of Public Health* 88 (1998): 623–29.

79. Reynolds M. W. L. Fredman, P. Langenberg, and J. Magaziner. "Weight, Weight Change, and Mortality in a Random Sample of Older Community-Dwelling Women." *Journal of the American Geriatric Society* 47 (1999): 1409–14.

80. Blair, S. N., and R. S. Paffenbarger. "Influence of Body Weight and Shape Variation on Incidence of Cardiovascular Disease, Diabetes, Lung Disease, and Cancer: Harvard Alumni Data." Paper presented at the thirty-fourth Annual Conference on Cardiovascular Disease Epidemiology and Prevention, Tampa, Florida, March 16–19, 1994.

81. Blair, S. N., J. Shaten, K. Brownell, O. Collins, and L. Lissner. "Body Weight Change, All Cause Mortality, and Cause-Specific Mortality in the Multiple Risk Factor Intervention Trial." *Annals of International Medicine* 11, (1993): 749–57.

82. Holbrook, T. L., E. L. Barrett-Connor, and D. L. Wingard. "The Association of Lifetime Weight and Weight Control Pat-

terns with Diabetes among Men and Women in an Adult Community." *International Journal of Obesity* 13 (1989): 723–29.

83. Lissner, L., P. M. Odell, R. B. D'Agostino, J. S. Stokes, B. E. Kreger, A. J. Belanger, and K. D. Brownell. "Variability of Body Weight and Health Outcomes in the Framingham Population." *New England Journal of Medicine* 324 (1991): 1839–44.

84. Guagnano, M. T., et al. "Risk Factors for Hypertension in Obese Women: The Role of Weight Cycling." *European Journal of Clinical Nutrition* 54 (2000): 356–60

85. Olson, M. B., et al. "Weight Cycling and High-Density Lipoprotein Cholesterol in Women: Evidence of an Adverse Effect." *Journal of the American College of Cardiology* 36 (2000): 1565–71.

86. Syngal, S., E. H. Coakley, W. C. Willett, T. Byers, D. F. Williamson, and G. A. Colditz. "Long-Term Weight Patterns and Risk for Cholecystectomy in Women." *Annals of Internal Medicine* 130 (1999): 471–77.

87. Fogelholm, M., et al. "Association between Weight Cycling History and Bone Mineral Density in Premenopausal Women." *Osteoporosis International* 7 (1997): 354–58.

88. Linblad, P., A. Wolk, R. Bergstrom, I. Persson, and H. O. Adami. "The Role of Obesity and Weight Fluctuation in the Etiology of Renal Cell Cancer: A Population-Based Case-Control Study." *Cancer Epidemiology Biomarkers Prevention* 3 (1994): 631–39.

89. Djuric, Z., L. K. Heilbrun, S. Lababidi, E. Berzinkas, M. S. Simon, and M. A. Kosir. "Levels of 5-Hydroxymethyl–2'Deoxyuridine in DNA from Blood of Women Scheduled for

Breast Biopsy." *Cancer Epidemiology Biomarkers Prevention* 10 (2001): 147–49.

90.   Hirschmann, J. R., and C. H. Munter. *Overcoming Overeating: Living Free in a World of Food.* New York: Fawcett Columbine, 1988.

91.   Polivy, J. "Psychological Consequences of Feed Restriction." *Journal of the American Dietetic Association* 96, no. 6 (1996): 589–92.

92.   Ernsberger, P., and D. O. Nelson. "Referring Hypertension in Dietary Obesity." *American Journal of Physiology* 254 (1988): R47–55.

93.   Koletsky, R., P. Ernsberger, J. Z. Baskin, and M. Foley. "Weight Cycling in Obese SHR Exacerbates Obesity and Hypertension." *Journal of the Federation of American Societies for Experimental Biology* 6 (1992): A1674.

94.   Levin, B. E., S. Stoddard-Apter, and A. C. Sullivan. "Central Activation and Peripheral Function of Sympatho-Adrenal and Cardiovascular Systems in the Zucker Rat." *Physiology and Behavior* 32 (1984): 295–99.

95.   Smith, G. S., J. L. Smith, M. S. Mameesh, J. Simon, and B. C. Johnson. "Hypertension and Cardiovascular Abnormalities in Starved-Refed Swine." *Journal of Nutrition* 82 (1964): 17–182.

96.   Wilhelmj, C. M., A. J. Carnazzo, and H. H. McCarthy. "The Effect of Fasting and Realimentation with Diets High in Carbohydrate or Protein on the Blood Pressure and Heart Rate of Sympathectimized Dogs." *American Journal of Physiology* 191 (1957): 103–10.

97.   Ernsberger, P., and R. J. Koletsky. "Weight Cycling and Mortality: Support from Animal Studies [letter]." *Journal of the American Medical Association* 269 (1993): 1116.

98.   Stunkard, A. J. "The Results of Treatment for Obesity." *New York State Journal of Medicine* 58 (1958): 79–87.

99.   Food and Drug Administration. *Consumer Affairs and Information: The Facts about Weight Loss Products and Programs.* Rockville, MD: Food and Drug Administration, 1992.

100. Miller, W. C. "How Effective Are Diet and Exercise in Weight Control?" *Medicine and Science in Sports and Exercise* 31 (1999): 1129–34.

101. Polivy, J., and C. P. Herman. "Diagnosis and Treatment of Normal Eating." *Journal of Consulting and Clinical Psychology* 55, no. 5 (1987): 635-44.

Chapter 16

HEALTH AT EVERY SIZE

Antidote for "The Obesity Epidemic"

*A focus on approaches that can produce health
benefits independently of weight loss may be the best way
to improve the physical and psychological health
of Americans seeking to lose weight.*

National Institutes of Health
Annals of Internal Medicine

Introducing the "New Paradigm"

A dramatically new perspective on resolving eating and weight struggles is now emerging. The thinking behind this perspective began in the 1970s as part of the women's movement. At that time feminist activists began to question the way in which women were being targeted differently than men regarding weight and health issues. In addition, in 1979 two major scientific reviews were published that questioned the effectiveness and social appropriateness of traditional weight loss treatment.[2,3]

Since that time, numerous books and research papers have challenged the basic assumptions of the biomedical emphasis on weight loss. In addition, the ethics of offering traditional weight loss programs are being questioned. From the combined work of many women and men from a variety of fields the nondiet/size acceptance movement was born. Over the last thirty years this movement has grown in popularity and developed into what is referred to by those of us involved as Health at Every Size (HAES), which is the term we will be using in this book.[4-8]

We strongly recommend that anyone working with people re-garding issues of eating and weight immerse themselves in the HAES literature. We particularly recommend the eating and body image work of Jane R. Hirschmann and Carol H. Munter (described in chapter 17), Ellyn Satter, and Geneen Roth, as well as powerful books on size work written by Pat Lyons, Cheri Erdman, and Marilyn Wann. There are also organizations that provide valuable information and support for both laypeople and health professionals. The National Association for the Advancement of Fat Acceptance (NAAFA) has helped many of us to move forward on size accep-tance issues. The Sports and Cardiovascular Nutritionists (SCAN), a subgroup of the American Dietetic Association, has begun including health at every size presentations as part of its annual conference and publications. The nationally recognized Renfrew Center for Eating Disorders is also using HAES at its treatment facilities around the country. (See "Holistic Resources" at the end of the book.)

Foundations of HAES

Although specific approaches within the Health at Every Size movement vary somewhat depending on the source, the philosophy and emphasis are remarkably similar. The basic conceptual frame-work includes acknowledgment of:

1. The natural diversity in body shape and size
2. The ineffectiveness and dangers of dieting
3. The importance of relaxed eating in response to internal body cues
4. The critical contribution of social, emotional, and spiritual as well as physical factors to health and happiness

Overall, HAES supports a holistic view of health that promotes "feeling good about oneself, eating well in a natural, relaxed way, and being comfortably active."[9] Table 16.1 contrasts the conceptual basis of traditional weight management approaches with those of Health at Every Size.[10]

Table 16.1. Traditional Weight Loss versus Health at Every Size

Traditional Weight Loss	Health at Every Size
Everyone needs to be thin for good health and happiness.	Thin is not intrinsically healthy and beautiful, nor is fat intrinsically unhealthy and unappealing.
People who are not thin are "overweight" because they have no willpower, eat too much, and don't move enough.	People naturally have different body shapes and sizes and different preferences for food and physical activity.
Everyone can be thin, happy, and healthy by dieting.	Dieting usually leads to weight gain, decreased self-esteem, and increased risk for eating problems. Health and happiness are not dependant on weight status and involve a dynamic interaction among mental, social, spiritual, and physical considerations.

Components of HAES

HAES provides health professionals with the opportunity to shift how we define and respond to people's food and weight-related struggles. In exploring the use of HAES, there are three major components to bear in mind. These components are outlined in table 16.2.

Table 16.2. Health at Every Size: Major Components

Component	Description
Size and Self-acceptance	Affirmation and reinforcement of human beauty and worth irrespective of differences in weight, physical size, and shape.
Physical activity	Support for social, pleasure-based movement for enhanced quality of life. Calorie burning and weight loss are not the goals of the activity.
Normalized eating	Support for discarding externally imposed rules and regimens for eating and attaining a more peaceful relationship with food by relearning to eat in response to physiological hunger and fullness cues.

Size and Self-Acceptance. The most important component of HAES is self-love and acceptance. Self-acceptance is an affirmation that, just as human worth is not based on race, color, or creed, it also is not dependent on body weight, shape, or size. Our obsession with thinness has spawned what may be the last culturally accepted prejudice against individuals who do not live up to our unrealistic societal standards. Like racism, sexism, anti-Semitism, and homophobia, this weightism:

Is based on visible cues, i.e., the fat person is discriminated against primarily because of the way she looks . . . defines an entire group of people numbering in the millions within a narrow range of negative characteristics and behaviors . . . elevates the status of one group of people at the expense of another . . . and serves as a vehicle for the bigot's own anxieties, frustrations and resentments.[11]

The result of this prejudice is rampant social, economic, and educational discrimination against larger individuals.[11-15] As with all forms of prejudice, however, it is not only the persecuted group that suffers. Women of all sizes suffer from an intense fear of fat that plays havoc with their self-esteem and promotes disordered eating and exercise behavior. Men suffer as well, "by participating in a culture that defines the worth of more than one-half the population in terms of physical appearance, rather than by the recognition of truly meaningful qualities such as honesty, compassion and love."[16]

The cornerstone of HAES, self-acceptance, involves honoring the natural diversity in the human form and challenging cultural weight prejudice. As health professionals we must begin by confronting our own prejudices and learning strategies to empower our clients to do the same. Fortunately, materials have been developed to assist health professionals with the process of understanding and combating their own weight prejudice.[17] These include a number of excellent books written by larger women health professionals who have struggled with the pain of growing up in a thin-obsessed culture.[11,18-22]

We would like to emphasize again that fear is a very poor motivator for change. Positive change is much more likely to come from self-love than from self-hatred; people seek to take care of themselves when they feel they are worthy of it. HAES sees self-acceptance and self-love as important prerequisites for enabling people to reach peace on issues of weight and health.

Physical Activity. Physical activity is widely recognized as an important element in human health, yet the majority of Americans of all sizes remain sedentary. Part of the problem may lie in the "old paradigm" approaches used to encourage people to become more active. As Thomas Moore writes in *Care of the Soul:*

> Usually we are told how much time to spend at a certain exercise, what heart rate to aim for, and which muscle to focus on for toning. . . . If we could loosen our grip on the mechanical view of our own bodies and the body of the world, many other possibilities might come to light.[23]

HAES focuses on promoting movement that is social, playful, and pleasurable and includes not just jogging, cycling, and exercise classes but activities connected with everyday living such as walking and gardening. Movement is encouraged for enjoyment, camaraderie, and improved quality of life, not calorie burning and weight loss.[24] Evidence supports the notion that physical activity can positively affect health and longevity regardless of weight status [25,26] and recent research suggests that "if you're fit . . . being 25 or even 75 pounds overweight is perfectly healthy. And if you aren't fit, being slim gives you no protection whatsoever."[27]

In addition, this alternative paradigm acknowledges the prevalence of sedentary living in our society as largely a cultural phenomenon that can be significantly impacted only by addressing cultural barriers.[28] This is especially true for larger individuals, many of whom are deterred from engaging in physical activity by fear of the ridicule and humiliation that they have endured as a regular, ongoing part of their lives.[29] For many such individuals, discovering movement in a size-friendly environment can be a means of beginning to rediscover and reconnect to the bodies they have been taught to hate and ignore.[30]

Normalized Eating. The externally focused, restrictive methods used by diet programs rarely succeed in helping people to become healthy eaters. There is strong evidence that human beings are capable of regulating caloric intake according to internal hunger, satiety, and appetite signals,[33,34] and that chronic food restriction such as dieting interferes with this process and actually increases the likelihood of overeating.[35]

Bigger People, Not Bigger Appetites

Traditional wisdom has it that larger people get that way because they eat a lot more than thinner individuals. Contrary to this belief, however, research on the caloric intake of larger individuals does not provide conclusive evidence that they eat more than their thinner counterparts.[29,31,32]

HAES refutes the concept of "good" and "bad" foods and discourages the use of externally-focused eating strategies such as calorie and fat-gram counting. Instead, individuals learn normalized eating. All foods are legalized and the focus is placed on reducing anxiety about eating, calories, fat, and so on. People also relearn how to eat in response to physiological hunger and satiety cues.[36,37] They are taught to listen to and trust their bodily signals as to what, when and how much to eat. We will address the nuts and bolts of teaching this kind of approach in the next chapter.

Individuals who adopt normalized eating may or may not see changes in their weight. However, this eating style is likely to improve people's health by reducing the anxiety, guilt, preoccupation with food, bingeing, weight cycling, and weight gain commonly associated with restricted eating (dieting). Although more scientific confirmation of this hypothesis is needed, initial research and intuitive experience are supportive of this conclusion.[38–44]

HAES recognizes that when people are struggling with food- and weight-related issues it is often symptomatic of underlying distress that cannot be relieved merely by delivering nutrition information and advice. As the following case study powerfully demonstrates, trying to help people with these kinds of issues and being sure to *do no harm* in the process necessitates a compassionate, truly holistic approach.

Case Study:

Filling up the Holes

A twelve-year-old girl was referred to us because her doctor was concerned about her weight gain. She walked into the office with her mom, and they both sat down on the couch. Usually we try to talk to the family together and then if possible to the mom and child separately. However, in this case the child looked very depressed and refused to say anything, so we talked to the mom and the girl together. We asked the mom to tell us what was going on. She said, "well, I just got divorced for the second time and we moved to this new town. We had to sell our house. We had two dogs, which we had to get rid of because now we are living in a small apartment."

It turned out that the little girl was sneaking food. Mom was finding candy wrappers hidden under the bed and behind the furniture. The mom continued, explaining that her daughter's aunt might be contributing to the problem. She often cared for the little girl while her mom was working. The aunt was a nurse who was terribly concerned about her niece's weight gain and was trying to control the child's eating. She was constantly telling the girl, "don't eat that, you'll get fat, it'll be bad for you," and so on.

We repeatedly asked the child if she wanted to say anything, but she just looked down at the ground and shook her head. Finally, the mom finished her story and asked us, "What do you think?" We said, "We think what you have here is a young child who has gone through more pain and suffering than many people go through in a lifetime." (She had lost her pets, her home and two fathers in eleven years and at her age she was likely convinced that much of this was her fault.) We continued, "This little girl is full of holes. She is using food to fill up those holes. If you take her food away, what will you have? A little girl full of holes. Of course, she will continue to try to fill up the holes."

So Mom asked us what we recommended. These were our recommendations. "First of all, nobody is to say a word to her about food or her body." Mom said, "Well, I can do that but her aunt, she's just adamant about this. She really wants to help." We were just as adamant: "Please send her aunt in to talk to us, and we'll explain why it is essential that she leave your daughter alone about these matters."

At this point, the girl, who had said nothing and showed no emotion for almost thirty minutes, all but jumped off her chair and out of her skin. She had a big smile on her face. Mom said, "Okay, I can do that. What else?" Our remaining recommendations were to find this girl some counseling help for her grief, her anger, and her fears and to teach the mother and the aunt how to set up a new food environment. They all needed to learn about eating in response to hunger and fullness and a more compassionate way of responding to emotional eating.

The adults in this scenario, the physician, the mom, and the aunt, were caring, intelligent people. The point is that the immediate reaction to the little girl's weight gain was to control her overeating and overlook her emotional pain: let's put a "band aid" on this "unhealthy behavior" and ignore what is going on in her life. More often than not, this makes things much worse. This girl was surviving in the moment the best way she knew how!

HAES:

Implications for Helping

Redefining Success

The underlying goal of traditional approaches to weight management is for people to be smaller, that is, to lose weight. This is an inappropriate and unacceptable goal for at least four reasons, which were discussed in the previous chapter.

- The relationship of weight loss to improved health is not supported by the literature.

- Weight loss is not (at the present time at least) a sustainable outcome for the vast majority of people.

- There is considerable evidence that promoting weight loss violates the underlying health care principle of "first do no harm."

- The desire to control weight (especially the weight of women) is rooted in the deep values of the patriarchal, dominator mentality.

The focus for health professionals in HAES is to empower their clients to live healthier, more fulfilled lives by honoring and caring for the bodies they presently have. Success with this process can be measured in a variety of ways, including the following.

- Improved quality of life and reduction of medical problems and health risks, independent of weight loss.[45,46]
- Decreased reliance on medications
- Quality and quantity of physical activity
- Body acceptance
- Normalized eating behaviors
- Improved quality of diet

Focus on Health

Removing the focus on weight does not imply ignoring health risks and medical problems. On the contrary, in accordance with the holistic principles we have discussed, this new paradigm approach strongly acknowledges that a person's experience with weight and health is part of a complex, dynamic interplay of social, emotional, ecological and spiritual as well as physical factors.[10] An exclusive focus on weight can obscure or even exacerbate these factors,[1,47,48] whereas removing this focus enables health professionals to view clients more appropriately as complex "wholes" that are more than the sum of their parts.

HAES proposes that people create health by healing disturbed relationships with food and making peace with their bodies, not by losing weight. This is a critical departure from traditional approaches.

Furthermore, it suggests that an appropriate healthy weight cannot be determined by a set of numbers on an ideal height and weight chart, associated BMIs, or body fat percentages. It can only be determined by observing the weight at which an individual's body settles as he or she stops dieting and strives toward living a fulfilled, meaningful life. HAES does not suggest that all people are currently at a weight that is the most healthy for their circumstances. It does, however, suggest that movement toward a healthier lifestyle will, over time for most people, produce a weight that is healthy for that person. Focusing on weight rather than health, on the other hand, is most likely to produce compulsive eating, weight cycling, and over time increased weight.

Medical Treatment

HAES does not suggest that health professionals should neglect the provision of effective health care for large people. When large individuals present with medical problems, health professionals should consider and offer the same approaches that they would for a thin person with similar presenting problems.[9] In the case of a thin person with essential hypertension, for example, conventional medicine suggests salt reduction, increases in aerobic physical activity, and stress management followed by medication, if necessary. Yet a larger individual presented with the same diagnosis is told to lose weight, despite all that is known about the likely unhealthy consequences of this prescription.

HAES can be followed regardless of the individual's presenting problems. Even with individuals experiencing serious conditions such as type II diabetes, hypertension, and coronary artery disease, where weight is commonly seen as such an important risk factor, research shows people's health status and risk can be improved without changes in weight. This is true even for individuals who remain markedly fat.[26,49,50]

Similarly, for extremely fat individuals, there is sparse evidence that traditional weight loss interventions are any more effective than they are with mildly or moderately fat individuals.[51] Because some extremely fat individuals are at increased medical risk, the use of these ineffective and potentially dangerous weight loss interventions are even more contraindicated. It is commonly argued that the risks of such interventions are outweighed by the risks of the excessive fatness. However, the large weight losses and regains that typically follow intensive interventions designed for extremely fat individuals may greatly increase mortality above that which would be expected in similar populations not participating in these interventions.[52] It may be, therefore, "ironic that most such deaths are blamed on the victim's overweight rather than the true culprit, radical attempts to lose weight."[53]

Show Me the Data!

Critics repeatedly cite the lack of data supporting HAES interventions as a major reason to continue with traditional approaches. However, these same parties also continue to recommend traditional weight loss programs *in spite of* their well-documented lack of success. Because the focus of HAES interventions is not on special foods, diets, pharmaceuticals, and so on, it is difficult to obtain resources to fund research that compares these programs to traditional interventions. In spite of these limitations, preliminary investigations suggest that HAES can help to reduce anxiety, normalize eating behaviors, and improve self-esteem in chronic dieters.[39,41–43] With individuals suffering from type II diabetes, hyperlipidemia, and hypertension such approaches improve self-esteem, increase feelings of self-control, reduce guilt, and decrease health risks.[38]

Perhaps most exciting is a recent study directly comparing HAES with a well-known and respected behavior/diet/exercise intervention.[44] In a six-month program followed by six months of maintenance, both the dieting group and the HAES group enjoyed similar improvements in metabolic fitness (cholesterol, triglycerides, blood pressure, etc.), psychological variables, and eating behavior, even though the dieting group lost weight and the HAES group did not. However, more than 40 percent of the dieting group dropped out compared to just 8 percent of the HAES group. Furthermore, the authors cautioned that "improvements in the diet group should be viewed with caution as previous studies suggest that improvements made in traditional weight loss programs are predicated upon lost weight, which is frequently not maintained." This study suggests that the writing is on the wall as far as traditional approaches to weight are concerned. It is only a matter of time before more studies reach the same conclusion: "A non-diet [HAES] program appears to be an effective alternative to diet programs in improving health."

Summary

Insanity can be defined as "doing the same things over and over again and expecting different results." Continuing to prescribe diets and weight loss programs is ineffective and potentially harmful. Health professionals should therefore refrain from doing so.

Traditional weight loss programs advocate exercise and re-strained eating and ignore the larger context of a person's life. With their inevitable failure, these programs cause shame and embarrass-ment and are likely to diminish further seeking of medical care.[38,54] Perhaps even more significant is the fact that traditional approaches continue to promote increasingly outdated Epoch II cultural values such as control over the body and the oppression of women. In the next chapter we will discuss in detail how to implement a specific HAES approach that is consistent with emerging Epoch III values and provides people more compassionate and successful help with their weight- and eating-related concerns.

References

We want to particularly credit Pat Lyons and Cheri Erdman for teaching us about weight prejudice and size acceptance in a way that only women who have lived the experience of being large in a thin-obsessed culture could. Through Lyons's work and her groundbreak-ing book *Great Shape: The First Fitness Guide for Large Women* (written with Debora Burgard), countless larger individuals have been able to reconnect with the bodies they have been taught to ig-nore and despise. Dr. Erdman's work with the support group Abun-dia and her insightful exploration of the process of size acceptance in her books *Nothing to Lose: A Guide to Sane Living in a Larger Body* and *Live Large! Ideas, Affirmations, and Actions for Sane Living in a Larger Body* have helped countless others to accept and love themselves just as they are. Because HAES differs in *many* fundamental ways from traditional approaches we also recommend that health professionals acquire information from a variety of sources such as those listed below.

1.   National Institutes of Health. "Technology Assessment Conference: Methods for Voluntary Weight Loss and Control." *Annals of Internal Medicine* 116 (1992): 942–49.

2.   Stunkard, A. J., and S. B. Penick. "Behavior Modification in the Treatment of Obesity: The Problem of Maintaining Weight Loss." *Archives of General Psychiatry* 36, no. 1 (1979): 801–6.

3.   Wooley, O. W., S. C. Wooley, and S. R. Dyrenforth. "Obesity and Women II: A Neglected Feminist Topic." *Women's International Quarterly* 2 (1979): 81–92.

4.   Satter, E. M. "Internal Regulation and the Evolution of Normal Growth as the Basis for Prevention of Obesity in Children." *Journal of the American Dietetic Association* 96, no. 9 (1996): 860–64.

5.   Berg, F. M. "Nondiet Movement Gains Strength." *Obesity and Health* 6, no. 5 (1992): 85–90.

6.   Omichinski, L. *You Count, Calories Don't*. Winnipeg: Hugs International, 1992.

7.   Parham, E. S. "Is There a New Weight Paradigm?" *Nutrition Today* 31, no. 4 (1996): 155–61.

8.   Robison, J. I. "Weight, Health, and Culture: Shifting the Paradigm for Alternative Health Care." *Alternative Health Practitioner* 5, no. 1 (1999): 1–25.

9.   Burgard, D., and P. Lyons. "Alternatives in Obesity Treatment: Focusing on Health for Fat Women." In P. Fallon, M. Katzman, and S. Wooley, eds., *Feminist Perspectives on Eating Disorders.* New York: Guilford, 1994.

10.   Robison, J. I. "Weight Management: Shifting the Paradigm." *Journal of Health Education* 28, no. 10 (1997): 28–34.

11.   Goodman, W. C. *The Invisible Women: Confronting Weight Prejudice in America.* Carlsbad, CA: Gurze, 1995.

12.   Fraser, L. *America's Obsession with Weight and the Industry That Feeds on It.* New York: Dutton, 1997.

13.   Gortmaker, S., A. Must, J. Perrin, A. Sobol, and W. Dietz. "Social and Economic Consequences of Overweight in Adolescence and Young Adulthood." *New England Journal of Medicine* 329 (1993): 1008–12.

14.   Rothbloom, E. D. "'I'll Die for the Revolution, but Don't Ask Me Not to Diet': Feminism and the Continuing Stigmatization of Obesity." In P. Fallon, M. Katzman, and S. Wooley, eds., *Feminist Perspectives on Eating Disorders.* New York: Guilford Press, 1994.

15.   Solovay, S. *Tipping the Scales of Justice: Fighting Weight-Based Discrimination.* New York: Prometheus, 2000.

16.   Robison, J. I. "Moving Away from Diets: A Professional Perspective." In K. Kratina, N. King, and D. Hayes, eds., *Moving Away from Diets: New Ways to Heal Eating Problems and Exercise Resistance.* Lake Dallas, TX: Helms Seminars, 1996.

17.   National Association to Advance Fat Acceptance. *Guidelines for Health Care Providers in Dealing with Fat Patients.* Sacramento: National Association to Advance Fat Acceptance.

18. Bruno, B. A. *Worth Your Weight: What You Can Do about a Weight Problem.* Bethel, CT: Rutledge, 1996.

19. Erdman, C. K. *Nothing to Lose: A Guide to Sane Living in a Larger Body.* San Francisco: Harper, 1995.

20. Erdman, C. K. *Live Large! Ideas, Affirmations, and Actions for Sane Living in a Larger Body.* San Francisco: Harper, 1997.

21. Bernell, B. *Bountiful Women: Large Women's Secrets for Living the Life They Desire.* Berkeley: Wildcat Canyon Press, 2000.

22. Wann, M. *Fat! So? Because You Don't Have to Apologize for Your Size!* Berkeley: Ten Speed Press, 1998.

23. Moore, T. *Care of the Soul: A Guide for Cultivating Depth and Sacredness in Everyday Life.* New York: Harper Perennial, 1994.

24. Lyons P., and D. Burgard. *Great Shape: The First Fitness Guide for Large Women.* iUniverse Press, 2000.

25. Krotkiewski, M., K. Mandroukas, L. Sjostrom, L. Sullivan, and H. Wetterquist. "Effects of Long-Term Physical Training on Body-Fat, Metabolism, and Blood Pressure in Obesity." *Metabolism* 28 (1979): 650–55.

26. Tremblay, A., J. P. Despres, J. Maheux, M. C. Pouliot, A. Nadeau, S. Moorjani, P. Lupien, and C. Bouchard. "Normalization of the Metabolic Profile in Obese Women by Exercise and a Low-Fat Diet." *Medicine and Science in Sport and Exercise* 23 (1991): 1326–31.

27.   Barlow, C. E., H. W. Kohl, L. W. Gibbons, and S. N. Blair. "Physical Fitness, Mortality, and Obesity." *International Journal of Obesity* 19, suppl. 4 (1995): S41–44.

28.   Robison, J. I., and M. A. Rogers. "Adherence to Exercise Programmes: Recommendations." *Sports Medicine* 17, no. 1 (1994): 39–52.

29.   Garner, D. M., and S. Wooley. "Confronting the Failure of Behavioral and Dietary Treatments for Obesity." *Clinical Psychology Review* 11 (1991): 729–80.

30.   Lyons, P. "Weight and Health: A New Approach for the New Year." *Wellness Management: Newsletter of the National Wellness Association* 11, no. 4 (1995): 1, 5–7.

31.   Rolland-Cachera, F., and F. Bellisle. "No Correlation between Adiposity and Food Intake: Why Are Working Class Children Fatter?" *American Journal of Clinical Nutrition* 44 (1986): 779–87.

32.   Striegel-Moore, R. H., and J. Rodin. "The Influence of Psychological Variables in Obesity." In K. D. Brownell, and J. P. Foreyt, eds., *Handbook of Eating Disorders.* New York: Basic Books, 1986.

33.   Davis, C. "Self-Selection of Diet by Newly Weaned Infants: An Experimental Study." *American Journal of Diseases of Children* 36, no. 4 (1928): 650–79.

34.   Johnson, S. L., and L. L. Birch. "Parents' and Children's Adiposity and Eating Style." *Pediatrics* 94 (1994): 653–61.

35.   Polivy, J. "Psychological Consequences of Feed Restriction." *Journal of the American Dietetic Association* 96, no. 6 (1996): 589–92.

36. Hirschmann, J. R., and C. H. Munter. *When Women Stop Hating Their Bodies: Freeing Yourself from Food and Weight Obsession.* New York: Ballantine, 1995.

37. Satter E. *Secrets of Feeding a Healthy Family.* Madison: Kelcy, 1999.

38. Armstrong, D., and A. King. "Demand Feeding as Diabetes Treatment." *Obesity and Health* 1 (1993): 109–10, 115.

39. Carrier, K. M., M. A. Steinhardt, and S. Bowman. "Rethinking Traditional Weight Management Programs: A Three-Year Follow-up Evaluation of a New Approach." *Journal of Psychology* 128, no. 5 (1993): 517–35.

40. Ciliska, D. K. *Beyond Dieting: Psychoeducational Interventions for Chronically Obese Women.* New York: Brunner/Mazel, 1990.

41. Omichinski, L., and K. R. Harrison. "Reduction of Dieting Attitudes and Practices after Participation in a Non-diet Lifestyle Program." *Journal of the Canadian Dietetic Association* 56, no. 2 (1995): 81–85.

42. Rosen, J. C., P. Orosan, and J. Reiter. "Cognitive Behavior Therapy for Negative Body Image in Obese Women." *Behavior Therapy* 26 (1995): 25–42.

43. Roughan, P., E. Seddon, and J. Vernon-Roberts. "Long-Term Effects of a Psychologically Based Group Programme for Women Preoccupied with Body Weight and Eating Behavior." *International Journal of Obesity* 14 (1990): 137–47.

44. Bacon, L., N. L. Keim, M. D. Van Loan, M. Derricote, B. Gale, A. Kazaks, and J. S. Stern. "Evaluating a 'Non-diet' Wellness Intervention for Improvement of Metabolic Fitness, Psychological Well-Being, and Eating and Activity Behaviors." *International Journal of Obesity* 26 (2002): 854–65.

45.   Atkinson, R. L. "Proposed Standards for Judging the Success of the Treatment of Obesity." *Annals of Internal Medicine* 119 (1993): 677–80.

46.   Robison, J. I., S. L. Hoerr, K. A. Petersmarck, and J. V. Anderson. "Redefining Success in Obesity Intervention." *Journal of the American Dietetic Association* 95, no. 4 (1995): 422–23.

47.   Brink, P. "Challenging Commonly Held Beliefs about Obesity." *Clinical Nursing Research* 1, no. 4 (1992): 418–29.

48.   Wooley, S. C., and D. M. Garner. "Obesity Treatment: The High Cost of False Hope." *Journal of the American Dietetic Association* 91, no. 10 (1991): 1248–51.

49.   Barnard, R. J., T. Jung, and S. B. Inkeles. "Diet and Exercise in the Treatment of Non-insulin-dependant Diabetes." *Diabetes Care* 17 (1994): 1469–72.

50.   Blankenhorn, D. H., R. L. Johnson, W. J. Mack, H. A. El Zein, and L. I. Vailas. "The Influence of Diet on the Appearance of New Lesions in Human Coronary Arteries." *Journal of the American Medical Association* 263 (1990): 1646–52.

51.   "To Diet or Not? The Experts Battle It Out." *Tufts University Diet and Nutrition Letter* 12, no. 8 (1994): 3–6.

52.   Drenick, E. J., G. S. Bales, F. Seltzer, and D. G. Johnson. "Excessive Mortality and Causes of Death in Morbidly Obese Men." *Journal of the American Medical Association* 243 (1980): 443–45.

53.   Herman, C. P., and J. Polivy. *Breaking the Diet Habit: The Natural Weight Alternative.* New York: Basic Books, 1993.

54. Olson, C., H. Schumaker, and B. Yawn. "Overweight Women Delay Medical Care." *Archives of Family Medicine* 3 (1994): 886–92.

Chapter 17

STANDING UP TO A DIETING SOCIETY
Applying the Philosophy of Health at Every Size

Women need to stop renovating their bodies and move in.

Jane Hirschmann and Carol Munter
When Women Stop Hating Their Bodies

If diets and weight management programs don't help people to resolve their eating and weight struggles, what does? As described in the previous chapter, we believe that the answer is Health at Every Size. We suggest that all health professionals stop teaching weight management classes and familiarize themselves with this alternative. It is that important!

The template in this chapter for applying HAES is based primarily on the work of psychotherapists and authors Jane R. Hirschmann and Carol H. Munter, who are best known for their book *Overcoming Overeating*. In 1988, it was Hirschmann and Munter's work that formed the basis for the first nondiet/size acceptance program offered as part of a corporate health promotion program anywhere in the country. In this chapter you will get a glimpse of the Overcoming Overeating approach as it was used in this worksite setting and perhaps develop ideas about using HAES in both your personal and professional life.

Common Questions and Concerns

Who Is the Overcoming Overeating Approach For?

The Overcoming Overeating approach is intended to help women and men, of any body size, who identify themselves as being in difficulty due to chronic dieting, compulsive eating, and body hatred. There are many fat people who *do not* have eating problems and there are a significant number of thin people *who do*. Regardless of body size, the focus is on helping people to live free of eating and body image struggles. This approach can also be effective for healing bulimia and binge eating disorder and can be taught to young people and adults as a way to prevent eating and weight struggles from developing.

Who Is Using the Approach?

Today, the Overcoming Overeating approach is used in clinical, corporate, academic, and community settings by a variety of professionals including psychotherapists, physicians, nurses, dietitians, and health educators. Health professionals are also applying this approach for treatment of diet-sensitive conditions such as diabetes and high cholesterol.

What Is the Approach Intended to Do?

The overall focus is to cure chronic dieting and compulsive eating by teaching a nonrestrained, internal cue eating style that helps reconnect the experience of hunger with eating. Through this process, individuals develop the ability to think about their problems instead of turning to food. The approach is designed to improve physical and emotional well-being by helping individuals to do the following.

1. Stop dieting and weight-loss-driven exercise behavior
2. Break free from the weight loss/overeating/weight gain cycle
3. Learn to eat in response to physical hunger, fullness and body cravings

4. Achieve a stable weight as close as possible to the body's natural weight (as determined by age, genetics, metabolism, dieting experience, and history of emotional eating)
5. Understand emotional hunger and learn a nonrestrained response
6. Explore movement for pleasure rather than weight loss
7. Rethink stereotypes and prejudices about fat people
8. End obsessive and negative body thoughts
9. Live a fuller life by reducing preoccupations with eating, exercise, and body size

What Are the Underlying Beliefs?

Several underlying beliefs are central to the Overcoming Overeating approach.

- ***Food is not the problem . . . food is the solution.*** Putting food off limits and the resulting cycles of restrictive eating followed by bingeing are the fuel that drives the problem. With this new approach professionals teach clients to bring food back into their lives and lift eating restrictions so they can end the scarcity thinking that has made so many foods emotionally charged.

- ***Harsh self-judgment about an eating or weight struggle never helps a person to move forward.*** To heal the difficulty, clients need assistance in breaking through the shame and sense of failure that have resulted from so many years of dieting. Once clients begin to see that they have not failed—that it is the dieting that has failed them—they can begin to move forward.

- ***A kinder view of emotional overeating is required.*** Clients must embrace emotional hunger and realize that it has helped them survive and cope with the distress in their lives. If they treat emotional hunger like the enemy and try to suppress or eradicate it, they will lose the opportunity to learn from it.

279

Doing Our Own Work First!

As health professionals many of us have eating, weight, body image, and exercise issues of our own. This is partly what drew us to our profession. We may have subconsciously believed that if we spent all our time teaching other people how to stay "in control of their food and weight" perhaps we could keep ourselves in control as well.

It is important to thoroughly explore the landscape of our eating life *before* we do this work with anyone else. A good starting place can be as simple as reading Hirschmann's and Munter's books (*Overcoming Overeating* and *When Women Stop Hating Their Bodies*), as well as the many excellent books and references listed in the previous chapter. The checklist in figure 17.1 can also be helpful for raising consciousness about issues that may need to be addressed. If any of the items below apply, it may suggest a good place from which to begin exploring and healing eating, weight, or exercise struggles. Remember, identifying and working on our own issues is how we become effective in helping others.

Self-Test for Eating, Body and Exercise Struggles

☐ I am ashamed of how I look.

☐ I think about food much of the time.

☐ I take laxatives or I vomit to eliminate food.

☐ I eat when I don't feel hungry.

☐ My eating habits make me feel bad about myself.

☐ My weight makes me feel bad about myself.

☐ I feel guilty about eating certain foods.

☐ I exercise primarily to lose weight.

☐ I exercise primarily to keep from gaining weight.

☐ I feel terrible, fat, ugly, lazy when I don't exercise.

☐ I have the same exercise routine every day no matter what.

☐ I feel anxious if I cannot adhere to my exercise schedule.

☐ I exercise when I am ill or injured.

☐ Exercise interferes with my family or work commitments.

Figure 17.1. Self-test for eating, body, and exercise struggles.
(You may find you need the assistance of a professional to do your own healing work on some of these issues. To find someone to assist you, call psychotherapists, social workers, and dieticians in your area and ask if they know of anyone who is supportive of HAES or trained in use of the Overcoming Eating approach.)

Introducing Clients to Overcoming Overeating

Because the Overcoming Overeating approach departs so dramatically from traditional weight-related programs, it is important to give clients thorough background information before teaching them the specifics of the approach. Exploring family and cultural influences and discussing the new research on weight and health should be done *before* teaching the actual mechanics of Overcoming Overeating. For most people, having this background information provides a meaningful rationale for adopting the radically different eating style that is advocated. A brief summary of the order and content of the topic areas for teaching this new approach is provided below.

Family Messages. Address how families often teach an eating style that is not helpful. People have learned to eat according to mealtime, to eat the portion they are given, to clean their plates, to eat to make other people happy, and so on. These behaviors disconnect us from hunger and lead to eating problems.

Cultural Messages. Address how the media inundates us with messages about food products, eating behavior, physical appearance, and exercise. Most of these messages are fat phobic and perpetuate unrealistic, unhealthy ideals for eating and body size.

Emotional Life Issues. Explain how overeating, dieting, and obsessive exercise diminish self-awareness and are often used as coping mechanisms in response to difficult life issues. Help people think specifically about the behaviors they rely on in their own lives and begin to explore the connection between these behaviors and underlying struggles.

Current Research. Compare the traditional research findings on the health risks of obesity with the newer perspective that presents an alternative view of obesity, weight cycling, weight loss, and associated health risks (see chapter 15).

A New Eating Style. Teach an internal cue approach that involves eating consciously in response to hunger, fullness, and body cravings and use of a nonrestrained approach for responding to emotional hunger. Legalization of "bad foods" and the skill of carrying a food bag are also key components that can help people effectively reconnect hunger with feeding and stop bingeing behavior.

Body Image. Teach people how to clean the closet, stop weighing and start looking in the mirror as they work on improving body image. Extensive work is usually needed around the concept of "bad body thoughts"—helping people understand that negative thoughts or feelings about their weight and appearance are never really about their body or fat; they are actually a metaphor for other life issues that need attention.

Movement. Help people explore a broad range of movement options. Encourage movement or exercise as a way to nurture the body, take personal time, and experience the joy of movement. Discourage the use of exercise to compensate for overeating, as punishment for weight gain, or to avoid feelings.

Responding to Others. Work with participants to give them coping strategies for interacting effectively with health care providers, coworkers, friends and family members who may resist their attempts to use this nontraditional approach to resolve their weight and eating struggles.

Teaching the Overcoming Overeating Approach

The following are examples of specific components that can be used to help people to explore and heal their eating/body issues. The nine basic teaching components listed below are based on the Overcoming Overeating work by Hirschmann and Munter and are meant to serve as a brief overview of the specifics of using their approach.

Component One: Creating a Positive Environment

As a first step, try making a commitment to do some or all of the exercises below.

1. *Dump the Diet.* Make a firm resolution that you will not go on another diet. Diets actually cause weight gain, and fuel eating, exercise, and body image problems. Explore the alternative: eating in response to hunger and fullness (see components 2 through 6 for a description of this eating style).

2. *Trash the Scale.* Throw out or put away the scale. "Weighing in" gives a piece of metal (the scale) the authority to tell you what you can eat and how you should feel. (If you cannot

stop stepping on the scale, try taping a piece of paper with the weight you can tolerate over the readout dial.)

3. ***Clean the Closet.*** Throw away, give away, or box up and store any clothes that are too small, too big, or unflattering as of today. Then treat yourself to at least a few new comfortable clothing items that fit at the size you are now.

4. ***Explore Movement.*** Explore different types of body movement or exercise that seem enjoyable. What would feel good to you? How often would you like to move? Make sure you want to move because it would be fun instead of because you feel you "should" in order to lose weight or compensate for overeating.

5. ***Consider the Possibility of a New Body Image.*** You do not have to change your body to begin feeling better about it! Buy a full-length mirror. Spend some time each day viewing your body in the mirror instead of avoiding looking at yourself. Focus on the body parts you like first and talk aloud to those parts, saying something like "I like you, arms—you are strong, and your skin is smooth and silky." Then, for the parts you have hated in the past, say something like "Stomach, I used to really hate you, but I now realize that you are an important part of me. I am trying to accept you as you are."

6. ***Contradict the Culture.*** Remember that in every area of your life you will be pressured to use exercise and dieting to change your body. Each time you choose to resist this cultural pressure, you strengthen your own internal resolve to live free of this obsession. You also help all women and all of humanity to move forward.

Component Two: Eating in Response to Stomach Hunger

The focus of this exercise is to help you become aware of true physiological hunger or "stomach hunger." (Stomach hunger is experienced by most people as a growling or rumbling sensation in the stomach. It can also be a feeling of shakiness or even nausea if you wait too long to eat.)

To do this exercise, you want to get hungry as often as possible during the course of one day. Choose a day in the next week when you feel relatively relaxed. A weekend day may be best, but a structured weekday may work for you also. Follow the instructions below as you begin this special day of eating. (You will need to carry food or have food near you throughout the entire day.)

1. As soon as you wake up in the morning, even before you get out of bed, check in with your stomach. Does it feel hungry? If not, go about the routine of getting up and notice every thirty minutes whether you are hungry yet.

2. Once you are hungry feed yourself within five or ten minutes. For now, eat only small amounts each time you feel hungry. Eat slowly, letting yourself truly experience the sight, smell, texture and taste of the food.

3. Proceed with your day, checking in with your stomach regularly and eating small amounts of food within five or ten minutes of feeling hungry. If you can, eat when you are feeling stomach hunger rather than for emotional reasons. (Remember to be kind to yourself if you eat from emotional hunger as well.)

4. As you do this exercise think about the times during the day when you normally would have eaten—because it was mealtime or because you were bored, anxious, lonely or tired.

At the end of the day, review your experience with this exercise. Think about the following.
  • How often did you experience stomach hunger?

- How did it feel to eat in response to stomach hunger? (How did the food taste? How did you feel when you were finished eating?)

- Was it difficult to eat from stomach hunger instead of eating for emotional reasons?

Component Three: Understanding Mouth Hunger

Mouth hunger is very different from stomach hunger. It is not a physical sensation, but rather a desire to eat for emotional reasons. Even though you are not physically hungry, you find yourself eating because the food "looks good" or "just because it's there." Eating past fullness is a form of mouth hunger as well.

There are two key steps to healing mouth hunger. These include (1) responding to mouth hunger in a new way, and (2) adopting a new attitude about mouth hunger.

Responding to Mouth Hunger in a New Way
When you notice you have mouth hunger, you have two choices.

First, if you think you can wait to eat *without feeling deprived*, you can can delay eating until you are truly stomach hungry. You simply say to yourself: "I feel like I can wait to eat until I am truly stomach hungry. In the meantime I will sit with my feelings or find something else nurturing to do for myself."

Second, if you think *you will feel deprived* if you wait to eat, then it is very important that you go ahead and eat and simply say to yourself: "Isn't it interesting that I'm feeling like I need to eat right now, even though I am sure that I am not truly stomach hungry. I wonder what is going on today that is bothering me? I am going to go ahead and eat, get myself the very best of what I want, and I will not say one mean thing to myself about it. And I trust that as I continue to eat in response to stomach hunger, and as I continue to respond to my mouth hunger without yelling at myself, I will gradually find that I need to eat for emotional reasons less often."

Adopting a New Attitude about Mouth Hunger
Remember, you are not a bad person when you eat for emotional reasons. You are merely caretaking yourself the only way you know how. As you involve yourself in the Overcoming Overeating approach, your mouth hunger will gradually diminish and you will naturally be able to eat in response to true physiological hunger more often.

Component Four: Matching Hunger to Food

Matching food choices to body cravings is an important part of healing eating problems. When you do not make a good match, and eat something you are not hungry for, it causes "forage eating." Forage eating is when you roam around the kitchen eating one thing after another because you have not gotten yourself what you really want.

To do this exercise, you will need to ask yourself the questions listed below each time you experience hunger. Try to sense what your stomach would like by visualizing the following.

- What would feel good in my stomach right now?
- What food would really satisfy me now?
- What am I in the mood to eat?

If you need more help deciding what you want to eat, ask yourself these specific questions.

- What texture would I like (crunchy, chewy, soft, liquid)?
- What taste would I prefer (sweet, salty, bitter, spicy)?
- What temperature food do I want (cold, hot, room temperature)?

Get the food you think you want, and take a few bites. Now pause and take a moment to check in with yourself to see if this food is actually what your stomach wants. If it is not the right food to alleviate your hunger, put it down and get something else to eat.

Component Five: The Food Bag

Carrying a food bag is a critical part of the Overcoming Overeating approach. Keep your food bag near you at all times. This enables you to respond to hunger very quickly and to make the best possible match to your body's cravings.

You should have your food bag and/or your food supply in your home, office, car, briefcase, and/or purse. It is best to stock your bag with a variety of foods (salty, sweet, liquid, solid, crunchy, and chewy). Choose some base foods that will not get stale quickly or require constant refrigeration. In addition, perishable foods such as fruits, vegetables, pastas, breads, and leftovers can be stocked in your food supply daily. It is important to note that food bag items are not just snack foods. Eating from your food bag will replace regimented meal eating, so it is important to keep it amply stocked with delicious foods on an ongoing basis. For example, you could carry toast, lettuce, bacon, tomato slices, and a mayonnaise packet to make a fresh BLT sandwich when you get hungry. Or you could carry sour cream, chives, and a potato to microwave when you want a fresh baked potato.

After you carry food with you for a few weeks examine how you are feeling about it. Initially, most people have a lot of resistance to carrying the food bag. They worry "what will people think when they see a person my size carrying food and eating frequently?" or they say "if I carry a food bag I will eat all the time." Others complain "I am hungry for things that are not in my food bag" or comment "it is too much trouble to pack the bag, I just don't have time." These are common concerns and most people can get past these doubts with time. Once they get through the initial period, they realize that it is very calming to have their food bag with them.

Remember, you have a right to eat whenever you are hungry. There is no reason to notice hunger if you don't have food with you to respond!

Component Six: Stopping When You Are Full

Each time you do this exercise, experiment with your sensation of stomach fullness. You can eat until you feel somewhat full or until you are stuffed. Be aware of how both of these conditions feel.

Choose three eating experiences in the next week to practice listening to your stomach for "full" signals. Follow the steps below.

1. Take a few bites of your food and then stop eating.
2. Ask yourself if you are still hungry. If yes, continue eating.
3. Continue this process of eating, stopping, and assessing your feelings of hunger and fullness.
4. When you decide you are no longer hungry, stop eating.
5. Remind yourself that you can have as much of this food as you want and that you do not have to stop eating until you feel sure you have had enough. This will help you stay calm and make you less likely to overeat past fullness.

For now, try not to be judgmental about where you need to stop eating. You may need to eat well past fullness for quite some time. This has to do with psychological rather than physiological fullness. As you continue to treat yourself in a caring, accepting way, you will gradually shift toward stopping your eating closer to when you are physiologically full. It is important to note that most people learn to recognize and respond to hunger very quickly. Learning to match food to hunger comes next. But being able to stop eating when full is something that comes much later in the process. It can take years. Be patient with yourself.

Component Seven: Legalizing Food

When you legalize food it means that in a psychological sense, all foods become equal. There are no longer "good" or "bad" foods. You stop labeling foods as "fattening" or "forbidden." Words like "calories" and "healthy" are no longer in your vocabulary. The best way for you to legalize food will probably depend on your current eating style. Two different approaches are described below. Choose the one that is best for you.

Legalizing-Option 1

If you have always had difficulty "sticking to diets" use this approach. Begin the process of legalizing by identifying the foods with which you most frequently have difficulty. After identifying your problem foods, figure out how much of each you could eat in one day. Now purchase at least three times this quantity and stock them at home, at work, and in your food bag. If some of these foods make you especially anxious, keep them with you at all times, so you know you can have them at any moment. And, very important to successful legalizing, you must restock your supply of problem foods *before* it begins to get low.

Legalizing-Option 2

If you tend to be very controlling and "disciplined" about your eating regimen it is best to use this alternative technique to modify the legalizing process. Begin the process by choosing just one or two of the foods with which you most frequently have difficulty. Arrange to eat a small amount of these foods on a daily basis. Gradually, as you feel less anxious, increase the availability of these foods and begin legalizing some additional problem foods. *Initially, it may feel too scary to include your problem foods in your food bag.* Over time, however, you should begin adding them to your food bag and carrying them in abundance.

As you experiment with legalizing foods be aware of the subtle ways in which you may sabotage yourself. These include the following.

- Buying foods that are not the ones with which you have a problem. (e.g., buying Hershey chocolate bars instead of the Snickers you really want).

- Buying your problem foods in large quantities but storing them in an inaccessible place (e.g., buying six gallons of ice cream but keeping five of them locked in a freezer in the basement).

- Providing yourself with an abundant supply of food but serving it to yourself according to traditional "portion sizes."

- Providing yourself with the foods you love but hiding from others when you eat them.

Component Eight: Eating Consciously and with Pleasure

Eating consciously helps you to be "in the moment" as you eat, allowing you to more fully experience the satisfaction and pleasure of eating. Choose a time in the next week to have a highly conscious experience with food. Below are some suggestions to help guide your experience.

1. Do this exercise when you are hungry (but not overly hungry!).
2. Choose a calm environment with a minimum of distractions (radio, TV, conversation).
3. Involve yourself in the process of preparing, serving, unwrapping, and/or cutting up the food.
4. Sit down, relax your body, and eat slowly, pausing periodically.
5. As you eat, focus on the visual aspects of the food.
6. Experience the smell and feel of the food while you eat it.
7. Tune in to each bite of food while it's in your mouth. Try not to focus on the bite to come before you have swallowed the food currently in your mouth.
8. Keep your thoughts on your eating. Try not to think about distressing situations or things unrelated to your eating experience.

It is very important that you do not use conscious eating as if you are on a diet or as a way to eat less! And there is no need to follow the eating consciously guidelines each time you have an eating experience. Use this exercise occasionally to help you learn to be in "the moment" with your eating.

Component Nine: Curing Bad Body Fever

Hirschmann and Munter point out that the healing power of this new eating style is further reinforced by working extensively on size acceptance and curing "bad body thoughts" (BBTs). BBTs are much like emotional hunger; they are an attempt to cope with distress. Many of us have become very good at making our bodies the target of our painful feelings. Rather than naming our problems, "sitting" with the feelings, or working to solve our problems directly, we have learned to distract ourselves by thinking incessantly about hating various parts of our bodies. Try using the four-step process below to interrupt your bad body thoughts and "cure" your bad body fever.

Step 1. Apologize to Yourself
Most of the things we say to ourselves about our bodies are so hateful that we would never say them to anyone else, even someone we did not like. It is important to apologize to yourself when you direct such awful thoughts and comments to your own body.

Step 2. Challenge the Authority of Your Bad Body Thoughts
Who says how a person's body is supposed to look? Remember your judgments are generated by unrealistic cultural standards reinforced by the media and the advertising industry. Take time to look around and notice the way peoples' bodies are really shaped.

Step 3. Set the Thought Aside
Remind yourself that painful thoughts about your body are not really about your body. In order to be free of these thoughts it is important to move on to figuring out the life information that is embedded in the thought.

Step 4. Learn from Your Bad Body Thoughts
When these thoughts occur, ask yourself the following.

- What were you doing, thinking, or feeling at the time the painful thought occurred? There is a reason why that painful thought occurred at that moment. Something was making you uncomfortable, and you made your body the target of the bad feeling you were having.

- What part of your body did you feel bad about and what words did you use to criticize yourself about this body part? It is important to realize that the words and feelings you direct at your body are really the words and feelings you are experiencing about specific difficult issues in your life.

Remember, bad body thoughts are never really about your body!

Understanding How and Why
the Overcoming Overeating Approach Works

For professionals teaching Overcoming Overeating it is very important to understand how the approach works.

The Power of the Hunger-Feeding Connection

As they begin this work, many clients are obsessed with food and miserably unhappy about their weight. They do not have any clarity about the issues in their lives that lie beneath the food and weight obsession. Since this is their initial level of consciousness about the problem, it is best to start working in this "food and weight" place.

When clients learn to (1) eat in response to physical hunger, (2) feed themselves lovingly without restrictions when they are emotionally hungry, (3) eat exactly what their bodies are hungry for, and (4) notice the exact moment of fullness, they can begin to eat in fine attunement with their bodies. Practicing these basics of internal cue eating and developing this attunement with themselves at the physical level begins to diminish the preoccupation with food and weight. As this preoccupation recedes, awareness about emotional life issues can begin to surface.

As they become calmer about food and more emotionally aware, clients are increasingly able to eat in response to physical hunger. This simple act of repeatedly eating out of physical hunger allows food to become less emotionally charged. In fact, emotional hunger recedes (on its own, without restricting it) in direct response to the increased number of stomach hunger feedings a person experiences.

The process of decoding and healing bad body thoughts is also essential for helping clients to give up the dieting that has fueled their eating problems and weight gain. (For a more extensive discussion of this very sophisticated portion of this work see Hirschmann and Munter's second book *When Women Stop Hating Their Bodies: Freeing Yourself from a Food and Weight Obsession.*)

Practicing internal cue feeding and decoding bad body thoughts helps people focus on the fears, pain, and struggles that have led them to so much dieting, overeating, and body hatred. Over time the compulsive eating and chronic dieting is *forever healed* and clients can begin to talk with great clarity about the emotions and associated life difficulties underneath the eating and weight struggle. People who are brave enough to embrace this approach can increasingly begin working directly on their life issues rather than needing to eat about them.

What about Nutrition Education?

We believe it is unwise to give nutrition information, even accurate nutrition information, to people who are locked in struggles with chronic dieting, emotional overeating, body hatred, and exercise addiction. These people cannot use this information, and it can actually make their eating problems worse. Given that such a large percentage of the population struggles with issues of food and weight, it is critical to keep this in mind when planning nutrition education programs, cafeteria programs, shopping tours, and cooking demonstrations.

First Things First!

If you are out on a boat with someone you love (who does not swim) and that person falls into the water, you would not consider running to the side of the boat to give them a lecture about the proper form of the crawl stroke. You would throw them a life preserver and help them back into the boat. Once they had calmed down, perhaps on the ride home, you might suggest that swimming lessons would be a reasonable choice before the next outing. This same principle is true with eating and weight struggles. A person "drowning" in their relationship with food cannot benefit from a lecture about how to eat nutritiously. We have to get them out of the water, so to speak, help them heal their compulsive eating, and then carefully give them nutrition information.

For wellness programs that adopt the HAES philosophy and/or the Overcoming Overeating approach we recommend screening potential program participants for problems with food, weight, or body image *before* placing them in nutrition-related programs. Things to check for include chronic dieting, emotional overeating, body image disturbance and exercise addiction. If any of these issues surface, healing the person's relationship with food, exercise and their body becomes the most important first step. Once a person has normalized their eating, and worked on body acceptance and exercise issues, they can begin to explore quality of diet issues.

For people who have never experienced food and body image struggles (a relatively rare situation) or people who have healed past eating issues, it can be helpful to provide information pertaining to quality of diet. It must, however, be done in a manner that does not reintroduce eating, weight, and exercise obsession. With this in mind, we offer the following suggestions.

- Quality of diet programs should be taught only by people thoroughly trained in the HAES philosophy who have resolved their own issues with food, body acceptance and exercise.

- Programs should reinforce eating as a pleasurable, relaxed experience. Nutrition information isn't helpful if used in a way that interferes with enjoying food.

- Programs should remind people to combine newly learned knowledge about food with evaluation of how foods taste and feel in their bodies. It does no good to choose the lowest fat hot dog if you hate the way it tastes and feel unsatisfied after eating it!

- Generally speaking, lists of calories, carbohydrates, fat grams, food exchanges, and so on lead people to be rigid and obsessive about their eating. We recommend omitting these items from regular program materials.

- Program language, images, and materials should be consistent with the HAES philosophy. At Conoco, the original name of the cafeteria wellness program was Eating Well. The name was changed to Choices after we adopted the Overcoming Overeating approach.

What about Diabetes?

Whether it is for medical reasons or weight loss, diets and restricted eating do not work! Special diabetic diets that restrict sugar and fat intake set people up for the same emotional eating and closet eating that weight loss dieters experience. The exciting news is that there is no need to subject people with diabetes to these kinds of dietary limitations. Certified diabetes educators, dieticians, and endocrinologists are now using the HAES philosophy and approaches such as Overcoming Overeating with such patients and experiencing excellent outcomes.

Learning to eat in response to hunger and fullness helps people with diabetes become more finely tuned to the exact amount of food their bodies need. Legalizing all foods and eliminating dietary restrictions helps these people break out of that same diet/binge cycle experienced by weight loss dieters. By normalizing their eating and becoming more in sync with their bodies the Overcoming Overeating approach helps people with diabetes eliminate the extreme high and low blood sugars that can follow from the compulsive, emotional eating that often results from strict medical diets.

The country's leading diabetes treatment center utilizing the HAES philosophy and the Overcoming Overeating approach is the Diabetes Care Center in Salinas, California. Dana Armstrong, R.D., C.D.E., and Allen King, M.D., have worked together as true paradigm pioneers in the use of non-restrained eating with people with both type I (insulin-dependent) and type II (non-insulin-dependent) diabetes. For more information about their treatment center see "Holistic Resources" at the end of this book.

Restrictive diets for treatment of high cholesterol and high blood pressure can also lead to compulsive eating, weight fluctuations, and body image problems. We recommend using programs based on the HAES philosophy to address all types of food related health problems. This helps people improve their health status and quality of life without leading to the undesirable outcomes often seen with medically restrictive diets.

What about Children?

Setting up a family food environment based on Overcoming Overeating (or any approach consistent with HAES philosophy) is an excellent way to prevent food, weight, and body image struggles in children. It is also a compassionate and useful approach to helping a child of any age who is already struggling with these issues, which we all know can be extremely painful in childhood. For a complete discussion of the use of Overcoming Overeating with children, we suggest reading *Preventing Childhood Eating Problems* by Jane R. Hirschmann and Lela Zaphiropoulos.

What about Wellness Programs?

Implementation of the HAES approach requires reexamining all aspects of health and fitness programming to avoid presenting an inconsistent or confusing message. Because HAES focuses on eating behavior, not weight loss, and encourages body acceptance, the following changes are helpful in wellness programs and fitness facilities (see chapter 18 for a more in-depth discussion of programming issues).

Eliminate from Programs
Scales in locker rooms
Body-fat testing
Weight loss classes
Weight loss competitions
Calorie or fat gram listings in the cafeteria
Good food/bad food lists on grocery tours
Food phobic and fat phobic language in exercise classes
Diet books and magazines in the wellness library

Add to Programs
Exercise classes for large people taught by large people
Large body size wellness staff members
Larger towels in locker rooms and protected locker space for large people
Books and magazines that feature HAES approach information in the wellness library
Programs, films, and videos on media, body image, size acceptance, and so on
Bulletin board materials that portray a variety of body sizes for healthy, active people

Summary

Embracing the Overcoming Overeating approach and the HAES philosophy can be one of the most challenging areas of health promotion "paradigm change." When we offer this work to clients each of us must examine the ways in which we ourselves have struggled with food, weight, and exercise issues. As challenging as this work is, however, it is critically important as well. Every time a woman is freed from her oppressive struggle with food and weight we contribute to liberating the intellectual, spiritual, and physical energy of one-half of the planet! This helps humanity progress just a little further from Epoch II towards Epoch III; such a significant and transformational outcome just from eliminating weight loss programs!

References

The Overcoming Overeating approach featured in this chapter was developed by Jane R. Hirschmann and Carol H. Munter. For over thirty years Hirschmann and Munter have spoken up for the rights of women and the need to reevaluate and challenge the oppressive culture of dieting and thinness that permeates our society. We strongly recommend reading all of their books as well as accessing their videotapes, audiotapes, Web site, and Overcoming Overeating Centers around the country. Full citations for their books, *Overcoming Overeating* and *When Women Stop Hating Their Bodies* are listed below, and additional information about Overcoming Overeating resources is listed in "Holistic Resources" at the end of the book.

1.   Hirschmann, J. R., and C. H. Munter. *Overcoming Overeating: Living Free in a World of Food.* New York: Fawcett/Columbine, 1989.

2.   Hirschmann, J. R., and C. H. Munter. *When Women Stop Hating Their Bodies: Freeing Yourself from Food and Weight Obsession.* New York: Ballantine, 1995.

3.   Hirschmann, J. R., and Lela Zaphiropoulos. *Preventing Childhood Eating Problems.* Carlsbad, CA: Gurze, 1993.

Part Six

BREATHING SPIRIT INTO
HEALTH PROMOTION

Chapter 18

DESIGNING A HOLISTIC PROGRAM
Softening the Old and Bringing in the New

*Those who say it can't be done should
get out of the way of those who are doing it!*

Joel Barker
The Business of Paradigms

In the 1980s no one in organizational health promotion was talking
about quantum physics, holistic mind/body medicine, or a new paradigm for humanity. Some of us just knew that the traditional biomedical "interventions" being used in our wellness programs were
not working. While some people clearly benefited from the programs
offered, there were many who did not. Regular program participants
sometimes took their participation too far, exercising when they were
ill and injured, or pursuing health guidelines in a rigid, driven manner. There were also many participants who repeatedly signed up for
programs only to drop out and relapse into old behaviors. Each time
they went through this cycle they increasingly felt a sense of shame
and failure. But perhaps the greatest concern was the fact that no one
who came to our traditional programs was seeing a connection between the state of their lives and the state of their health. They would
complain in the locker room to co-workers about their marriage, their
children, their finances or their job, but never see that their pursuit of
health in the Wellness Center might be related to all of that.

In order to begin offering programs that addressed these concerns
we had to begin exploring new information and resources from outside the field of traditional health promotion. We had to seek out
conferences, trainings, and mentors in areas such as psychology and
social work, alternative medicine, psychoneuroimmunology and the

new sciences. These diverse fields of study began to give us new ideas for redesigning our wellness programs. We did not know until later that we were going through a "paradigm shift."

As we began to transition to holistic approaches, there were no other worksite programs to look to for ideas. There were no evaluation data to prove that a holistic approach was the right way to go. What guided us on this new path was our intuition and a deep sense of caring for the individuals in our health promotion programs.

Specific Program Modification Ideas

The sections below outline the typical areas of programming covered in traditional biomedical health promotion programs. Under each topic area are listed specific suggestions for softening or transitioning traditional program designs to include more holistic types of themes and activities. All of the suggested program modification changes in this chapter have been implemented in holistic programs around the country. Some programs have adopted only a few of these ideas; others have implemented many of them. Keep in mind that each of us can do as much or as little as our comfort level allows.

Life Center
(Instead of Fitness Facility)

For those that have one, the physical facility is often the most visible symbol of the program. It is therefore very important to "soften" the facility. Move away from a strict emphasis on physical health, cardiovascular conditioning, and strength training. It is also helpful to create resource and support areas throughout the facility that encourage relaxation and socialization and that help people explore a broad range of health and life issues.

- Modify the fitness facility by adding aquariums, plants, audiovisual offerings, chair massage areas or table massage rooms, meditation rooms, and a food bar (with more than just stereotypically "healthy" foods).

- Create pleasurable bulletin boards that portray people of all body sizes and ages involved in a wide range of life activities (napping, playing, snuggling, reading—not just jogging).
- Provide exercise clothing for a full range of body sizes and provide large towels in the locker room so that all people will feel accommodated.
- Provide separate locker facilities for fat people who want a protected environment.
- Do not install scales for weighing.
- Eliminate (or at least cover) books and magazines that feature "perfect body" images. Offer readings and a resource library that address many mind/body/spirit, and ecological topics (e.g., *National Geographic* rather than *Shape*).
- Create healing spaces for private one-on-one education or counseling. Have soothing music, sacred objects, artwork, plants, and candles if possible.
- Encourage health promotion staff to move away from dressing in traditional fitness center uniforms such as warm-up suits or running shorts.

Life Center Staff
(Instead of Professional Trainers and Aerobic Instructors)

Wellness programs are traditionally staffed by biomedically trained, middle class, thin, young, white, stereotypically fit looking people. Wellness program participants, however, often represent a wide spectrum of ages, economic status, races, religions, body sizes and fitness levels. For Holistic Health Promotion programs it is important to create a more diverse staff that can effectively and compassionately relate to the needs of many types of people.

- Add older staff members.
- Add larger body size staff members.
- Add staff members from diverse racial, religious, ethnic and economic backgrounds.

- Add staff members with training in holistic areas: counseling, psychology, mind/body medicine, complementary/alternative therapies, consciousness research and so on.

Movement Offerings
(Instead of Exercise Classes)

Create experiences for exploration of the mind/body/spirit connection through movement. Move away from competitive classes focused on reshaping the body and seek alternatives to promoting exercise as a way to compensate for overeating.

- Develop cardiovascular offerings that incorporate emotional expression, connectedness to the earth, and whole-body movement styles (e.g., the NIA technique developed by the Rosas and The 5 Rhythms of Gabrielle Roth).
- Add nontraditional offerings (jazz, ballet, ballroom dancing, rollerblading, golfing, etc.).
- Add offerings that teach holistic concepts (yoga, tai chi, meditation, martial arts).
- Use positive instructional statements and work toward creating a cooperative, fun environment.
- Seek alternatives to negative body talk and food conversations.
- Add body image and positive self talk to warm-up and/or cool-down time.
- Eliminate perceived exertion and heart rate monitoring and encourage people to tune in to their bodies instead.
- Create variety in instructor body sizes and ages (incorporate older and fat instructors).
- Minimize revealing instructor dress.
- Add classes specifically designed for less fit or older participants.
- Add classes specifically for fat participants (preferably taught by a fat instructor who knows what it feels like to move in a large body).

Eating Behavior/Quality of Diet
(Instead of Weight Control and Nutrition)

Offer programs that address chronic dieting and body dissatisfaction among people of all sizes. Help people see how weight obsessions and body dissatisfaction are connected to emotional life struggles. Teach quality of diet from an internal cue, "body-based" focus.

- Screen for disturbed eating, exercise addiction and body image problems.
- Replace weight loss and weight maintenance programs with Health at Every Size offerings that address chronic dieting and body hatred.
- Offer classes and workshops showing how media and advertising images influence eating and exercise behaviors.
- Eliminate weigh-ins, use of pig logos, and other shaming strategies and images.
- Eliminate the taking of body composition, weight, and BMI measurements. They are unscientific, uncompassionate, and iatrogenic.
- Eliminate weight loss contests.
- Create food service programs that expose people to a wide range of foods.
- Eliminate calorie counts, fat gram listings, and portion control information in all food materials.
- Add cooking demonstrations, food sampling, and grocery shopping tours that emphasize the pleasures of eating. Move away from a focus on heart disease, cancer, weight loss, and good food/bad food lists.

Life Simplification or Life Enhancement
(Instead of Stress Management)

Move away from a negative focus on stress that emphasizes "controlling" symptoms. Add programs that help people address the origins of stress and give them ideas and support for expanding and enhancing their lives. Provide new holistic information about the relationship between life struggles and the development of illness and pain. Inform people about integrating alternative and traditional health care systems. Sample topics for such programs might include the following.

- Alternative/Complementary Therapies and Choosing a Provider
- Blending Alternative and Traditional Health Care
- Holistic Medical Self-Care
- Family of Origin Issues
- Understanding Addictions and Compulsive Behaviors
- Parenting/Step-Parenting/Single Parenting/Adoptive Parenting
- Relationships/Marriage Satisfaction/Divorce/Blended Families
- Gender-Based Communication Styles
- Legal Wellness
- Financial Wellness
- Sleep/Rest/Play
- Life Simplification
- Identifying and Responding to Stereotypes and Prejudices (regarding age, gender, race and body size)
- Elder Care/Aging/Death/Conscious Dying
- Healthy Touch/Massage/Self-Massage
- Healthy Pleasures (music, art, humor, relaxation, etc.)
- Vision Screening and Holistic Vision Care
- Advertising and Health Values
- Workplace Changes and Career Development Issues
- Over the Counter and Prescription Drug Use

Life Balance Questionnaire
(Instead of Health Risk Appraisal)

Move away from authoritative and shaming computer feedback and an exclusive focus on disease, physical health, and behavioral control. Create assessments that look for positives and see the whole person and the systems in which they exist.

- Add psychological, social, and spiritual questions.
- Add questions that address the systems in which people live. Include family, work, and community issues that influence a person's health.
- Add questions about perceived health and happiness.
- Add questions about a broader range of lifestyle and health issues, including the following.

purpose in life	economic well-being
emotional style	attitudes/beliefs
contact with nature	intellectual stimulation
touch/sexuality	rest and play
social support	meaning in work

- Focus on positives: what people are doing *right* for themselves.
- Do not give actual age versus risk-age feedback (this can set up an expectation for illness).
- After administering a health risk assessment, provide people with counseling, follow-up programs, and resources to help them with issues they choose to address.

Wellness Extravaganza
(Instead of a Health Fair)

Move away from the exclusive emphasis on physical health, illness detection, and symptom control (disease fairs). Create a pleasurable experience that exposes people to new holistic therapies and give them ideas for moving towards a more enjoyable, meaningful life.

- Add booths staffed by holistic providers: chiropractic, home-opathy, acupuncture, biological dentistry, music and art therapy, energy work, reiki, massage, reflexology, aromatherapy, and so on.
- Add a booth on emotional life issues (with self-scored screening tests for relationship problems, depression, phobias, addictions, etc.).
- Eliminate weight loss booths and body fat testing.
- Eliminate cholesterol-testing booths (or at least be sure to give *complete* information about the issues surrounding cholesterol testing accuracy, significance, and HAES-based treatment options).
- Screen for compulsive eating and body hatred problems.
- Add a booth that offers chair massage or teaches self massage.
- Add a booth by a local bookstore that has books on a broad range of topics related to well-being.
- Add a booth by a local music store to let people sample and learn about the different types of music that might bring them pleasure.
- Add a booth by an area grocery store/whole foods market for sampling new foods.
- Add a booth with information from the American Association of Retired Persons (AARP) and information on elder care facilities and programs.
- Add a booth on parenting resources and learning disability issues.
- Add a booth for holistic vision screening.

- Add a booth by a recreation and sports store on recreation clothing/equipment/activities.
- Add a booth by a travel agency on affordable vacations and quick getaways.
- Add a booth with information on financial planning and legal advice.

Fitness Evaluation/Exercise Prescription

We feel it is best to eliminate fitness evaluations and exercise prescriptions whenever possible. When it is not possible there are modifications that can help minimize their conflict with the spirit of holistic programming.

Fitness evaluations and exercise prescriptions, especially upon entry into a wellness program are very intimidating for many people. Certainly physically fit individuals may love to be tested, but these people are already joining wellness programs. For the sedentary and less fit people, testing may be a huge initial barrier that keeps them from joining. We have often heard people say that they did not join a health promotion program because they wanted to avoid the fitness evaluation and exercise prescription. They say these tests feel very shaming, pointing out all the places where they are not "good" or "healthy enough." Even worse, fitness evaluations can make a person's body hurt. Arms, stomach, hamstrings, and the back may be sore the next day. It is not helpful for a person's first experience with the health promotion program to be one that makes the body hurt! Another problem is the fact that both fitness evaluations and exercise prescriptions perpetuate the biomedical feel of a program, placing visible emphasis on physical health to the exclusion of emotional, social, and spiritual health issues. This is inconsistent with Holistic Health Promotion. For those of us who must continue to offer these types of tests and recommendations as part of our programs we offer some suggestions for softening the impact.

- As a tester, wear nonstereotypical professional dress (no warm-up suits, running shorts, or clipboards and whistles).

- Address participant test anxiety before and during testing (ask participants how they are feeling about the testing and outcomes).
- Soften guilt-oriented results interpretation and emphasize the positives (people who have been sedentary would not be expected to do well on these tests—and fitness has a significant genetic component).
- Elicit participant feedback about past health experiences, movement preferences, and lifestyle issues. And listen, listen, listen!
- Explore options/choices and minimize the dispensing of authoritative, "expert" advice.
- Validate a full range of activity levels and preferences.
- Teach people how to listen to their bodies and tune in to internal cues while exercising.
- Support the pursuit of "flexible and varied" participation in physical activity or movement.
- Use fitness testing and exercise prescription time to begin raising awareness about the new holistic paradigm for understanding health and healing.
- Remember that, as difficult as it might feel given our training, it is perfectly all right for someone to choose not to exercise, stop smoking and so on.

Competitions/Incentive Programs

These types of programs pit people against themselves or others. They are "jump through the hoop," and "chase the carrot" types of strategies through which a person is supposed to develop a long-term interest in running by getting a short-term, unrelated prize such as a T-shirt. This concept is at odds with a holistic approach that seeks to foster cooperative, supportive relationships among people as well as motivation through increased consciousness of internal needs. As with fitness evaluations and exercise prescriptions, it is best to eliminate this type of programming. If elimination is not possible, try the modifications below.

- Sponsor individual incentive promotions rather than group competitions.
- Reward varying levels of accomplishment, not just the person who runs the farthest or fastest.
- Reward a broad range of behaviors, emphasizing the importance of balance in life.
- Place a ceiling on the amount of activity rewarded.
- Use smaller rather than larger rewards (although traditional wisdom assumes that larger rewards result in better outcomes, research suggests the opposite).
- Use noncontingent rewards (rewards not tied to any predetermined behavior) whenever possible (i.e., put a small gift on all participants' desks before they come to work in the morning as a reminder of upcoming programs or as thanks for participation).

It is important to note that one of the biggest drawbacks to incentive programs is the fact that they actually reward and promote addictive behaviors. When people are given prizes and recognition for running, swimming, or cycling more than others, what is being rewarded is an excessive level of activity. The person most likely to win this type of award and receive recognition is the person who obsessively pursues this level of activity. When our health promotion programs run these types of contests we are actually encouraging extreme and addictive behaviors. Compounding the problem is the fact that we also typically have nothing in our traditional programs that heightens awareness about compulsive/addictive behaviors such as exercise dependence or chronic dieting.

Beyond Program Modifications

The information presented above provides ideas for making a traditional wellness program more holistic. But it is important to remember that even with holistic modifications the traditional focus is usually still on trying to impact "individuals" using the "shotgun" approach. Programming is offered to the entire population without targeting groups of people with unique or more urgent needs. Traditional programming that targets individuals for behavior change, in isolation from the environment and the relationships in which they exist, will always have significant limitations. An alternative for the health promotion programs of the future is to incorporate more systems-based programming.

Breast-Feeding Education: A Systems Approach

In traditional programs the health topic of breast-feeding is typically addressed by having a yearly brown bag presentation on the benefits for the mother and child. There might also be an article in the newsletter or a pamphlet in the health promotion facility. Unfortunately, if a couple finds out they are pregnant the month *after* the brown bag, the resources they can access may be limited. In addition, there may be nothing in place once the baby is born to help the woman breast-feed successfully at home and work. This is significant since it has been shown that private, clean areas in which to pump, adequate equipment, and good social and emotional support are critical for women who are breast-feeding at work.[1-3]

A systems-based, holistic approach would have breastfeeding information, a lactation counseling hotline, and workplace lactation equipment available *year round*. Some work sites have successfully implemented this model by partnering with the manufacturer of electric breast pumps to set up "lactation stations" and counseling.[1] These services make the work site environment lactation friendly. High-powered, efficient pumps are leased by the company. These pumps can also be assigned to employees for take-home or travel use. A lactation consultant is made available to answer questions and provide emotional support. By providing better pumping equipment; clean, private, accessible areas for pumping and counseling and emotional support, a health promotion program can greatly increase the chances that a working mom will be able to breast-feed successfully in a stress-reducing environment. As a result, mother, baby, and the organization will benefit. With a little flexibility and creativity all wellness program offerings can adopt this type of more holistic, systems-based approach.

Questions and Fears

Many organizational health promotion programs are beginning to experiment with holistic programming concepts. Some programs adopt only minor modifications. In other cases programs are completely re-created based on holistic thinking. In both cases, however, there seems to be a fairly common set of concerns and questions that arises during the transition. Here are some of the most common ones.

1. Can holistic programming be used only with a new start-up program or can it be used to change an existing traditional program as well? Successful holistic approaches have been created in both start-up and existing traditional programs. In either case, success will depend on becoming familiar with key aspects of the environment before planning a path forward. Important aspects to consider include the following.

- Does the organization have a liberal environment open to change?
- Do the people planning the health promotion programs have a strong connection to senior management?
- Is the health promotion staff open to holistic concepts and enthusiastic about program change?
- Is anyone in the organization well connected to the local mental health and alternative/complementary medical community?
- Does the organization already have initiatives that encourage personal growth and development?

2. What is the best way to determine if there should be a gradual transition to holistic concepts or a dramatic shift in programming? Once again, the best way to decide how to handle this issue is to ask "how conservative or liberal is the organizational environment?" A more liberal environment may comfortably accept either a new program based on holistic concepts, or a rapid transition of a mature program from biomedical to holistic concepts. In more conservative environ-ments, both start-up and ongoing mature programs may need to slowly modify biomedical programs and gradually introduce holistic concepts. For example, a high-tech firm that is constantly experiencing change and cultivating new ideas may be an excellent place to launch an entirely new holistic program. On the other hand, a conservative hospital that has all its operations rooted in biomedical thinking may be a place where a gradual transition to holistic programs would be a better choice.

3. Where do we look for holistic programming ideas if only a few organizations have started doing this? Fortunately, there are now corporate, hospital and academic programs as well as public health programs that are using holistic approaches. For example, one of these, the Kailo Program, is described in detail in chapter 21. Looking to these established programs can provide an excellent source of ideas. It is important to remember however, that holistic program design does not lend itself to the kind of "paint by number" strategies that are used in the traditional model. There are not, nor should there ever be, cookbook-type guidelines specifying how to set up a holistic wellness program. The program that each of us creates comes in great part from the healing process we go through as we embrace the new holistic information ourselves. It is of course helpful to see what others have done, but in the end it must come to a large degree from our own hearts and minds.

4. Isn't it going to require a bigger budget to implement holistic programming? No! More money is not required. What is required is a shift in resources. For example, the money that was used to buy T-shirts and caps for competitive incentive programs can now be used to pay presenters to do brown bags on mind/body medicine, aromatherapy, or financial wellness. The money that was earmarked for fancy health risk assessments and fitness evaluations can be used to create a "relaxation station" in the wellness center or to subsidize chair massages throughout the work complex. The "bottom line" is that if you have enough money to run a traditional biomedical program you have enough money to run a holistic one.

5. *Do we as health professionals need to be completely grounded in these new concepts before we can begin transitioning our programs?* One of the foundations of the holistic approach is the belief that everything in life, including our professional experience, is a "work in progress." There is no such thing as waiting until we "know enough" to get started. If the holistic perspective seems compelling then it is time to jump in! Of course, it makes sense to develop at least an initial familiarity with the basic principles of quantum physics, chaos theory, mind/body medicine, and holistic health. (This book is designed for exactly that purpose.) Beyond that, following our intuition and cultivating our personal growth and healing work is the biggest determinant of how effective any of us will be. It cannot be emphasized enough that our personal wellness is the cornerstone of our professional compassion and effectiveness. This is certainly not about being perfect (or "optimally" healthy). However, if we are unhappy or depressed; in an abusive relationship; addicted to food, alcohol, exercising, or dieting; or just chronically exhausted from going too fast, doing too much, and caring for others to the detriment of our own health, then it is critical that we begin working on our own issues as we offer ourselves as a healing ally to others. The bottom line is that creating new holistic approaches comes from within each of us. The more we can access our intuition, listen respectfully to others, and do our own healing work, the more opportunities we will all have to generate compassionate, useful programming that frees us from the limitations of biomedically based, traditional health promotion.

Holistic Programming Materials

The following are examples of a range of materials used in wellness programs that have "gone holistic." Included are several types of brown bag marketing flyers, a HAES workshop promotional brochure, a general wellness program information piece, a resource library description and a grocery shopping tour promotional piece.*

These sample materials are presented in this book to provide examples of how topics and language shift when moving in a holistic direction. Please note that it is important to re-examine *all language* used with clients and move away from any controlling, judgmental or shame-based terminology. It is also critical to make sure that the images and artwork used in marketing pieces, educational materials and bulletin boards reflect the new language, information and themes of the holistic model.

Take a few moments and ask yourself the following questions. Do your newsletter articles just have images of young, thin people jogging or do they also feature people of all ages and sizes walking, gardening, hiking, bicycling and so on? Are your bulletin boards filled with articles about eating low-carb foods with images of broccoli and apples everywhere, or do they feature articles about the HAES philosophy and show people of all sizes enjoying a wide range of foods? What are your conversations with program participants and clients like? Do you "sympathize" with them for the ways in which they "confess" that they have been "bad" for not exercising or for eating too much? Or do you offer a gentle contradiction to such an old and unhelpful view of these types of behaviors? The process of bringing holistic concepts into our programs requires us to rethink and recreate all of the ways in which we reach out to people.

*We would like to acknowledge that the sample materials on the next few pages are modified versions of materials originally used in the Conoco Wellness program from 1988 to 1994. Many creative people on the Conoco Wellness staff helped to develop these materials and associated programs. Those individuals include: Linda Spreen, Kathy White, Donna Sullivan, Mary Sue Abernathy, Bob Ealing, and Rusty Krause.

Learn

The Art

OF SELF-MASSAGE

Tension? Headaches? Trouble relaxing?
If you'd love a massage but don't have the time
and don't want to spend the money, this is your
chance to give yourself a wonderful gift!

The Academy of Massage will demonstrate:

- Self-massage techniques that are easy to remember and apply

- How to target the specific areas that are typically prone to tension and tightness

- The difference between massage and acupressure and where specific pressure points are located

- How to reduce tension at your desk, in your car, before a stressful meeting, etc.

Come and relax and bring your lunch.

ADVERTISING
AND
YOUR HEALTH

Advertising impacts us in a variety of ways.
We are exposed to advertising through television, radio,
billboards, newspapers and magazines on an ongoing
basis. Many of the messages conveyed by these forms of
advertising are responsible and helpful
Yet some messages, especially those related to health,
can be misleading.

COME TO THIS LUNCH TIME SERIES
AND:

Explore the nature and influence of advertising messages
in our culture

Experience and discuss samples of health-related
television commercials and print advertisements that can
be misleading

Assess how you and your family have been influenced by
advertising messages

BRING YOUR LUNCH

DRINKS WILL BE PROVIDED!

ARE YOU TIRED OF FEELING GUILTY ABOUT EATING THE FOODS YOU LOVE?

If you're sick of soup and salad and weary of weighing in, this **Eat for L.I.F.E.** workshop can change the way you think about food forever.

This workshop can enable you to:
— give up dieting forever
— discover that you eat less when you don't diet
— learn to distinguish physiological from emotional hunger
— move beyond preoccupation with food to a fuller life

Program

Rethinking the Problem
— The diet/binge/weight gain cycle
— Cultural messages about food and body size
— Family messages about food and body size

Free to Eat
— Legalizing and equalizing food
— "Stomach" (physiological) versus "mouth" (emotional) hunger
— When, what, and how much to eat

Everyday Eating
— Food bag ideas
— Tips for eating consciously
— Reconnecting with the joy of eating

The Body/Mind Connection
— Emotional life and food
— Self-acceptance in action
— Transforming body image

Please note: There will be no weigh-ins and no physical testing in this workshop.

A NEW DIMENSION IN WELLNESS

Our new corporate Wellness Program is about what people CAN do. It is not a program about what they SHOULD do!

We believe people are born into the world with an innate ability and desire to be well. We are not here to make people feel guilty about how much they weigh, the foods they eat, or how much they do or do not exercise. We are here to accept everyone, just the way they are, and support them in their efforts to learn more about themselves. The Wellness Program provides an opportunity for employees to explore what wellness means to them in a cooperative, pleasurable, and caring environment. If you are interested in discovering more about your personal wellness, join us on the wellness journey!

The Wellness Program includes classes, workshops, literature, and counseling in the following areas.

Whole person wellness (body, mind, emotions, spirit)

Parenting and work/family relationships

Pleasurable movement opportunities

Eating behavior

Stress release and relaxation

Massage therapy

New food exploration

EXERCISE DOESN'T HAVE TO HURT
to be good for you!!!!!!!!!!!!!!!!!

A BROWN BAG DEMONSTRATION OF FOUR NEW EXERCISE CLASSES

New research shows that exercise on many different levels is very beneficial!

Come and see some exciting new class demonstrations that might be just what you've been looking for!

EVERYBODY EXERCISE. An exercise class designed to nourish the body—NOT PUNISH IT! Emphasis will be on creating a nonjudgmental, pleasurable environment for movement among people of varying fitness levels, ages, and body sizes. This class deemphasizes exercise to reshape the body or as a punishment for overeating.

REMBRANDT WOMEN. A movement class for women of size, with emphasis on providing a nonjudgmental, pleasurable environment for moving and self-acceptance while de-emphasizing exercise to reshape the body or as a punishment for overeating.

LOW-IMPACT MOVES. Low-impact aerobic moves for 45 minutes will revitalize your day! Also included are exercises utilizing specific muscle groups with light weights and/or the Reebok step.

Instructors and class participants will present a short demonstration of each class and answer any questions the audience may have. (The audience will not be asked to participate in the movement.)

Bring your lunch, relax, and enjoy what might be a wonderful new way to move your body!

You don't have to sweat! You don't have to change clothes!
All you have to do is BE THERE!

323

THE WELLNESS RESOURCE LIBRARY

is a collection of
reading materials, audiotapes, and videotapes relating to
wellness issues. A complete resource listing, by title and
author, is available at the Wellness Center reception desk. The
topics are listed below.

RESOURCE MATERIALS

MIND-BODY-SPIRIT

INTERPERSONAL RELATIONSHIPS

EATING BEHAVIORS

ORGANIZATIONAL EFFECTIVENESS

PREGNANCY/CHILD CARE

RECREATIONAL ACTIVITIES

SELF-ESTEEM/SELF-IMAGE

WOMENS' ISSUES

AEROBIC CONDITIONING AND CLASS VIDEOS

ACTIVE PARENTING

BACK CARE

GENERAL WELLNESS ISSUES

HUMOR

"MAKE A BIG SPLASH"

HOW TO SURVIVE A DAY AT THE BEACH IN YOUR SWIMSUIT

A lunchtime brown bag designed for full-figured women to increase your comfort level in your swimsuit.

The presentation will include:

Concrete strategies to increase your comfort level in a swimsuit in public.

Participation in experiential exercises designed to identify your individual blocks to body/self-acceptance.

Who should attend? Any woman who identifies herself as a full-figured woman and wants help feeling comfortable in her swimsuit.

Bring your lunch!

IF YOU'RE MAKING
NEW YEAR'S RESOLUTIONS. . .

Resolve to
Be Kind to Yourself!

- Be gentle, kind, and patient with yourself! Treat yourself as you would someone you really love.

- Support yourself! Think of some new ways to give yourself support. Reach out to friends and allow them to support you. It is being strong to ask for help when you need it.

- Praise yourself! Criticism breaks down the inner spirit. Praise builds it up. Tell yourself how well you are doing with every little thing.

- Take care of yourself! Listen to your own needs for a change. Think of ways to nurture yourself physically, emotionally, and spiritually.

- Think positively about yourself! Stop terrorizing yourself with negative thoughts. Picture yourself succeeding in the areas that challenge you.

- Resolve to give yourself more pleasure and enjoyment in the future.

YOU DESERVE IT!

SUPERMarketing

A BROWN BAG SEMINAR

A guided grocery shopping tour without going to the grocery store!

Learn to save time and energy while expanding your knowledge of foods and their preparation.

Why learn about SUPER Marketing?

To know about and taste the newest foods available in the grocery store

To increase your understanding of food labels and their value. (If any)

To save money and time while feeling good about the food you buy.

To discover convenient foods and preparations without sacrificing the fun and enjoyment of great-tasting foods.

—Bring your lunch—

THE SANDWICH GENERATION

UNDERSTANDING AGING & ELDER CARE

A Four-Part Brown Bag Series

NEW WAYS TO LOOK AT OLDER ADULTS

A look at the developmental stages of aging—
physically, emotionally and psychologically—and
how older adults can cope constructively.

FACING THE MAJOR AILMENTS

The physical and mental implications for the elders
and their caregivers will be discussed, especially
balancing work with family pressure.

WHO IS THE "SANDWICH GENERATION"?

Identifying conflicts between caring for parents
and children—while remembering spouses
and significant others. Dealing with important
decisions and setting limits.

CARING FOR THE CAREGIVER

The conditions that create overload, types of care,
and successful family support will be presented.
Resources available will be summarized.

Bring Your Lunch!

THEME SESSION
UNDERSTANDING
EMOTIONAL HUNGER

When you notice your hand reaching for food and you know you're not hungry, do you

Tell yourself to wait, and not to eat until you're truly hungry?

Eat but feel fat and yell at yourself for eating?

Eat but think about exercising or dieting to work off the calories?

Emotional eating has always been viewed as the enemy. We have all been taught to **eat celery sticks, just ignore it,** or **distract ourselves** when we have emotional hunger. We are suppose to **go for a walk, read a book,** or **take a bath** to keep ourselves from eating. But for most of us these strategies have never "worked," and we end up overeating in the end.

Come to this Theme Session and explore some alternatives! We will discuss nurturing strategies that can help you respond to emotional hunger in a positive way and help you end your eating problems <u>forever</u>. **REMEMBER, emotional hunger is not the enemy ... it is the clue that helps you solve the mystery of who you are and what you want in life!**

BRING YOUR FOOD BAG. WE WILL PROVIDE DRINKS.

"Healthy Pleasures"
A Brown Bag Series

In the coming months, the Wellness Group will be offering a variety of brown bags dedicated to encouraging a relaxing and enjoyable lunchtime break. We hope you will find one or all of the following opportunities especially interesting and will choose to join us!

Music to Your Ears
Accomplished musicians perform

Movie Month
Look for your favorites

Funny Business
A comedy/humor brown bag

Relaxation
Relax and enjoy

... and more!

Watch for flyers with dates and times, coming soon!

WHAT WOULD IT TAKE TO MOVE YOU?

Exercise! Exercise! Exercise! #@*%!! Over recent years we have heard a great deal about how important it is to exercise. Yet, only 8% of Americans participate in a regular program of vigorous activity. The good news, however, is that new research indicates **that even very small amounts of activity** enhance physical and emotional health. The research also shows that participation in activities that create pleasure and cooperative social opportunities is associated with high self-esteem. So when you think about activity and your health, remember all the kinds of activities in which you can participate. Think beyond the traditional activities (i.e., walking, running, swimming) that are usually associated with exercise.

HOW ABOUT . . .

TAI CHI

COUNTRY WESTERN DANCING

BALLROOM DANCING

MARTIAL ARTS   BALLET

JAZZ

TAP

YOGA

Summary

Today discussions of quantum physics, shifting human consciousness, and holistic health are starting to occur more often at health
promotion conferences. Some organizations are also beginning to
work these new ideas into their wellness programs. It is critical to
understand that the holistic approach is based on the belief that it is
who we are, not what we do that makes the most difference in our
attempts to help people to grow and heal. There is no cookbook for
the top ten things to do to make a holistic program a success. For all
of us, doing our own healing work is the most important thing we
can do to facilitate the process of helping others.

References

1. Katcher, Avrum L., and Mary Grace Lanese. "Breast-Feeding
    by Employed Mothers: A Reasonable Accommodation in the
    Work Place." *Pediatrics* 75 no. 4 (1985): 644–47.

2. Cohen, Rona, and Marsha Beck. "The Impact of Two Corpo-
    rate Lactation Programs on the Incidence and Duration of
    Breast-Feeding by Employed Mothers." *American Journal of
    Health Promotion* 8, no. 6 (1994): 436–41.

3. Auerbach, Kathleen, G. "Assisting the Employed Breastfeed-
    ing Mother." *Journal of Nurse-Midwifery* 35, no. 1 (1990):
    26–34.

Chapter 19

MEASURING OUTCOMES

What about Evaluation and Cost Containment?

Researchers analyzing cost data find that
health risk status accounts for only a small fraction
of the variability in health care costs (6–8%).

W. Lynch and D. Vickery
American Journal of Health Promotion

The #1 Concern

Health care cost containment has been the issue of urgency for most health promotion professionals. This is because for the last twenty years decision makers in organizations have been told that "for every dollar spent on health promotion, there will be several dollars of savings in medical claims." Reduced absenteeism, less employee turnover, better productivity, and improved morale also have been repeatedly promised. In today's quantitative and fiscally oriented Epoch II organizations, management expects to see proof that these outcomes are being achieved in return for their support and financial investment. Proving the existence of these specific benefits, however, has been difficult. As Ken Gerhardt, an executive at Conoco, Inc., said years ago, "trying to quantify the cost savings directly attributable to a health promotion program is like trying to put cellophane around warm Jello!"

Fortunately, a holistic evaluation and health cost containment process can successfully address some of the difficulties encountered with more traditional approaches. Four aspects of evaluation and cost containment change dramatically as a result of adopting a more holistic process.

1. *The variables of interest change.* The evaluation process no longer focuses on just physical health measures. Psychosocial, ecological, and spiritual variables also are assessed and examined in the context of physical health measures.

2. *The population of interest changes*. Rather than assessing the health risks of an entire population, evaluation and cost containment efforts in a holistic program focus primarily on identifying and intervening with the small group of individuals who incur the greatest costs for most organizations. These are the people who are in the most distress physically and emotionally and therefore need the most help.

3. *The response to evaluation results changes*. Traditional health risk appraisal results are no longer used as a motivation for behavior change. Instead, sophisticated, ongoing, systems-based programs and counseling are offered to individuals who are identified as high risk. Interventions are voluntary, and people are counseled about their options for medical and mental health services rather than having restricted access to services imposed on them as a way of controlling costs.

4. *The philosophy changes*. The underlying beliefs that guide the evaluation and intervention process are (as would be expected) very different in the holistic model. Reduced emphasis is placed on evaluation results and multiple ways of assessing or "knowing" what is true are embraced. There is no longer a reliance on quantitative data alone to define reality.

New Variables of Interest:

Beyond Traditional Health Risk Appraisals

Because it is something that has "always been done," many health professionals assume that traditional health risk appraisals (HRAs) are a valuable component of health promotion efforts. A critical look at the research, however, suggests that these tools do not work well for creating individual behavior change or as a means of predicting and assessing health risks in a population.

What Is the HRA?

HRAs are designed to assess a person's risk for illness by asking questions about lifestyle practices such as quality of diet, activity level, stress, smoking, alcohol use, and use of seat belts. In addition, demographic data and biomedical variables such as blood pressure, weight, and cholesterol are often measured. An algorithm that involves using computerized equations that combine lifestyle answers with biomedical values is then used to assign an individual a "risk age" that can be compared to his or her biological age. HRAs have traditionally been employed in four ways.

1. They have been given to people on an individual basis in an attempt to "evaluate" their health status, raise awareness, and create behavior change. A confidential computer-generated report of results, including normative data and suggested strategies for behavior change, is mailed to each person.

2. They have been used for program design. It has been thought that population-wide data collection can identify the risk-related needs of specific groups, thereby enabling health promotion professionals to plan their programs accordingly.

3. They have been used to predict the expenditures an employer may be at risk for incurring in relation to medical claims areas such as back pain, cardiovascular disease and cancer.

4. Aggregate data collection with HRAs has also been used by health promotion programs on a pre- and post-test basis to evaluate the effects of implementing a wellness program.

HRAs: The Research

Unfortunately, the literature does not support the effectiveness of traditional HRAs for any of the above uses. For example, with regard to behavior change the research shows that "There is little evidence that the use of HRA alone is sufficient to produce long-term changes in health-related behaviors or health-risk outcomes."[1] Furthermore, HRAs do not appear to provide an effective means of predicting health care costs. In their work over many years with Steelcase, a large manufacturing company, Yen, Edington, and Wittig discovered that "Smoking, physical activity, blood pressure, and cholesterol were all nonsignificant predictors of medical claims costs."[2]

The traditional focus on biomedical risk factors in health promotion has been justified by the high prevalence of cardiovascular disease (CVD). It has always been assumed that since half of all deaths are caused by CVD this must a major component of work site health care costs. Again, however, the research does not back up this assumption. As Yen and Edington explain:

The costs of cardiovascular disease, accounted for 14 percent of the total employees' medical claims costs . . . [and] the health related measures, which have been used to identify risks for cardiovascular diseases may not significantly associate with total medical claims costs in a working population because of the small percentage of the costs associated with cardiovascular disease.[3]

Clearly, these findings have important implications for the development of health promotion interventions as well as for evaluation and cost containment efforts. Yen and Edington also suggest that:

> The recognition of this limitation may be critical to the future of worksite health promotion/wellness programs. It may prevent an overestimation of program-related savings on employer health care payments and help to set realistic goals for health care cost containment.[4]

Interestingly, this same research suggests that a perceived health index may be a better predictor of health care costs. Thus, "A person's positive perception in life, job, personal health, and stress combined in a 'perception index' derived from HRA responses significantly predicted costs in six of the nine models."[4] Needless to say, this finding is consistent with the latest research on the relationship between "perceived health" and health outcomes.

A New Population of Interest

The Pareto Group

The behavior change and evaluation process in organizations has typically been a shotgun type of approach targeting toward the entire employee population. However, it is usually only a small group of employees, the Pareto group, that incurs the majority of health care expenses in an organization. Interventions must be directed toward these specific individuals in order to improve the effectiveness of claims reduction efforts.

The term *Pareto group* comes from the Italian economist Vilfredo Pareto, who observed that in most countries a small number of people hold the largest distribution of income. The same dynamic appears to exist in the distribution of claims costs in organizations. The Pareto group is the small group of employees that utilizes the majority of employee health benefits. (Note that "benefits" includes group health medical coverage, workers' compensation, and short-

337

and long-term disability compensation.) This finding has major implications for health promotion evaluation, as work site health consultant Harold Gardner observes.

> Less than 20% of employees incur 80% of the benefits cost (the
> Pareto group). As a result, average or mean employee benefits
> cost, which is commonly reported, tells you very little. Unless
> employers can identify and provide effective intervention to the
> Pareto group, there is little hope of successfully controlling em-
> ployee benefits costs.[5]

A research study that looked at health care claims costs at the U-
Haul organization illustrates the Pareto group dynamic.

> Phoenix-based U-Haul International, Inc. had 18,600 employees
> and dependents in 1989, generating nearly $19 million in health
> care expenses: A mere 392 people accounted for $7.7 million of
> that total.[6]

These and similar findings in other organizations (such as Federal
Express and Burlington Industries) illustrate the importance of identifying and intervening with Pareto group members as part of any
effort to reduce health care claims costs.[6,7]

Unfortunately, traditional biomedical variables such as those
used on standard HRAs do a very poor job of predicting membership
in the Pareto group. Early work in this area by pioneers such as Harold Gardner, suggests that *both* psychosocial and biomedical variables must be evaluated to identify employees likely to belong to this
higher-cost group. Typically, the variables found to predict Pareto
group membership include the following.

Back pain	Chemical dependency
Depression	Disability benefits use
Smoking	Job satisfaction
Lost work time	Perceived health
Pregnancy	Disciplinary action
Social support	Tenure with organization

The HERO study examined health care expenditures from more than 46,000 employees of six large organizations over a three-year period. Contrary to expectations, they found that "Two psychosocial factors, depression and stress, accounted for the greatest difference between low- and high-risk individuals."[8] Again, not surprisingly, the people struggling with these issues are likely to be those in the Pareto group, people who are rarely identified or supported by traditional health promotion approaches.

Don't Forget Dependents and Spouses

Responding to the Pareto group dynamic in an organization increases the likelihood that employee medical claims will be reduced. However, it is important to be aware that the majority of claims expenditures are often incurred by spouses and dependents. Evaluation and intervention efforts are significantly limited if *only employees* are included. Spouses and dependents have typically not been included because they can be a difficult and expensive group to reach with programming. If reduction in claims costs is the goal, however, this population cannot be overlooked. For example, Yen, Edington, and Wittig's Steelcase data indicate that:

> Spouses accounted for 35% of all the health care claims, dependents 25%, and employees 40% of the claims. If the goal of a health promotion program is to reduce health care costs, then the program should be available to all who are covered.[9]

Identifying and Reaching out to the Pareto Group—Wherever They May Be

By increasing the focus on psychosocial issues and including spouses and dependents it is likely that Holistic Health Promotion programs will be better able to identify and support those most in need (the Pareto group) with the most efficient use of resources. Organizations working with the Pareto group concept are experimenting with the best ways to reach the individuals who make up this group. Some use a self-report, holistic health assessment to help identify those who are having severe problems in key psychosocial areas. Other institutions use a very sophisticated process of linking organizational databases to track absenteeism, job performance, medical claims data, and use of employee assistance programs. Employees who show up across the categories are identified as Pareto group members and may be invited to participate in supportive interventions.[6,7]

Responding Differently to Evaluation Results

The industry standard in attempts at cost control is to regulate access to health care. "Case management" of high-risk individuals has been aimed at limiting the use of benefits that show a pattern of incurring excessive costs. This "regulation" is enforced at both the user and provider ends. A newer approach, however, seeks to put health care decisions back in the hands of the consumer by providing high-risk Pareto group employees and dependents with holistically-based support and counseling. (Counseling is provided by specially trained physicians, master's-level nurses, and psychologists or social workers who can help clients understand all treatment and *nontreatment* options.)

This counseling enables individuals to make more informed decisions about benefits usage. Evidence suggests that this leads to a reduction in costs. Group medical services cost data have shown significant comparative cost reductions ranging from 15 to 45 percent under such programs, depending on the intensity and timing of counseling supplied and the severity of health needs of the study subjects. As Dr. Harold Gardner, writing in the journal *Business and Health* in 1986, observes, "Individual acceptance of cost control programs that promote genuine choice is far greater than attempts to regulate access and providers."[10]

Personal Decision Making in Action

An excellent example of a personal decision-making process that promotes genuine choice is a case study mentioned in the *Business and Health* article cited above. A fifty-six-year-old man was diagnosed with pancreatic cancer. He was matched with a holistic counselor, and a trusting relationship developed. Over a period of six weeks and hours of face-to-face discussions and telephone counseling, the man's options for treating the disease and managing his health were explored. Through the counseling and information gathering process this man learned that medical experts recommended aggressive invasive therapy that included removal of the pancreas, intraoperative radiation, and biliary bypass surgery, followed by chemotherapy. There was, at the time, a 35 percent mortality rate for this treatment, with severe morbidity and loss of health among survivors.

While being supported by his counselor, the man reviewed these options and decided the risks and health-deteriorating effects of this treatment were too high. Despite pressure from his friends and family, his counselor helped him stick to his decision to avoid the standard treatments. He chose instead to pursue health-preserving measures that would protect his quality of life as long as possible. To control the diarrhea that results from pancreatic cancer, he reduced the fat in his diet. He took vitamins and improved the nutritional quality of his diet to maintain his weight. He started exercising and meditating. He sought medical treatment only for the side effects of his cancer. He continued to work part-time and focused on maintaining a high quality of life for as long as possible.

In this case the individual's health care costs were less than $1,000 over an eighteen-month period. Traditional treatment would have cost at least $50,000. Yet this case demonstrates that an individual may of his or her own choosing save on health care costs, without cost savings being imposed by the employer.

A Holistic Philosophy about Evaluation

One of the most challenging obstacles when working from a holistic perspective is the difficulty of moving Epoch III values forward in what is still an Epoch II society. Nowhere is this challenge greater than with regard to evaluation and cost containment issues. Today's organizations are still entrenched in dominator society deep values. As the latest rash of corporate crime so devastatingly demonstrates, they continue to pursue endless financial gains regardless of the cost to human and environmental capital and rely exclusively on "rational" thought and quantitative assessments to define reality and solve problems. Therefore, efforts to evaluate health promotion programs are overly reliant on quantitative assessments and attempts to "control costs."

As we explore evaluation issues from a holistic perspective however, we can begin to see and do things differently. From quantum physics and chaos theory we have learned that it is virtually impossible to predict and control complex systems such as human beings and organizations. Thus, the goal of attempting to pin down the economic contributions of health promotion programs may be illusive at best. As Dr. Steve Aldana, writing in *The Art of Health Promotion*, concluded after a recent review of the financial impact of work site health promotion programs, "We will likely never know the actual economic impact of health promotion programs."[11]

Professionals working in Holistic Health Promotion can help management begin to define reality and solve organizational problems using not just objective, quantitative assessments but subjective, qualitative, and intuitive measures as well. It is also important to emphasize with decision makers that health care cost reduction is not the only aim and outcome of interest to be pursued by health promotion. Human quality of life, organizational relationships, community function, and environmental stability are also key areas in which to measure potential improvement.

Can health professionals successfully persuade key decision makers that Holistic Health Promotion is a good organizational choice? We think that the answer is yes! The next chapter provides information and ideas for helping with just that process.

References

1. Anderson, D., and M. Staufacker. "The Impact of Worksite-Based Health Risk Appraisal on Health-Related Outcomes: A Review of the Literature." *American Journal of Health Promotion* 10, no. 6 (1996): 499–508.

2. Yen, L. T., D. W. Edington, and P. Wittig. "Prediction of Prospective Medical Claims and Absenteeism Costs for 1,284 Hourly Workers from a Manufacturing Company." *Journal of Occupational Medicine* 34 (1992): 428–35.

3. Yen, L. T., D. W. Edington, and P. Wittig. "Associations between Health Risk Appraisal Scores and Employee Medical Claims Costs in a Manufacturing Company." *American Journal of Health Promotion* 6 (1991): 46–54.

4. Yen, L. T., D. W. Edington, and P. Wittig. "Corporate Medical Claim Cost Distributions and Factors Associated with High-Cost Status." *Journal of Occupational Medicine* 36 (1994): 505.

5. Gardner H. H. Presentation to American Journal of Health Promotion Conference, Colorado Springs, April 1994.

6. Woolsey, C. "Health Care Cost Control." *Business Insurance,* February 17, 1992.

7. Owens, Patricia M. "Another Approach: The Human Capital Model at Federal Express." In *Annual Review of Disability Management, 1991.* Washington Business Group on Health and Institute for Rehabilitation and Disability Management, 1991.

8.   Gardner, H. H. "When 'Patients' become 'Consumers.'" *Health Cost Management* 3, no. 1 (1986): 26–33.

9.   Edington, D. W., and L. T. Yen. "Is It Possible to Simultaneously Reduce Risk Factors and Excess Health Care Costs?" *American Journal of Health Promotion* 6 (1992): 403–9.

10.   Gardner, Harold H. "Putting Health Care Decisions in the Hands of Consumers." *Business and Health,* October 1986.

11.   Aldana, S. G. "Financial Impact of Worksite Health Promotion and Methodological Quality of the Evidence." *The Art of Health Promotion* 2, no. 1 (1998): 1–8.

12.   Goetzel, R. Z., D. R. Anderson, R. W. Whitmer, R. J. Ozminkowski, R. L. Dunn, and J. Wasserman. "The Relationship between Modifiable Health Risks and Health Care Expenditures." *Journal of Occupational and Environmental Medicine* 40, no. 1 (1998): 843–54.

Chapter 20

MAKING THE CASE WITH MANAGEMENT

Helping Decision Makers Understand Holistic Approaches

All truth passes through 3 stages.
First, it is ridiculed.
Second, it is violently opposed.
Third, it is accepted as being self-evident.

Arthur Schopenhauer

Many health professionals hold the opinion that the management of organizations will never fund or support Holistic Health Promotion programs. It is assumed that holistic programs will be seen as touchy-feely, New Age, pop psychology. They don't focus on biomedical risk factors, they don't address the "bottom line," and they are perceived as being unscientific and difficult to evaluate. Ironically, as detailed earlier in this book, the philosophy and strategies used in Holistic Health Promotion actually are based on the latest scientific findings. Quantum physics as well as recent developments in sophisticated fields such as mind/body medicine and leading-edge consciousness research provide the basis for holistic theory and approaches. Furthermore, as we have discussed in previous chapters there is growing evidence that holistic programs *can be evaluated* and may actually be more effective than biomedical programs in reducing health care costs. So the challenge to those of us speaking with management becomes "how can we contradict incorrect cultural assumptions about holistic health and create a more abundant vision for what is possible?"

When preparing for management presentations, there are seven key areas from which to draw to make the case for Holistic Health Promotion. The characteristics of the organization, the attitudes and beliefs of management, and the intuition of those preparing the presentation should be the guiding factors in deciding which of these areas will be most helpful.

Key Concepts for Management Presentations

Use the Hard Sciences to Help You!

The *bad news* is that the vast majority of organizations are still completely rooted in reductionist, Epoch II humanity. Therefore, Epoch II beliefs and research still drive the decision-making process. The emphasis on determining truth and reality through measurement continues to be the primary focus in these organizations. The *good news* is that the research coming from the new sciences provides an excellent way to present "scientific data" that make use of quantitative and qualitative research to define a holistic reality.

It is important to note here that the holistic philosophy supports the importance of *deemphasizing* the use of measurement to determine reality. However, since our predominately Epoch II organizations have not yet embraced this new philosophy, management presentations must sound scientific and data based in order to "meet them where they live," as the saying goes. By using the data coming out of the new physics, as well as information from psychoneuroimmunology and consciousness research, a research-based, scientific-sounding case can be made for supporting holistic approaches.

Over time, as acceptance of the holistic approach grows among management, there will be increasing openness to combining scientific data with human subjective experience and intuition to make organizational decisions. In the beginning, however, presentations that employ Epoch II language are likely to be most successful.

Illustrate the New Sciences in Action

The field of holistic health has attracted exploding interest and an enormous following in recent years. However, new concepts such as healing through prayer and the mind/body connection can sound unbelievable to some people. These concepts can be especially hard to embrace among individuals in management who have become "fact based" due to the influence of working in Epoch II organizational environments.

That is why it can be useful to follow your presentations on quantum physics and psychonueroimmunology with applied examples of how this new information helps us understand seemingly unexplainable phenomena in holistic health. For example, the physics principle of nonlocality helps us understand how distant healing through prayer may be possible and research from psychoneuroimmunology helps us understand how attitudes and emotions can so powerfully affect the physical body. There are many opportunities to illustrate these types of connections between new scientific findings and the healing experiences we increasingly hear about.

Dabble and Document

One way to build a convincing case for embracing holistic programs is to have already successfully implemented some! To be more specific, health professionals in some programs have influenced management by quietly offering a few initial holistic programs and carefully measuring participant response. At Conoco, whenever there was a new holistic program participation rates would rise as much as 400 percent. For example, traditional weight management classes usually attracted about 30 participants. When nondiet/size acceptance classes were offered, over 250 employees signed up to participate. Organizations are always more apt to fund programs that generate higher levels of interest and ongoing participation. Showing these types of results from a few initial holistic programs may help garner support for adding more programs of similar philosophy over time!

Be a Copycat

One of the most powerful pathways for getting the ear of business leaders is through contact with management from other organizations who have successfully tried holistic programming. These types of interactions can be carried out by phone, letter, email, or even through site visits. It is especially useful when communication can be arranged with management in the same industry. Participation data, program satisfaction and adherence rates, and cost containment data from these holistic programs shared "management to management" are extremely influential in the decision-making process in most organizations. Even when top executives do not have time to share their experiences, it can be beneficial to obtain information from someone lower down in the organization; a human resources person or a wellness department staff member.

Address the Issue of Cost Containment . . . Holistically!

Along with the issue of measurement, there is nothing Epoch II organizations care about more than reducing costs and increasing material wealth. The holistic model provides an excellent opportunity for powerful discussions with management on the issue of costs. Two main areas are very important to cover regarding the cost containment issue.

First, it is important to take management through the traditional thought process regarding biomedical model risk factors and the assumed association with costs. As part of this discussion it is necessary to refer to the data showing that traditional risk factors *do not* predict a statistically significant portion of the variance in the health care costs incurred in most organizations.

Second, it is also critical to familiarize management with the influence of the Pareto principle regarding health care costs in organizations. Once management understands that the 20 percent of employees who make up the Pareto group are creating 80 percent of the health care costs in the organization, they will be very interested in knowing more about identifying and intervening with these individuals.

It is important to emphasize to management that (1) the psycho-social variables measured in holistic programs are by far the best predictors of membership in the Pareto group, and (2) holistic programs that address the broader aspects of the human experience are best equipped to intervene and make a real difference in the lives, health, and health care costs of these people.

Share Biomedical Data (If You Dare)

While there is a great deal of research regarding biomedical health promotion, the majority of studies show that it does not work! Point out to management that traditional exercise, weight loss and smoking cessation interventions have very high dropout rates. In addition to failing to create the desired outcomes, traditional programs also have been shown to create unintended and undesirable consequences. For example, participation in weight loss programs can lead to repeated weight cycling, eating disorders and exercise addiction.

Depending on the situation within the organization, *it may or may not* be useful to share this type of discouraging health promotion data with management. If management has a history of being open-minded and progressive, then using these data in a management presentation should help create acceptance and a preference for holistic approaches. However, if management has a history of being conservative (such as in many medically-based environments), it may be best not to share these data. The only way to get support for a holistic program may be to start with a more traditional biomedical approach. In this case it would clearly not be helpful to share all the failures of the biomedical model at this point. Get in the door with a more traditional approach, get the program going and then gradually transition to more holistic approaches as opportunities present themselves.

Tell the Human Side of the Story

Preparing for a management presentation, especially for senior management, can be intimidating. In the autocratic environments of today's organizations, it is easy to get caught up in thoughts and fears about how much power and influence these executives have over the lives of others. But it is important to remember that executives are human beings, too. They have husbands, wives, children, parents, coworkers, and friends. You can count on the fact that both they and the people in their lives have been touched by physical illness, emotional struggles, and spiritual dilemmas. During management presentations on holistic philosophies, it is useful to ask people to consider their own lives and the lives of loved ones in the context of the information being presented. Asking people to connect with the human side of their own experience is often a powerful strategy for breaking through "rational, analytical" resistance to the holistic concepts being presented.

The ideas discussed above may be helpful when considering preparation of management presentations. Whether to use some or all of them will depend on an intuitive reading of the organization's culture and knowledge of the personalities involved. Beyond these specific ideas for appealing to management, there is an additional issue that has a huge impact on health professionals in organizations, although it is seldom addressed. This is the issue of organizational power.

The Little Fish in the Big Pond

Perhaps the most fundamental issue faced by health promoters in organizations and communities is the issue of power. In most organizations, health promotion is one of the most poorly funded programs, positioned far down on the "food chain" within the organizational lineup. Furthermore, Holistic Health Promotion programs present members of the organization with a new view of humanity, a new view of business, and a new set of deep values. It is very difficult to drive this type of deep value change from the lowest, least funded spot in the organization. This is not to say that it should not be attempted. However, it is very important that we realize how daunting this task is and how critical it is that those of us doing this work support each other. It can take a huge toll on individuals who day after day struggle to bring Epoch III, holistic philosophies into Epoch II organizations.

Summary

Everything about our current Epoch II organizations is set up to support reductionist, dominator types of systems that seek endless improvement in material gains regardless of the human and environmental consequences.[8] These organizations continue to define reality exclusively on the basis of data gathered through quantitative methods. It is a sizable challenge to bring Epoch III values and Holistic Health Promotion into these environments. However, it is possible to move management and health promotion in a more holistic direction. The next chapter provides a powerful case study of just how successful "going holistic" can really be!

References

1.   Conrad, P. "Who Comes to Worksite Wellness Programs? A Preliminary Review." *Journal of Occupational Medicine* 29 (1987): 317–20.

2.   Edington, D. W., and L. T. Yen. "Is It Possible to Simultaneously Reduce Risk Factors and Excess Health Care Costs?" *American Journal of Health Promotion* 6 (1992): 403–9.

3.   Golaszewski, T., et al. "The Relationship between Retrospective Health Insurance Claims and a Health Risk Appraisal Generated Measure of Health Status." *Journal of Occupational Medicine* 31 (1989): 262–68.

4.   Lynch, W., et al. "Health Risks and Health Insurance Claims Costs: Results for Health Hazard Appraisal Responders and Nonresponders." *Journal of Occupational Medicine* 35 (1993): 28–33.

5.   Yen, L. T., et al. "Associations between Health Risk Appraisal Scores and Employee Medical Claims Costs in a

Manufacturing Company." *American Journal of Health Promotion* 6 (1991): 46–54.

6.   Yen, L. T., et al. "Corporate Medical Claim Cost Distributions and Factors Associated with High-Cost Status." *Journal of Occupational Medicine* 36 (1994): 505.

7.   Yen, L. T., et al. "Prediction of Prospective Medical Claims and Absenteeism Costs for 1,284 Hourly Workers from a Manufacturing Company." *Journal of Occupational Medicine* 34 (1992): 428–35.

8.   Wheatley, M. J. *Leadership and the New Science: Learning about Organizations from an Orderly Universe*. San Francisco: Berrett-Koehler, 1994.

Chapter 21

KAILO

An Organizational Case Study*

Kailo is a shining example of Mercy's values. We have taken risks and proven our approach works. This is not fluff. In most organizations wellness programs are the first to go when things get tight. At Mercy, Kailo will be the last.

Jim Fitzpatrick
Mercy Medical Center
CEO/President, 2003

*Caring for ourselves
as well as we care for our patients*

✝ mercy medical center–north iowa

* *Kailo is the name of the nontraditional, hospital-based work site wellness program at Mercy Medical Center–North Iowa. Kailo is*

nontraditional because it is one of the first employee wellness pro-grams in the country to fully embrace a holistic approach to work site health promotion. This chapter was written by Kelly Putnam; executive director and creator of Kailo. In her own words, she de-scribes the process of developing, marketing and evaluating the Kailo Program.

The Kailo Story

How did we get here from there?

As I begin telling the Kailo story, I must be clear about one thing. If you're hoping that the secret recipe to "going holistic" is contained in this chapter, I'm afraid you'll be sorely disappointed. There simply are no guaranteed steps or a definitive set of directions for adopt-ing a holistic approach to work site health promotion. Oh, if only it were that easy! It just isn't possible to apply a "cookie-cutter" men-tality to holistic wellness, and we would never suggest using a one size fits all approach to organizational wellness. We believe each workplace, like each person, is unique. We believe each workplace, like each person, possesses an internal wisdom that when tapped can provide the rich resources needed for healing and health. Thus, our purpose in sharing our story with you is not to prescribe any "right" way to go holistic but to offer one organization's experience in mov-ing toward wholeness.

I wish I could tell you our decision to move in a holistic direction was the result of some spiritual awakening or superb intuition. The truth is, it was *customer service.* Yup, that's right. We became pio-neers in work site health promotion by *listening to our customers—* the 2,800 women and men who work at Mercy. They are the ones who put us on this path. And we are forever grateful.

In 1996–97, we conducted employee surveys and focus groups and logged nearly fifty hours of one-on-one interviews with Mercy managers. Once all the data were collected and analyzed, four major themes emerged.

1. *Psychosocial Issues.* The first and strongest theme in the data was that psychosocial issues were the primary health concerns for our employees. Believe it or not, we did not hear much about people wanting to lower their cholesterol or body fat. We didn't even hear much about people wanting to lose weight. What we *did* hear was this: 57 percent of employees perceived the stress in their lives to be out of control; 51 percent reported that they had experienced depression in the past six months; over 70 percent were sleep deprived; and nearly 20 percent admitted to living with domestic violence. In addition, we heard time and time again that the presence and quality of relationships played a key role in determining how resilient our employees were in dealing with major stressors in their lives.

2. *The Value/Fun Factor.* The second and third major themes we lumped together and called the "value/fun factor." Our employees expressed an intense need to feel valued in the organization in which they work, not just for what they show up and *do* every day but for who they are as *whole* people—with families and feelings, dreams and disappointments, souls and sorrows. In addition, our employees expressed a strong desire to have more fun on the job—to relax what had become in their eyes a very "corporate" culture as a result of Mercy's recent expansions and mergers.

3. *Barriers to Participation.* The fourth major theme addressed barriers to employees participating in a Mercy wellness initiative. Employees were honest enough to tell us that if we wanted them to attend programs and activities, they would have to be on company time and their immediate supervisor would have to be supportive. *Whew!* As any work site wellness coordinator is probably already thinking, this was a tall order! For starters, securing and justifying any wellness budget is difficult enough without asking an organization to cover the additional indirect costs of paid time for employees to attend. And what about all that psychosocial stuff? As a traditionally trained work site health promotion practitioner, I was very uncomfortable with these data in particular. I knew how to set up cholesterol screenings, interpret

355

health risk appraisals, and teach diet and exercise classes. *I knew nothing about depression and domestic violence!* Mercy did not need a wellness coordinator, I thought to myself, they needed a therapist!

Our next step was to review the current literature on work site health promotion and survey some of the country's best practices. What we discovered was disheartening to say the least. For starters, despite a lot of lip service being paid to mind/body/spirit approaches, the models we studied were decidedly focused on reducing biomedical risk factors for disease—not a good match for the psychosocial and relational distress our employees were experiencing. Second, the traditional programs seemed to be plagued with problems: low participation, inadequate funding and staffing, and a lack of planning, evaluation, and meaningful outcomes. More bad news!

At this point in the process, it became obvious to us that if we were going to have a wellness program that truly addressed our employees' needs we were going to have to create it from scratch. We took a deep breath, pooled our collective experience in women's health, mental health, and health promotion, and widened our search for help. It was about then that we learned of a whole new way of tending to the health of our employees.

A New Approach

Holistic? Is that with an h or a wh?

From the moment I heard about the holistic approach to health promotion, I was hooked. This was an approach that truly was about wellness, not just preventing disease. It was about giving equal time to physical, psychosocial, and spiritual aspects of health in a meaningful way. It was about honoring relationships and purpose and meaning in life as the major determinants of health. It was about building authentic connections with people. *It made perfect sense.*

Reenergized with the prospect of creating a program around a holistic philosophy, we began to develop Kailo. In addition to the holistic approach, we borrowed ideas from positive psychology, relational theory, solution-oriented therapy, gender expertise, employee assistance programs (EAPs), Pareto theory, and organizational development to fortify our concept.

Campaigning for Administrative Support

You want how much money to do what?

With the research and development phase nearly complete, it was time to begin campaigning for budgetary support from our senior leaders. We scheduled individual appointments with each member of our administration and presented our data and our ideas for a new kind of wellness initiative. Their concerns were no different than the concerns of senior leaders in any organization. They wanted to know why a wellness program was necessary, how much the initiative was going to cost, and what kind of return they would get on their investment.

With a written business plan and budget proposal in tow, we made a formal presentation to our senior leader team and addressed their concerns. We presented the employee data. We had thoroughly researched our costs—both direct and indirect. And as for a return on investment we outlined an extensive evaluation plan that included tracking participation, satisfaction, improvements in perceptions and attitudes toward health and life satisfaction as well as a plan for measuring by-proxy cost savings.

Clearly, the most compelling evidence we had supporting the development of a comprehensive wellness initiative was the employee data. Our leaders were seriously concerned about the high levels of stress, depression, fatigue, and relationship issues our staff was experiencing and concluded that despite precarious financial times in health care Mercy couldn't afford *not* to take better care of its employees.

Mercy Medical Center–North Iowa is the largest provider of health care services in a fourteen-county region and the largest employer in Cerro Gordo County. The main campus is located in Mason

City, Iowa, but the health care center encompasses over fifty satellite sites, including primary care clinics, affiliated rural hospitals, home care facilities, and hospice units.

In order to reach Mercy's 2,800 employees spread out over fifty sites in fourteen counties, we requested and received a $225,000 annual operating budget to cover three full-time staff positions and program and marketing costs. In addition, we were granted "paid time" for staff to attend and participate in wellness activities – an indirect expense of approximately $90,000 per year.

But securing the money was only part of the package. We also made a bold request of our senior leaders to actually participate in Kailo on a regular basis. To make sure they showed up, we invited them to introduce all of our speakers during the first couple of years of the program. They not only showed up, but they became engaged in the process and in turn requested that Kailo staff become engaged in strategic initiatives such as leader training, nursing recruitment, and organizational development. This integration has been a key factor in Kailo's ongoing success.

Marketing Kailo

Can we talk?

One of the most important lessons we learned in designing and implementing Kailo is that any work site wellness effort is only as strong as its marketing strategy. You may be thinking, "how could we possibly be talking about such meaningful subjects as purpose and meaning in life, relationships, spirituality, and something as crass as marketing all in the same breath?" Our reply would be "how could we *not* talk about it?"

Like it or not, we have a culture that responds to marketing. And a huge piece of Kailo's success is due to our extensive efforts in this area. But our approach to marketing, like our approach to health promotion, is nontraditional.

Marketing is typically based on a philosophy of exchange. In commercial marketing, the exchange is usually goods or services for money. In social marketing, which is most often used in health education and promotion, the exchange is information, education, or incentives for behavior change. In marketing Kailo to Mercy employees, however, we are not concerned with making money or changing behavior. Our exchange is based on having a two-way conversation with our employees in order to establish an authentic connection and build a long-term relationship with our audience.

Although many marketing campaigns focus on building positive relationships, the end goal is usually to sell more product or increase the likelihood of behavior change. The end goal of Kailo's marketing strategy, in contrast, is the relationship itself. As Holistic Health Promotion practitioners we believe social connectedness and support are the most important predictors of health and well-being. We define a successful marketing campaign as one that inspires conversation and authentic human connection that transcends the wellness program, and even the workplace, and trickles into the homes and communities of our employees.

Yeah, it sounds great doesn't it? What we quickly learned is that it is very difficult to have a meaningful conversation without trust. And Mercy employees, quite frankly, did not trust us in the beginning. We suspected that launching a wellness program during some very tough times for health care was going to be a bit of a bumpy ride, but we had no idea how bumpy! Our employees were tired, stressed out, cynical, and skeptical. Budgets were shrinking, and everyone was being asked to do more with less. How could we even begin to break through the negativity? How could we get their attention? How could we begin to gain their trust? This was the challenge.

Figures 21.1 through 21.4 show the promotional brochure and fliers we used for our initial program offerings. In keeping with the holistic philosophy, care was taken to avoid the use of fear, guilt, and shame-based messages. Rather, we used honest, respectful and sometimes humorous messages to begin a long conversation with our employees. We wanted them communicate to them "We hear you. Many of you are struggling. You are not alone. We are in this together."

Figure 21.1 We'd like you to join us—
the front panel of the Kailo membership enrollment brochure

What is Kailo?

Kailo, an Indo-European word meaning to be whole, uninjured, or to be of good omen, is Mercy Medical Center - North Iowa's employee wellness initiative.

Kailo is a gift of time, company time, to do some good things for yourself. You'll get to know "Kailo Breaks" as participative, relaxing, healthy escapes.

But before you jump to any conclusions, look at all that Kailo isn't.

What isn't Kailo?

• No aerobic classes.

• No incentive contests.

• No weight-loss programs.

• No mass health screenings.

• No tofu and tree bark recipes.

• No preaching, no judgmental attitudes, no height/weight charts, no food police, no guilt-trips, no self-righteous finger pointing, no goal setting.

No kidding.

The benefits of joining Kailo.

(Or, why you should interrupt a perfectly chaotic life to join another wellness program.)

Kailo Breaks. Monthly wellness activities you can attend on our time, not yours.

Recreational Rebates. Join a health club/ fitness center in your community. Kailo will rebate you up to $50 per calendar year on the cost of membership.

Free Health Screenings. Cholestrol, blood pressure, and more. Always optional, always confidential.

Kailo for One. Customized wellness services.

Kailo Birthday Club.

Kailo Library.

Fun. Camaraderie. Prizes. Giveaways. Company Time. Massages. Laughter. Personal growth. An excuse to get away from work.

Kailo™
Caring for ourselves as well as we care for our patients

Figure 21.2 What is and isn't Kailo?— the inside panel of the membership brochure describing a very different approach to work site wellness

Figure 21.3 "Kailo Schmilo"—
using humor to disarm employee skepticism

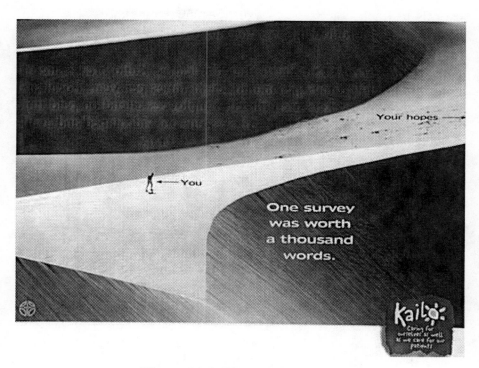

Figure 21.4 "Desert Hopes"—
communicating to employees that their psychosocial needs
had been heard and help was on the way.

Kailo Programming

Why would I interrupt my perfectly chaotic life to join a wellness program?

Mercy employees join Kailo by filling out a survey packet that allows us to track outcomes. In exchange for their time, Kailo members received the following programs and services free of charge.

- *Kailo Breaks*. Similar to lunch'n learns, Kailo breaks are offered eight times per month, eight times per year. Local and national speakers are utilized. Employees attend on paid time and are treated to lunch. All sessions are videotaped and available for checkout through the Kailo Library.

- *Intensive Workshops*. A more in-depth form of Kailo breaks, these workshops cover a wide range of wellness topics, including body image and spiritual development.

- *Recreational Rebates*. Kailo members who join health clubs or pay for fitness classes in the community can earn up to fifty dollars per calendar year toward the cost of club dues or class fees.

- *Health Screenings*. Blood pressure, cholesterol, and bone density heel scans are offered annually.

- *Kailo Library*. Over 1,500 titles of books, videos, and audio-cassettes are available for checkout. Our library can be accessed by visiting the Kailo office or logging onto Mercy's Intranet.

- *NIA Classes*. NIA is a form of mind/body exercise that combines elements from yoga, the martial arts, and modern dance. NIA is a kinder, gentler alternative to traditional aerobic classes and appeals to participants at all fitness levels.

- ***Kailo Birthday Club.*** Each year Kailo members receive a birthday present.

- ***Other Stuff.*** On-site minimassages, walking club, silly contests, and so on.

At first glance, Kailo's programming may not look all that different from other wellness programs. But look closer. What you won't find here are some of the hallmarks of traditional work site health promotion—HRAs, weight loss classes, and incentive or point systems (what we call pinch and pay programs), just to name a few. What makes Kailo so fundamentally and philosophically different from other wellness programs are the basic assumptions of our concept.

- We do not focus on reducing biomedical risk factors for illness. We focus on bolstering physical, psychosocial, spiritual, and relational factors that support health.

- We honor relationships and purpose and meaning in life, rather than health risk appraisal scores, as the most powerful predictors of health and well-being.

- We base our outcomes on participation, customer satisfaction, and improvements in perceptions and attitudes toward work and life satisfaction rather than behavior change and biomedical indicators.

- We value connection over competition.

Despite their initial skepticism, it did not take long for Mercy employees to begin to embrace Kailo. Our first year was tremendously rewarding. Nearly 90 percent of our employees joined the program. Participation in Kailo breaks averaged over 450 employees each month, and satisfaction scores were consistently hitting 95 percent or better.

Kailo for One

Because sometimes life is not a group activity

Although the overall Kailo program was going very well, it quickly became apparent to us that we could be doing more to offer our customers support on an individual basis. So in 1999 we launched Kailo for One.

Kailo for One integrates Holistic Health Promotion with a nontraditional model for delivering an employee assistance program (EAP). Although Mercy already had a wonderful EAP program, it was terribly underutilized. When asked why they were not accessing EAP our employees listed a variety of barriers: (1) lack of awareness that the service existed, (2) stigma attached to going to EAP (this is the place you go when you are in trouble with your boss or you have a drug or alcohol problem), (3) confidentiality concerns, (4) inconvenient hours of availability, and (5) a limited number of sessions.

Again taking a customer-driven approach, we created Kailo for One as an alternative, not a replacement, for our traditional EAP. We remarketed the service as customized wellness instead of counseling or coaching. We located the Kailo for One office in the wellness office, not the counseling office. We gave our social worker a "makeover," having her dress in Kailo attire rather than business suits and attend all Kailo functions as part of the wellness staff. We offered unlimited sessions, same-day appointments, and appointments on second and third shifts.

We don't know how you would go about marketing such a service, but to us the answer was obvious—penguins! *Why penguins?* The story below, which appears in the Kailo for One brochure, explains it best.

Penguins spend their lives battling some of the harshest weather on the planet—ice, snow, wind, and brutal cold. Left alone in these conditions, they would surely perish. Huddling in masses called scrums, the penguins take turns standing on the edge, using their bodies to shelter the rest. When an outside penguin begins to grow weary, it is gently folded into the inner warmth and comfort of the scrum and another penguin takes its place. It is both their strength as protector and their willingness to be protected that allow them to survive.

What a perfect metaphor for Kailo for One! As health care providers, we are very good at standing on the outside of the scrum. What we tend to struggle with is self-care, admitting that we sometimes need to be on the inside, receiving help and support and getting warm. The penguin story gently reminded our employees that the only way we are going to survive as an organization is if we care for ourselves as well as we care for our patients.

Another reason we selected penguins as the "spokesanimal" for Kailo for One is their undeniable charm and sense of humor. Penguins, we surmised, could communicate sensitive or emotional issues in a very nonthreatening way. Figure 21.5 shows one of the fliers we used to introduce Kailo for One to Mercy employees.

Figure 21.5 How would you remarket your employee assistance program? We decided penguins were the obvious choice, because sometimes life isn't a group activity—Kailo for One's informational brochure cover.

Outcomes

This holistic stuff sounds great, but does it work?

Mercy employees' response to Kailo has exceeded our wildest dreams. Five years after the program's kickoff, our participation and customer satisfaction scores have never been stronger. Our outcomes, as measured by a holistic life assessment, Life's Odyssey™, indicate that our employees are thinking and feeling more positively about their health and well-being (for more information on Life's Odyssey, see "Holistic Resources" at the end of the book).

Life's Odyssey is a seventy-item, self-scoring questionnaire that asks participants how they perceive their health in seven dimensions of wellness: life and health attitudes; social connectedness; emotional well-being; physical well-being; rest, pleasure and play; purpose and meaning in life; and self-care. We chose the Life's Odyssey as the primary tool for measuring our long-term outcomes because of its nonthreatening, nonpunitive language and its balanced representation of physical, psychosocial, and spiritual health factors.

Figure 21.6 shows a comparison of Mercy's aggregate Life's Odyssey scores collected in 1998, 2000, and 2001. As the figure illustrates, there is a positive trend in median scores across all seven dimensions of Life's Odyssey. This indicates that in general Mercy employees' perceived health has improved since Kailo's inception. This is no small outcome given the research suggesting that perceived health is one of the most reliable predictors of actual health!

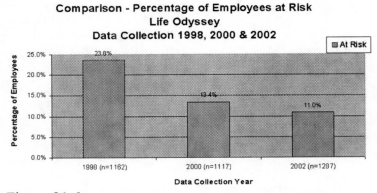

Figure 21.6

Figure 21.7 shows a comparison of the number of employees who scored 30 or below, out of a possible 50, in four or more dimensions of the Life's Odyssey. These participants could be considered "high risk," meaning that they are much more likely to have higher rates of absenteeism and presenteeism and to generate more in employer paid health care claims costs. As you can see, Mercy has experienced a dramatic reduction in the percentage of employees scoring in the high-risk category.

Comparison - Life's Odyssey
Median Score By Dimension
Data Collection 1998 - 2002

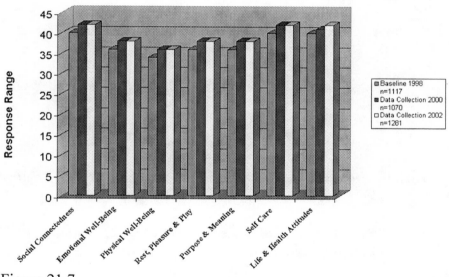

Figure 21.7

Other outcomes associated with Kailo include the following.

- A by-proxy cost-savings estimate of over $200,000 associated with reducing depression among Mercy employees. (By-proxy cost savings are figured by multiplying the number of employees Mercy demonstrated went from depressed to non-depressed by benchmark estimates of per employee savings in health care claims and regained productivity associated with eliminating depression).

- A 171 percent increase in EAP utilization in the first year of Kailo for One, followed by an additional 67 percent increase in the second year.

- Seventy-six percent of employees agree that Kailo is a valuable benefit of working at Mercy ($N = 1,173$).

- Fifty-two percent of employees agree that Kailo has had a positive impact on how they view their health ($N = 1,169$).

In addition, Kailo has received the following awards and recognitions.

- Joint Commission for Accreditation of Healthcare Organizations (JCAHO), "Best Practice," 1999

- Wellness Councils of America (WELCOA), Gold Well Workplace, 1999.

- Trinity Health Excellence and Innovation Award, 2001

- Iowa Psychological Association, Psychologically Healthy Workplace Award, 2002

- Wellness Councils of America (WELCOA), Platinum Well Workplace Award, 2002

The Ultimate Outcome

We're talking the BIG picture here

Five years ago, we probably would have said that the ultimate outcome of a Kailo-like approach would have to be the improved psychosocial well-being of Mercy employees. Our rationale was that if our participants began thinking and feeling more positively about their health they would naturally gravitate toward more healthful physical practices as well, sort of a wellness from the inside-out rather than the outside-in approach.

Today, we have come to believe that the ultimate outcome is much more than how many people show up at a Kailo break, how many people increase their Life's Odyssey scores, or even how much money we've saved the organization. The ultimate outcome is far more meaningful. Unfortunately, it is also far more difficult to measure. In fact, it's not really an outcome at all—it's the *process* of creating and maintaining supportive, life-affirming relationships with other human beings. That's what it's all about. That's the *real work*. There is no more powerful outcome in health promotion for practitioners and participants alike.

A Final Thought

The most meaningful distance between two points is never a straight line

Adopting a holistic approach to health promotion is not a linear process. It's messy and complex and unclear. It's intertwined, interconnected, and interrupted frequently by challenges from the old paradigm. Just like the pioneers of the Old West, the path is anything but certain. It winds and turns and dips and, yes, sometimes it even disappears for a while. There are mountains of resistance and rivers of doubt along the way. But one thing *is* certain. A new land of rich, meaningful opportunity awaits any health promotion pioneer who chooses to explore what the holistic approach has to offer.

Are you ready to be a pioneer?

EPILOGUE

Throughout *The Spirit and Science of Holistic Health*, we have stated our belief that social injustices such as racism, poverty, and violence underlie much of the physical and emotional suffering experienced in our own country and around the world. Although an in-depth commentary on the impact of national and world politics on social oppression is beyond the scope of this book, we would be remiss if we did not acknowledge the importance of these issues in relation to health.

This book has provided a rationale and suggestions for shifting organizational health promotion programs from biomedical to holistic approaches. However, much of what affects the health of individuals occurs outside of the confines of organized wellness programs. For example, it is certainly important for health professionals to explore the ways in which PNI research helps us to understand the emotional issues that underlie asthma attacks. We must also be aware, however, that close to *a quarter* of the mostly poor, black children in West Harlem now suffer from asthma. This is four times the national average and is likely related to the fact that they live in an area that is home to 2,400 diesel buses and six of the city's seven diesel bus depots.[1] Moreover, living in substandard housing filled with mold and other allergens can only exacerbate their condition. Clearly, mind/body medicine cannot help these children if nothing is done about the economic and political environment that perpetuates these living conditions.

This tendency to ignore the less measurable but more fundamental causes of people's suffering is a legacy of the seventeenth-century mechanistic worldview and the resulting biomedical focus of health care. Thus, for example, it is also not surprising that most of the research conducted to date on health differences between the races has focused on genetic and biological explanations. Now a growing body of research suggests that such health disparities may be strongly influenced by these less measurable factors like racial prejudice and discrimination.[2,3]

We have dedicated an entire section of this book to detailing the new Health at Every Size approach to healing weight and eating problems. At the same time, however, food selections for our children are being limited as fast food franchises provide an increasing percentage of school lunch offerings. Why are these companies being invited into our schools? The answer is that we have not been willing to provide adequate financial support for public schools, which must turn to fast food revenues to generate funds for critically needed educational programs.[4]

Social and political policies often lead us astray even when we think we are doing the right thing. An excellent example is our misguided attempt to help children with learning differences. Our culture is to be applauded for finally standing up to the big tobacco companies and forcing them to stop marketing their products to children, who then become lifelong customers. However, at the same time we are failing to stand up to the pharmaceutical companies and the health establishment when they aggressively market Ritalin, Adderall, and other stimulants to parents and their children. Recent studies suggest that as many as 10 percent of school-age children (who once again may become lifelong customers) are being prescribed these powerful, psychiatric drugs. In some parts of the country, this number is as high as 20 percent among boys, who are more likely to act out in the classroom.

As a culture, we find it easier to pathologize these children and control them with psychostimulants than to fund development of flexible and creative educational environments and parental support programs that can nurture children with normal, yet diverse behavioral needs. Meanwhile, our schools continue to face overcrowding and teacher shortages that force parents to succumb to pressure from the schools and aggressive pharmaceutical industry campaigns to medicate their children so that they will "fit in." Ironically, these attention-focusing medications are chemically similar to some of the drugs that we are trying to eliminate from "illegal use" by society.[5]

As important as these issues (and many more like them) are for the health and well-being of adults and children in the United States, they pale compared to the issues affecting people in many other parts of the world. Holistic health as described throughout this book cannot even be entertained by individuals who live where famine, AIDS, war, and terrorism are the order of the day. We must remember that in some parts of the world it is not even considered a crime to rape or murder a woman or a child. Indeed, in many places women, who are still considered to be the property of men, are unable to obtain an education, vote, work, own resources, or participate in society in a meaningful way.[6]

We want to remind readers that these inequities and their attendant human suffering are all products of the Epoch II, Dominator values that still govern most cultures worldwide. These values promote political and social systems based on violent hierarchal control, oppression of people based on their differences, and the endless pursuit of material gain at the expense of the health of humanity and nature.

We may find ourselves thinking that as health professionals we can do nothing to address social injustice and world problems. This is not true. We can all make a difference. Whether it is getting involved with worldwide activist organizations such as Re-evaluation Counseling (see "Holistic Resources" for information) or simply listening without judgment when someone comes to us concerned about his or her blood pressure or weight, we can make a difference that contributes to the emergence of more peaceful, just, and health-promoting Epoch III cultures.

In closing, we would like to emphasize again that doing our own work is the most important part of helping people to heal and grow. We believe that the same holds true for healing on a global level. While there are many avenues for helping available to all of us, perhaps the most powerful route to change is suggested by Wayne Muller in his book *Sabbath*.[7]

Ultimately, we have just one moral duty: to reclaim large areas of peace in ourselves, more and more peace, and reflect it towards others. The more peace there is in us, the more peace there will also be in our troubled world.

References

1. West Harlem Environmental Action Inc. (WE ACT), 271 West 125th Street, Suite 308, New York, NY 10027–4424. e-mail <www.weact.org>

2. Williams, D. R. "Race and Health: Basic Questions, Emerging Directions." *Ann Epidemiol* 7, no. 5 (July 1997): 322-33.

3. Mckenzie, K. "Racism and Health." *Student British Medical Journal* 11 (2003): 2–3.

4. Schlosser, E. *Fast Food Nation: The Dark Side of the All-American Meal.* Boston: Houghton Mifflin, 2001.

5. Breggin, P. R. *Talking Back to Ritalin: What Doctor's Aren't Telling You about Stimulants and ADHD.* Cambridge, MA: Perseus, 2001.

6. World Health Organization. World Report on Violence and Health, October 2002. ISBN 9–241–54561–5. e-mail: <publications@who.int>

7. Muller, Wayne. *Sabbath: Finding Rest, Renewal, and Delight in Our Busy Lives.* New York: Bantam, 2000.

REFLECTIONS

People Who Have Helped to Clear the Way

You must be the change you want to see in the world.

Mahatma Gandhi

We have both been fortunate to meet many brilliant and compassionate people through our work. Over the years these individuals have become not just colleagues, but trusted friends as well. This chapter contains short stories written by these special people. Their stories address both personal and professional aspects of their journey to holistic healing. We hope their experiences will be as inspirational and educational for you as they have been for us.

Kay Ryan

Professor and Vice President of Institutional Effectiveness at Nebraska Methodist College

My educational background is very medical and health oriented. I am a nurse with a masters in health promotion and a Ph.D. in community and human resources. I worked in critical care for a number of years before I decided that if you really wanted to "save lives" you would have to get to people WAY before they showed up in critical care— but that isn't the beginning of the story.

I was the oldest of two children who were lucky enough to have a dad who truly believed we were the greatest gifts he had ever been given. My dad was the youngest of thirteen children. He thought playing was a vocation and passionately pursued it. We were his dream come true: built-in playmates!

My dad was that unusual creature who thought that schoolwork should be left in school and he adamantly defended our family time to teachers, principals, and anyone else who dared to encroach. He was a blast! He picked us up from school every day, and that's when playtime started. We were on a mission to live life fully and have fun (all the same thing). We took this very seriously AND we learned a lot along the way.

My dad always had headaches, and sometimes they were crippling. He tried to tell many physicians that something was terribly wrong, but with the medical science of the times unable to explain his symptoms he inevitably met with the "just your nerves" diagnosis. Finally, after years and years of symptoms, he went temporarily blind and was diagnosed with a brain tumor. He went to the Mayo Clinic to have surgery and was sent home to get his affairs in order and live out his last few months. Most people would have taken this very seriously—and maybe he did—but not in a traditionally serious sense. He made up his mind to make each minute count, and he openly honored his two sacred priorities: to love and to play.

Against all odds, we had ten years. We laughed and we played and we learned. Most of all, we loved each other. We were happy and busy and together.

If I could paint you a picture of wellness, it would be the picture of my dad and my brother and I on a brisk fall day sitting in a pile of leaves with our backs against the trunk of a sturdy tree saying "Aaaah, this is the life!"

What I know about true health is this: your physical condition is just one piece of the puzzle. It's your life that reflects your health.

I have learned that true health promotion is not really about telling people what to do (or more often what not to do). It is about helping people have rich, happy lives—like the one I was given by my dad. By all means, we should value this great gift of life and take good care of it. But stuff happens to people—there are things beyond our control. The goals, as I see them, are to be kind and to be happy.

Holistic health promotion is about being kind to ourselves, being kind to the people we hope to help, being kind to the organizations and communities we serve. We can do this in all kinds of ways and sometimes that includes tackling the hard problems of life—the things that get in the way of being happy and healthy. Health promotion doesn't look any one prescribed way to me—it's very much based on what is needed to be holistically healthy: socially, physically, intellectually, spiritually, and emotionally. I can tell you that it's a blend of science, creativity, and caring.

As I have worked with organizations in my career in health promotion, I have noted that people who are valued seem to value themselves more. I believe health promotion has a unique and powerful potential to build in that valuing piece to organizational culture.

As I work with students, I hope to teach them to consider the whole picture: the holistic individuals they will serve, the lives and families they need to consider, the organizations and cultures that serve as mirrors to them, and the communities they ultimately impact. That is the scope and the power of health promotion—to make lives kinder and happier!

For my own life, I acknowledge the path of learning that I have been privileged to experience and that has shown me that a happy life is about being the best we can be—even in the face of adversity. As I learn more about what makes people truly happy, I know that it is very much about what we can do for others. I think that health promoters can be healers in all kinds of ways but that is a vocation—not just a job. I encourage the spirit of healing in my students, and that goes way beyond the "thou shalt nots" of traditional health promotion practice of days gone by. It really all gets back to how we inspire people to sit in the leaves with their backs against an oak tree and say (with great meaning) "Aaaah, this is the life!"

Kay Ryan is a registered nurse with a master's degree in health education and a Ph.D. in community and human resources. Currently, Kay is Professor and Vice President of Institutional Effectiveness. She also publishes and presents internationally on the topic of whole person wellness.

Kay was previously awarded the Dr. Jean Beyer Distinguished Professorship for holistic health education and last year received a visiting fellowship from the National University of Ireland in Galway, where she and her son lived and worked for a semester. Kay is the mother of three. She lives in the house in which she grew up in Omaha, Nebraska. Kay is passionate about her family and friends, her work, and Irish music. She plays the bodhran, the Irish drum. (402-354-4953, kryan@methodistcollege.edu)

Terry Golden

Family Physician and Captain in the U.S. Public Health Service

As a young child I remember sitting on my front steps watching the other kids playing together. They all knew exactly what they were doing. They seemed to have a purpose and a sense of urgency in their play. But it wasn't that way for me. I didn't know where I was going, or what purpose I had, and I certainly had no sense of urgency. For the first time I recognized my differences from others. Perhaps it was the first awareness of my emerging individuality or contrasting my self-image with how I perceived others. In retrospect, it may have been a vague awareness of time passing or just being in the moment. Later I would discover that concepts of self, relationships, and time awareness evolve from learned societal values and that many of those values are formed from a belief system based on the scientific model. It wasn't until much later that I realized how quantum physics was about to rewrite my life journey.

Since the age of enlightenment there has been an intimate relationship between core societal values, individual social values, and the scientific method. "Science" seemed to present such a more organized way of mentally cataloging the various phenomena observed by man. So by the time of the Industrial Revolution, the scientific process was woven into most societal structures. This trend has continued as science has explained and controlled more and more of the "unknowable."

Then I learned about quantum physics theory, which seemed to thrive on the unknowable, dependent, complementary relationship. In fact, at the quantum level, duality, probability, and complementarity form the foundation of everything that exists in the material universe. Quantum physics tells us that relationship is a primary process. Nothing occurs in the universe without something interacting with something else.

This is in marked contrast to classical scientific theory where relationship (effect) was a by-product that could be manipulated or caused/prevented by combining the proper ingredients. Thus, the universe was purely a mechanical phenomenon that whirred along when the right mix came together even by happenstance and where creativity was irrelevant. Thus, the quantum concepts of complementarity and relationship had a profound impact on me. I now had a crude blueprint for my life.

This shifting scientific paradigm (from Newtonian physics and scientific process to quantum possibility) is beginning to reveal a very different picture of us as conscious participants in this universal process of creativity through relationship (synergistic interdependence). These new ideas of science are beginning to influence the way health scientists examine and frame the ways we relate to our own bodies. The most important development in this realm may be the important connection between the spirit, mind, and body. Nature does not recognize the separation of spirit, mind, and body that some humans artificially created. Research suggests that there is a powerful connection between our creativity (expressed by the presence or lack of synergistic relationships) and our health. The more synergistic relationships the healthier the individual. The difficulty seems to be that the creativity generated by a true synergistic (interdependent) relationship is dependent upon the individual coming to the relationship fully aware of who they are. Nature goes to great lengths to genetically ensure uniqueness in each of us. But society goes to great lengths to make each of us the same. However, society is changing, and we are perhaps entering an age where uniqueness and creativity are highly valued and deconstructing and reduction are seen as less useful.

As we journey into the "Information Age," many recognize that the quantity of information available creates complex demands. In my opinion one of the greatest emerging demands is to bring diverse minds together to create the processing ability (skill) to handle today's more complex demands. Not many diverse minds thinking the same, but a collection of minds blending their diversity into one mind. A truly synergistic relationship demands that we come together not despite our differences but because of them. By bringing together complementary skills, recognizing differences, and instilling

381

a true desire to do our part we can create the necessary response to meet the demand.

For these reasons, relationship skills are rapidly becoming necessary if we are to evolve as a society. Individuals who lack relational skills will suffer from the increasing stress of attempting to interface with the informational society, and those who lack the education necessary to cope with the technological demands will experience even greater stress.

One positive benefit of the recognition of the mind-body connection is that medical practitioners now recognize that stress is a growing epidemic in our postindustrial society and the root cause of many illnesses. However, we're still grappling with this concept as a society. So few people seek or accept treatment aimed at stress and emotional causes, while at the same time medicine is grappling with approaches to these patients within the standard medical model. Unlike our "scientific remedies" there is no "one size fits all" cure for stress-related illnesses. Thus, the key to coping with the human problems caused by continued progress suggests the need for interventional creativity and individualized treatment much in keeping with quantum theory.

- Living mindlessly, we live a life of fear and chance, governed by our instinct for survival.

- Living mindfully, we live a life of love and choice, governed by our instinct for unity.

The social core values of competition, predictability, linear thinking, and reliance on external authority that evolved from our classic sciences is giving way to new social core values of cooperation, probability, nonlinear thinking, and reliance on internal authority based on the new model of science.

Only by aligning mind, body, and spirit can we achieve true interdependence. True interdependence (relationship) is a critical ability for individual and social health. If optimizing our potential is an integral part of our holistic definition of health, relationship or synergistic interdependence is critical to that process. All relationships become true living organisms, whether it's composed of two people or a whole community. Like the individual, the relational organism (family, organization, or community) must be aware of its own unique identity and path. This relational organism must be mindful of its obligation to itself and the unique individuals who make it up.

The relational organism provides an opportunity for individuals to explore and develop their uniqueness and individuals bring their unique qualities to the larger organism. This must be a mindful (conscious) process to succeed. Each must be willing to invest psychic energy into the other's interest. Relational organisms (groups, families, communities) are always held together by the cohesive forces of matter (physical needs) and psychic (emotional and spiritual) energy. Unfortunately, all too often in medicine we recognize and value the physical but ignore the emotional/spiritual.

Aligning ourselves with our greater purpose by optimizing our unique potential for creativity also aligns us with the universal principle of creativity. To develop a road map for this journey we need only look into the research on our own brain physiology and understand the core social values evolving from the new science. Only by understanding our biology, especially our brain physiology and the importance of truly synergistic relationships, can we reach our fullest potential and help those in our care.

Healing is truly an internal process but is only fully activated through relationship. We must understand that each of us possesses the ability to heal ourselves. That ability is enhanced when we strive to be the truly unique and authentic people we were meant to be and recognize that our relationships are potential sources of strength, creativity, and ultimately healing. As we honor our authenticity and relationships, we activate our internal source of healing. We cannot achieve synergistic relationships as secondhand people. We are evolving into an interdependent society, and our biology was set up to accomplish that goal. The health of the one is intertwined with the health of the many.

Dr Golden is a Board Certified Family Physician with over 20 years of clinical, academic, and administrative experience including building and managing programs with a national scope for the Federal Government. He is currently a Captain in the U.S. Public Health

*Service (PHS), and served as a U.S. Army Medical Officer until
1991. As a PHS physician, he was detailed to the U.S. Coast Guard
for 6 years and served as the Chief, Health Promotion and Substance
Abuse Program. He has extensive knowledge of readiness issues for
military, uniformed service personnel and civilians across multiple
environments. He also has extensive experience working with health
professionals from a variety of disciplines including medicine, nursing, and environmental health. (goldenfin@aol.com)*

Cheri K. Erdman

Professor Emeritus at College of DuPage, author and activist

Let's go back fifty-some years to 1953. I am five years old and in
kindergarten. I am a gifted child with a high IQ. I love school. And I
am fat. My teacher, who cares about me, is concerned about my
weight. She is fat, too, and maybe she wants to save me from a lifetime of shame. Whatever her intentions, she puts in motion an event
that changes my young life forever: she convinces my parents to put
me in a residential treatment facility for children with "special nutritional needs." In other words, I was sent away from home to be put
on a diet. I was there for more than a year. My parents say they vis-
ited me once a week on Friday nights, that I lost twenty-five pounds,
and that I seemed happy enough.

I don't remember. I have to take their word for it because I recall
very little of those thirteen months. In fact, I only have one clear
memory from that entire year. I was out on the playground with the
other kids. It was a bright spring day. Something made me look up
from where I was swinging. In the distance, past the fence that separated the playground from the entrance to the camp, was a familiar
car. My heart beat faster as I realized that it belonged to my parents.
I ran over to the chain-link fence and peered out, hoping to catch a
glimpse of my mother. I saw, instead, my brother Patrick. He saw me
too. With longing we looked at each other from the prisons that separated us—a fence, a locked car, a camp for special kids, adults who
thought they were doing what was best, and a society that was be-

ginning to hate fat people so much that it had devised a place to put fat kids away until they lost weight.

I will never forget what longing feels like because I was clenched in its hold forever as Patrick and I watched each other. I saw it in his four-year-old eyes, too. The void of being separated from each other grew larger than ever. The emptiness filled me.

Being at fat camp affected me in many ways. Its first and primary impact was that it put my relationship with my body at the forefront of my awareness of who "I" was. Not only did I have a body, *my body had me*. The struggle between my body-self and the other parts of myself continued for the next thirty years, with body obsession tainting everything else I accomplished. Its message? "Because you're fat, it doesn't matter how smart, creative, fun, and loving you are."

Fortunately, the intelligent, creative, fun, and loving parts of me did not roll over and die under the tyranny of my body-self. They stayed alive and showed themselves in big ways—they had to be *big* for me not only to notice them but to allow their accomplishments to override the ever-present sense of not being good enough because of my weight.

Fortunately, during my professional education I stumbled across psychosynthesis, a holistic psychology of personality development that includes recognition of spirituality as integral to being fully human. Learning about psychosynthesis gave me a framework to understand who "I" was in terms of my subpersonalities (parts of myself) and how to balance and harmonize these parts. It also taught me how to use my will as a way to take active responsibility for my life. And it emphasized that the development of my personality was connected with my recognition and development of my spirituality. This gave me a way to make meaning of my experiences and give purpose to my life.

When I worked with the psychosynthesis concept of subpersonalities I learned about myself in several ways. My intelligent part assisted me in completing my doctor of education degree. My creative part helped me write two books. Those two parts collaborated in my successful career as an educator and counselor. My fun and loving parts made sure I had many loyal friends and a strong marriage. And yet, through all of this, my body-self remained fat. "I" (the director of these parts) had to take notice: I *have* a body and I am *not* my body.

My next step was learning to balance my body, intellect and emotions in expressing who I was in the world. My body, though important to take care of and respect, was not the ALL of me. I began to give my body less dominance in my thoughts (by not obsessing) and emotions (by not shaming, blaming, or guilt tripping myself). I began to respect its need to eat in a way that is right for me and take pleasure in moving. Now when I look in the mirror I see a fat woman who takes care of herself, not a fat woman who needs to lose weight.

The psychosynthesis concept of the will looks nothing like the Victorian "willpower" we believe is the motivation behind all changes. This will does not identify with the agendas of any of the subpersonalities. It is the energy that is available to take action from a place that sees the best and highest purpose for the whole being. It asks me, "Am I willing?" not "Should I?" or "Can I?"

Learning about the will gave me this insight: I was not a failure because I could not keep lost weight off. I saw that losing weight was the agenda of the part of me that bought into cultural messages that I "should" be thin or I am not good enough, no matter what else I accomplish. When I asked myself if I was willing to do the things I had to do to *lose weight* (for the umpteenth time!), I said no. But I *was* willing to take responsibility for my body in ways I could be successful at changing; like eating right, moving and meditating. I was also willing to take responsibility with the other aspects of my life, directing the parts of me who could assist in self-acceptance regardless of weight and to go forward with my life *in the body I already have*.

The higher self (or spirituality, creativity, intuition, God, or however one defines this energy) in psychosynthesis has allowed me to understand that the experiences I have had as a fat person have given my life a purpose. My life purpose is to teach, counsel, and assist others who have faced discrimination around weight. I have also broadened my purpose to include working against any kind of discrimination be it race, gender, sexual orientation or any of the myriad ways society says people do not fit in.

And, finally, I have created this special meaning out of my fat camp experience. When I remember the six-year-old fat girl who continues to live in me, I imagine her with all of her feelings of being abandoned and rejected in the name of "for her own good," and I want to say this to her: thank you for being brave enough and strong enough to withstand the separation from your family. Thank you for being resilient enough to bounce back. Thank you for giving me compassion. Thank you for bearing and nurturing the seeds of my future profession. Thank you for being fat, because if you weren't, I wouldn't have the rich life I do today.

Through the holistic lens of psychosynthesis, I have finally learned and accepted that I have a body and I am more than my body. Much, much more.

Cheri K. Erdman, Ed.D., is a professor and counselor at the College of DuPage in Glen Ellyn, Illinois, and author of the books, Nothing to Lose: A Guide to Sane Living in a Larger Body and Live Large! (abundia22@yahoo.com)

Brian Luke Seaward

Author, speaker, executive director of Inspiration Unlimited

For as long as I can remember, I have had an interest in service, helping others achieve their highest human potential. It was Mark Spitz, who in 1972 won seven gold medals in swimming, who inspired me to swim competitively in high school. I thought I wanted to be a swim coach, but my professional interests quickly turned from coaching swimming to cardiac rehabilitation-coaching of a different sort. The four years at the University of Maine at Orono with an exceptional professor who mentored me through the labyrinth of course work and politics, in turn, laid groundwork for a master's degree in exercise physiology at the University of Illinois, Champaign-Urbana.

My mission was to save the world from heart disease and with unbridled enthusiasm I hit the ground running. It was during my first position working in a cardiac rehabilitation program in La Crosse,

Wisconsin, that I realized my mission was misdirected. Even with the best of intentions, protocols, and sincerity, cardiac patients in rehabilitation eventually (and often quickly) died. It didn't take long to realize that it wasn't rehabilitation but prevention where I felt I could make the biggest impact. My biggest complaint with the focus of fitness programs was its shortsightedness and the exclusion of the mind, emotions and spirit.

While in Wisconsin, I met Elizabeth Kubler-Ross, M.D., a person who influenced my career significantly. As the keynote speaker for the 1981 American Holistic Medicine Association conference, she spoke eloquently of the ageless wisdom of wellness, where the whole is greater than the sum of the parts, with the parts being mind, body, spirit, and emotions. Kubler-Ross validated my thoughts that human spirituality was the cornerstone of wellness, yet Western culture has ignored this fact for nearly four hundred years. In my conversations with her afterward, she encouraged me to follow her lead as one of the pioneers in health promotion by helping her reintegrate human spirituality back into the health care industry. I accepted the challenge gladly.

In 1983, I began a self-directed program at the University of Maryland in a field that had no name. Today it goes by several names: health psychology, psychoneuroimmunology, holistic wellness. I wanted to look at the integration, balance, and harmony of mind, body, spirit, and emotions. The best I could do was psychophysiology (mind-body). I was told that in graduate school people didn't study the whole picture. Rather, they, in the footsteps of René Descartes, divided and dissected the parts to minutia to become experts in practically nothing at all. I raised a lot of eyebrows with my mind-body-spirit approach to health, but luckily not enough to become an enemy of the academic state. Instead, I was lauded for starting a highly successful campus wellness program, which bore the fruits of my academic pursuits.

With a position on the faculty of American University in Washington, DC, I began what some people have called my seminal work, a holistic textbook on stress management entitled *Managing Stress*. When published in the spring of 1994, it was hailed as the first holistic health textbook of its kind. Perhaps what made it unique was an entire chapter on the topic of stress and human spirituality. Where other textbooks gave tacit mention of human spirituality (with a mere sentence) or neglected it entirely,

Managing Stress not only had an entire chapter, but nearly every chapter held a resonance of mind-body-spirit integration. Kubler-Ross and Jung were only two of my mentors. I have been greatly inspired by the works of Larry Dossey, Rachel Naomi Remen, Deepak Chopra, Patch Adams, Michael Talbot, Richard Gerber, Norman Cousins, Viktor Frankl, Matthew Fox, Mietec Wirkus, and scores of other luminaries whose wisdom and grace have cultivated my journey of enlightenment.

With a deep interest in community- and corporate-based wellness programs in the 1990s, I made several presentations to many Fortune 500 companies, at first under the topic of stress management. Not too long afterward, I was asked by the wellness directors of Quaker Oats, Conoco, and Hewlett Packard to give presentations on the topic of stress and human spirituality.

Looking back on my career in the field of health care and health promotion, what have I learned? I have learned that there are wonderful people who follow their hearts and change the world, one person at a time. I have learned not to be afraid of what I believe in and through the best diplomatic channels make efforts to raise consciousness so that we can all achieve our highest human potential. At the time I was forging my career, there were certainly moments of challenge, but in hindsight it all seems extremely well orchestrated. I have no doubt that I have the best spiritual guidance. A closer look into my past reveals a childhood blessed with an adventurous spirit and two alcoholic parents. Having been raised by alcoholic parents might not seem like a blessing (and indeed at times it seemed more like a curse), but through the gift of hindsight, I realize that this, too, gave me wisdom to integrate human spirituality into the wellness paradigm. Freud would have said (in a thick German accent) "Since he couldn't save his parents, he decided to save the world." Carl Gustav Jung (my hero) more aptly would have said, "He has taken the wealth of experiences from childhood to forge the strength of his own spirit" (thanks Carl!). My greatest resistance has been from those individuals who are stuck in fear-based (egotistical) thinking. They see that the holistic approach as threatening to their belief systems. My greatest support has come from like-minded individuals in various pockets of the country who intuitively know the holistic approach makes the most sense. As Kubler-Ross said, "To deny the aspect of the spiritual dimension in health, and life, is to lead to dysfunction." Dysfunction is the national adjective in America today, not just in health care but in nearly every aspect of society.

Because of politics in the academic setting I left Washington, DC, to return home to Boulder, Colorado, in 1993, where I now consult, write, and teach part time at both the University of Colorado-Boulder and the University of Northern Colorado-Greely. In some regards, without the political restrictions of academia my career has reached new heights.

If someone were to have told me back when I was in undergraduate school that I would be giving lectures in corporate America about spiritual well-being or seminars to physicians about the dynamics of complementary medicine I would have thought they were crazy. But times are changing and the paradigm of reductionism, so deeply entrenched in American society, is giving way to the ageless wisdom of holism, where, indeed, the whole is greater than the sum of the parts.

If I were to be so bold as to take a peek at the future of health care, health education, and humanity as a whole, this is what I would see.

- Primary and secondary educational systems that nurture creative as well as critical thinking

- Higher educational systems that honor the holistic nature of life. As futurest and author Marilyn Ferguson once stated, "It's time to put a stake in the heart of the Cartesian principle!"

- Health care educators and practitioners who are trained holistically honoring the integration, balance, and harmony of mind, body, spirit, and emotions

- Health care centers where patients have a choice between allopathic, holistic, or a combination of the two

- The elimination of politics in health care, particularly regarding the food industry

- Honoring the global ecology before the global economy

In every age, wellness has been more than diet and exercise. It is my wish that aspiring health educators and health care practitioners follow not only their minds but their hearts as well and honor the ageless wisdom of the real wellness paradigm, where the whole is considered greater than the sum of the parts, honoring the integration, balance, and harmony of mind, body, spirit, and emotions.

We are living in interesting and challenging times. For the first time, the pace of technology has exceeded the balance of responsibility required to use it safely. At the time of this writing, the human genome project has just been completed, yet more commentary in the news focuses on the ethics involved with potential misuse than the potential for treating illness and disease. We have much to learn from the elders who hold sacred the ageless wisdom of health and well-being. Best wishes and inner peace.

Brian Luke Seaward, Ph.D., is internationally renowned for his work in the field of holistic stress management, human spirituality, and mind-body-spirit healing. He serves on the faculty of the University of Colorado-Boulder and the University of Northern Colorado. Luke is the executive director of Inspiration Unlimited, a health promotion consulting firm in Boulder, Colorado. He is the author of several books, including Stand Like Mountain, Flow Like Water and Stressed Is Desserts Spelled Backward. (www.brianlukeseaward.net 303-678-9962)

Walter Elias

Health care consultant specializing in care management President, Elias and Associates

In the late 1970s, I was a freshly minted Ph.D. in anthropology, part of the baby boom generation looking for spots in academic departments. Unfortunately, the next demographic wave was much smaller and academic departments were constricting. So one day I was searching the bulletin board of the Health Sciences Center at the University of Arizona when I came across an ad for an evaluator for a health education research project. I wasn't completely sure what an evaluator was, but it sounded like something I as a trained social scientist could do. The head of the project had been in the Peace Corps and had worked with anthropologists in South America. She liked the breadth of perspective an anthropologist brings. She gave me a chance.

So in the late 1970s I became the evaluator for a Kellogg Foundation funded research project in Tucson, Arizona, called "Well Aware about Health." We were evaluating the impact of a health risk appraisal (HRA), lifestyle counseling, and health education interventions on a fee for service clinic and an HMO population. Given the fact that we were a small group running the project we all had overlapping roles. One of my tasks was to organize the lifestyle counseling aspect of the interventions.

After not too considerable a thought process I started calling around to see if I could find the appropriate people. For those participants who were high risk because of sedentary lifestyle I hired an exercise physiologist. For those participants who were high risk because of elevated cholesterol, I hired a nutritionist. For those people who were high risk for hypertension, I hired a physician. For the smokers, I hired a smoking cessation expert. For those who were overweight, I brought in a Weight Watchers lecturer. And so on and so forth.

Individuals filled out their HRAs in group meetings, listened to a generic group lecture on how to interpret their results, and then were given the option of one-on-one counseling and health education classes. After our first group results sessions we were ready for the first counseling participants.

I knew something was wrong from the very beginning of these sessions. We had very unhappy clients and counselors. After about a week of counseling sessions the staff counselors asked for a meeting with me. "We're the wrong people," they said. I wasn't sure what they meant, but it soon became clear. One after the other started relating stories of their counseling sessions.

"How can you ask me to lose weight when my son just ran off to Haight-Ashbury?" (this was still the seventies you know). "How can you expect me to stop smoking while I'm going through this nasty divorce?" "You expect me to not eat a gallon of ice cream a night," said another participant, describing how she was just fired from her job. "I'll start exercising as soon as I figure out how to juggle three kids, a full-time job, and being a single Mom," was another comment.

It finally dawned on me that when the participants signed up for "counseling" they were expecting help with some of these emotional problems. Their life stresses and their high-risk health behaviors were somehow related. My goodness, there seemed to be a mind attached to the body! I had neglected a basic need of the participant. The existing counselor staff agreed to resign, and in their place I hired therapists and counseling psychologists. Everyone seemed happier, participation increased, and our results improved. To my knowledge this was the first time that a community-based wellness program delivering services to clinic populations offered psychological counseling to complement health education interventions.

Later I wondered why I never saw this model replicated in corporate health promotion programs. It seemed intuitively obvious now that I had seen it in operation. I began to work for an HRA company and then later for one in health communications. I got to see an awful lot of programs in my traveling. Most of what I encountered was of the HRA/health education class variety with some moving into more of a communications-based approach. All were basically the traditional medical model transposed into a corporate setting. In one corporation I was even told, "there is no stress here at XYZ Company." This was the epitome for me of the mind/body separation I was observing in corporate wellness programs. Years later, I began meeting a few forward thinking holistic health professionals who were starting to advocate use of mind/body/spirit approaches in corporate settings. These people agreed with me that there was something inherently wrong with the traditional model around which most of corporate health promotion was constructed.

This experience happened over twenty years ago. Yet the original biomedical designs of health assessment and evaluation programs remain the standard in most organizations today. Health risk appraisals are still the predominant tool used, and physiologists, nutritionists, and other "physical-health-oriented" professionals are most often recruited for counseling.

Walter Elias is President of Elias & Associates, Inc. a Minneapolis based consulting firm specializing in care management (disease & demand management and prevention). He is currently working with the Agency for Health Care Research on Quality (AHRQ) on a hospital quality project regarding cardiovascular procedures and surgery and with the Academy for Health Services Research on a rural health project. He also is the evaluator of the Schlumberger corporate wellness program. Other experiences include the design and development of health risk appraisal instruments, worksite health promotion programs, and extensive program development work in e-health care. (952-546-0229, 952-546-1499 wselias@msn.com)

Linda Bedre-Vaughn

Teacher of deep listening, activist and healer, Founder of *A New Way*

I felt called, and my life seemed to flow that way - to assist people in healing from deep wounds inflicted by families and society - some unconscionable but most unintentional.

It all started as the oldest of six, living in rural East Texas, running free in the woods among the trees connecting with the earth, spirit, light, stars and the sky. However, life involved learning skills in managing a childhood few would consider optimal - caring for young ones and managing adult family chores at four, being exposed to violence, poverty, neglect, torture and passivity. As I grew, I became the competent one, the one people looked to for solutions and consistency. I seemed to be able to mediate situations and stood up against mistreatment.

And, I left as soon as I could. I married at nineteen, had two children, and underwent two serious surgeries, all before I was twenty-three. I finished college, became certified to teach and was divorced at twenty-nine. I felt unable to raise two young children on a teacher's salary with no child support, so I became involved in marketing and sales.

Years later, after another (brief) marriage and divorce with a violent alcoholic, I became involved in twelve-step programs and experienced a spiritual awakening. I became willing to trust, let go, and allow life to flow. This has taken much practice - starting and restarting, making fresh new mistakes and learning to change. Accepting me.

Around 1985, no longer in deep denial, I "discovered" that I was the child of an alcoholic and became involved with Adult Children of Alcoholics. At this time I was also introduced to the insights of Re-evaluation Counseling (RC), an international project based on peer relationships whereby people listen deeply to one another in classes and one-on-one sessions. In this way people assist each other in healing and in reclaiming their thinking and clarity in order to eliminate all forms of humans hurting each other and our universe. Releasing stored hurts emotionally is healing and leads to thoughtful relationships in all areas of our lives. We can become leaders in whatever endeavors delight our hearts.

By 1989, I was informally teaching RC classes in the evenings. RC has a policy that you may use their information in any way you would like as long as you do not represent yourself as teaching official RC certified classes. As my classes became larger, people began to ask if I would be willing to see them individually and I said, "Why not?" (In Texas there was no requirement at that time to have a license to "counsel" as long as a person did not represent themselves as a person who in fact was required to have a license, such as a therapist, psychologist, doctor, etc.) However, in 1993 the Texas legislature required all people who "counsel" others to be licensed. The clergy and lay ministries of Texas lobbied and were excluded from the bill, and so I became a nondenominational minister. That was the beginning.

Today, I work from home with my friend and partner, Michael. Here I find I can nurture and care for myself more easily as I see seven to nine hours of clients per day. I also facilitate a monthly women's group, a monthly men's group, a weekly class and facilitate workshops.

I look forward to devoting more time to writing. I travel, find time for sacred silences, play with my grandson and enjoy my family and a large group of friends. I have weekly body/energy work, practice QiGong and when I need it, emotional release sessions. My health care practitioners are considered complementary or are traditional healers and curanderas. Michael and I regularly visit our home in the mountains of Jemez Springs, New Mexico, for rejuvenation, relaxation and work with healers in the area.

I have integrated into my practice some basic RC insights, continuing education from mental health/social worker's courses and twelve-step programs, knowledge from my personal guides/teachers, integration of some ancient perspectives from Chinese, homeopathic and herbal medicines, Ayurveda, aromatherapy, subtle energy and vibrational medicine disciplines. I have studied cultural and spiritual practices of selected indigenous peoples. I continue my personal healing encompassing everything from my conception through the reclaiming of my own heritage and empowerment as a woman. These insights and experiences combine to inform how I interact with people. I had to process through the "embarrassment" of not having official credentials and instead noticing the results with the people with whom I interfaced. I am especially grateful for the insights of RC as it has allowed me to handle confusion, criticism, and transference issues. My burnout is minimal and my energy remains consistent.

Many people referred to me are survivors of the mental health system. These individuals have been "diagnosed" and labeled with all sorts of maladies - depression, panic disorders, multiple personalities, other dissociative disorders, compulsive/obsessive behavior, borderline personality, psychotic behavior, bipolar disorder, or manic-depressive. They usually have been given drugs or shock treatment as a temporary substitute for any real assistance or healing. The majority of these women and men, have been profoundly abused as children. They are very confused about their goodness and intelligence. Most have been searching many years for information or a process to assist in reclaiming their lives. As they begin their work, they feel discouraged, lonely, hopeless, or self-righteous. But they are living with pain that can be released.

First I listen; people sometimes cry moments after sitting down. With each session, as I listen, they release more feelings and gain more clarity. If appropriate I assist with information within the context of their abuse. But more importantly, a safe space is created to facilitate the deep, physiological release of emotions. I notice that developing a connection with spirit (whatever the concept), quiet time, expressing creativity, energy and body work, balanced nutrition, fun, and relaxation are necessary in the process of recovery and healing. Most people have to reclaim many areas in their lives.

The stories that I listen to are sometimes difficult to hear, and yet it is imperative that a person talk with a compassionate person about what was done to them (or what they have done to someone else). Each person needs to process the feelings attached to the information. Expressing feelings in a physiological way balances the human. Drugs put a cap on this process and interfere with healing. Although drugs may sometimes be helpful as a temporary measure, they are not a substitute for interaction with a caring person who listens in a way that elicits deep emotional release. Usually it is not necessary to verify or validate the story; if a person "believes" it and releases feelings for a while, the truth will emerge as denial disintegrates. Working toward acceptance and forgiveness leads to understanding. Forgiveness is a gift we are given as we come out of denial, heal, and reclaim our lives.

It is difficult to hear the stories - like the young woman I worked with for several years who as a small girl had been traded by her father many times as a sexual favor for drugs he used; or, others who had been threatened with death, terrorized or whose pets had been killed in order to silence them. As appalling as these events are, the hardest client to reach is the one coming from a quietly manipulative, seemingly loving and conforming home, where the mistreatment is very covert. This person is usually deep in denial. They have a difficult time recognizing and defining hurtful behavior - subtle betrayal, conformity, emotional incest, criticism, perfectionism, hidden family secrets and behaviors done "for your own good." For example, this type of client may say "we only got whacked once or twice, or they just mostly yelled, or they isolated me when I made a mistake or sent me to bed with no supper or they just had to look at me, you know, with that look." Many intergenerational patterns (origins forgotten) have been passed on to new generations, not as genetics but as energy patterns. For instance, "a great-grandparent had affairs or drank, there have been several suicides in our family, or we were taught to be afraid of or blame certain other people based on skin color, religion, or other arbitrary criteria."

Most of my clients internalize their abuse and rigidly cope using addictive behavior or substances, including prescription drugs. Others feel trapped, immobile and terrified, surviving day to day. I know that anyone who abuses another disconnects from their humanity in order to hurt someone. And I am grateful and awed that not everyone who has been hurt passes it on. All perpetrators that I have worked with have been previously abused. I offer this not as an excuse, as each perpetrator is accountable, but as an explanation that as survivors we are responsible for our healing and for stopping the legacy of abuse. If we really examine our behavior, most of us notice that we have, in fact, passed hurts on to others or ourselves in some way.

As I am present with clients, I listen with compassion, stay consistent, give information and hold out hope for them. I encourage and facilitate the deep physiological emotional release of feelings - rage, sadness, terror, shame and watch as thinking clears up, lives and relationships change, hope and renewal become evident. Clients attach to me just long enough to develop trust, often for the first time in their lives. I encourage each person to take full charge of their life and relationships in thoughtful and caring ways. At some point, I encourage clients to explore and to take their healing a step further, to work to change institutions and systems - mental health, legal, economic, religious, educational, health care, government and the institutions of racism, classism, sexism, ageism, poverty, hunger, environmental devastation, and the pull to greed in all of its malignant forms. Most people I have worked with express passionately, "What am I here to contribute, what is my purpose, or how can I make a difference?"

How do I do what I do, I really do not know. First of all, I know that it is a spiritual endeavor, and I show up willing to be open and compassionate. It is also a culmination of my experiences, my own work and the insights that I have used with the thousands of people with whom I have been privileged to work. I think that there is an energy transfer, like a figure eight that goes back and forth between me and the client that is grounded in spirit. A calm centered place in me touches the chaotic place inside of the client so they can feel that calm place for themselves. I stay connected to my concept of spirit and attempt to put my ego aside and keep the intent of kindness, compassion and healing in mind. In closing, I would like to say that I help people remember that when we are connected to each other we are respectful. How then can we do any harm? How then can we be less than thoughtful?

Linda Bedre-Vaughn cofounded A New Way in 1989 and listens to people with compassion and insight. Linda works in Houston, Texas, with her partner, Michael Vaughn, where they encourage, teach and support couples, young people and individuals through sessions, classes and workshops to respond with kindness, courage and re-spect. They facilitate the client in processing not only family of origin but also societal and institutional conditioning. The personal healing that results leads to well being, empowerment and excellent relationships with others. Thinking well can extend to one's community and assist in developing broad cultural perspectives and in eliminating sexist, racist and other conditioning. They teach parents to interact with their young people in "play listening" sessions as an alternative to medication. They encourage all of their clients to eliminate dependence on prescribed medication in lieu of healing. (713-802-1139, anewway@earthlink.net)

Pat Lyons

Author, speaker, activist, public health nurse

I grew up hating myself because I was fat. Teasing began at age five, and from thirteen to thirty-one my life was consumed by yo-yo dieting and the depression that followed each failed weight loss attempt. At thirty-one I realized I was just enduring my life, rather than living it. With the help of a friend, who got me started in yoga, I began a self-help course of healing fueled by feminist politics, sports psychology, and holistic health practices. I began as an *N* of one in my own research projects. Today, at fifty-five, I am healthy and happy. I am also still fat. But I don't hate myself or my fat body. I also don't apologize or try to be invisible. In fact, I've not only "come out" as a fat woman but have put a bull's eye on my chest as a leader in the size acceptance movement. I do whatever I can to reduce weight prejudice and improve access to health care and self-care for fat people. It is ironic that in overcoming the deep pain and shame of childhood, I've found life work that brings me meaning, satisfaction, and joy.

That does not mean it has been easy. After writing and developing programs based on *Great Shape: The First Fitness Guide for Large Women*, my work has been both celebrated and condemned by practitioners of both traditional medical and holistic health modalities. Fat phobia is deeply entrenched in the culture. Neither fat people nor health care providers want to believe the truth: that people naturally come in different shapes and sizes and that fitness and health are for every body, not just thin folks. It is not enough to simply switch from a biomedical to a more holistic model if prejudices and biases remain unexamined and untouched. "You can never be too thin or too rich" and other white, middle class biases still dominate both health paradigms. Being poor in America is still the leading cause of ill health, and many poor people, including high percentages of fat people, have little access to either paradigm. So, as we move forward to challenge traditional biomedical thinking, it is important to address our own learned cultural biases openly and do whatever we can to unlearn them.

Someone sent me an e-mail recently that really stuck with me: surviving oppression is not the same as being free. In my thirty-five-year career in public health education with oppressed and marginalized communities I've learned that my most important job is to support people in thinking for themselves, respecting themselves, and trusting their own experience. It is certainly what has worked for me, and I'd like to share an excerpt from my book *Great Shape: The First Fitness Guide for Large Women* (Morrow, 1988; iUniverse.com, 2000) to give you a sample of that process.

Great Shape: Challenging the "Thin Is Best" Paradigm

When I started running at age thirty-three I was a five-foot eight-inch, 190-pound, two-pack-a-day smoker with a scary cough. I played tennis fairly regularly but could only run a block at a time nonstop. Every day I'd run a block, go home, smoke a cigarette, and congratulate myself that I'd been out there trying. After about a month I was running two to three blocks and smoking fewer cigarettes. I started reading everything I could get my hands on about aerobic exercise, women's sports, feminism, sport psychology, nutrition, and wellness, and finally came to believe that I could actually make a difference in my health. Although I'd been a nurse for many years, I knew mostly about illness and medical treatment; I didn't actually know much about becoming or staying healthy. I began really learning about health by trying to become healthy myself, and running seemed like the most direct route to improvement. I figured I'd lose weight, too, if only I could run far enough or fast enough. About the third month of running I quit my twenty-year smoking habit, something I'd tried unsuccessfully to do on several previous occasions. What a reward! Still, it took a year before I could run a mile. In another year I was able to run three miles and began fantasizing about running the San Francisco Bay to Breakers race. Could it be possible? The next thing I knew it was Bay to Breakers Sunday, and I was facing the Hayes Street hill. . . .

I finished the 7.6-mile course in one hour forty-five minutes. There are those who say "real" runners go much faster than that, but what did I care? I wasn't even supposed to be able to run. I was *la-*

beled obese by medical types, and three months after I'd started running I read in a fitness book that people more than thirty pounds "overweight" shouldn't run, that they should lose weight before running. Fortunately I read that *after* I'd discovered the challenge, exuberance, and rewards of running, or I might never have had the Bay to Breakers to celebrate. I was fat but I was *fit,* and no one could take that away from me.

My health had improved dramatically since my first days of running. My resting pulse went from one hundred to sixty; my blood pressure, while always normal, lowered slightly; seemingly endless bouts of depression, that I'd experienced for years, lifted; my cigarette-related colds became virtually nonexistent; and my flexibility, strength, and lung power improved enough to play softball at the third base position and to backpack to over ten thousand feet. I threw away my scale and stopped dieting once and for all and concentrated on eating whole, nutritious foods. All things considered I was much healthier at age thirty-five than I was at twenty-five, the year I weighed 139 after a crash dieting spree. But despite all these positive changes and being at the peak of my activity level, running, skiing, playing softball, and backpacking, I never attained my "ideal" weight. I was in the best shape of my life but at 185 pounds and 35% body fat I had not become magically thin. The truth was apparent: I could be *fit* and healthy, but I'd always be fat.

I ran in three more Bay to Breakers races over the next five years, the last time weighing 215 pounds after spending a year filled with more time writing than running in grad school. That last time, there was a woman a little larger than I running very near me. We smiled at each other in a shy, almost secret, knowing way that acknowledged we were breaking the rules, flouting the stereotyped expectations people have of us. Fat people are lazy. Fat people hate to exercise. Fat people don't deserve respect. Fat people can't be healthy and *fit.* Oh yeah?

It is said we teach what we are trying to learn, and certainly this has been true for me. From my earliest feminist reading I'd been encouraged to find my voice. Working in women's health and family planning I learned that body sovereignty is central to health and that people must challenge existing norms and work together to ensure respectful health care. As a public health nurse for five years on a Paiute-Shoshone Indian reservation I learned how shame has been used as a weapon to force people into submission and assimilation. I also learned about the value of social support, unbending community spirit, and their interplay with the limits of "white man's medicine." Incorporating sports psychology and holistic practices and perspectives into my life helped liberate me from a narrow physical definition of health and surpass limits of all sorts. In searching for role models I found fat women who, in their writing and by their example, convinced me that it was my ideas about fat that needed to change, not my fat body. Because of my work on social justice issues, I knew that no one could be free as long as anyone was oppressed. I also found that fat people were at the bottom of the social ladder and that many would rather continue dieting to try to escape being fat than work toward liberation. Sad but true. But I found I had no choice—I'd found my tribe, fat women, and in them found my life's work.

In the years since writing *Great Shape*, I've developed many successful programs for large women willing to shift their focus to health and well-being rather than weight loss and have spoken to thousands of health professionals interested in incorporating these ideas into their practice. Even though the scientific evidence has backed us up 100 percent, in getting *Great Shape* back into print recently it surprises me that our ideas remain controversial. I see both greater support and greater resistance. Through it all I continue to emphasize the same principles with both health consumers and professionals: (1) show up and be yourself, (2) speak up and express yourself and (3) support and mentor each other in advancing these new ideas. Whenever I am at a loss about how to proceed, I simply return to these clear guidelines. They inspire me to keep going. Regardless of the federal "war on obesity" and the billions of dollars pitted against our size acceptance efforts, the truth is I've always enjoyed being a rabble rouser. Doing this work gives me plenty of opportunity to live up to my principles. It suits me. It frees me. I hope it frees you as well.

Pat Lyons, RN, MA, has been a public health nurse and educator for more than thirty years. She holds a master's degree in psychology and is a member of the steering committee for the University of California-Berkeley Center for Weight and Health. (510-763-7365, plyons@earthlink.com)

Deborah Kern

Speaker, author, and wellness coach

When I began my journey in the health field in 1978, my focus was primarily on the physical aspects of health. I spent over eight years teaching patients how to lower their cholesterol, their blood pressure, and their body fat, while telling them to increase their exercise levels. As a health educator, I was trained to inundate my patients with information about how to create these positive health changes without even acknowledging the possibility that their mental, emotional, social, or spiritual being might be affecting their physical being.

Likewise, in my own life I was unaware of the connection between mind, body, spirit, and emotions. In my desire to create the healthiest life possible, I taught aerobics every day after work and competed in 10K races on the weekends. I monitored my fat intake and maintained a very low body fat percentage. I had the "right" house and the "right" job and participated in the "right" church and volunteer activities. But when my husband told me he no longer wanted to be married, I was completely blind-sided. Why was I taken by surprise? Because I was so busy doing the "right" things, so focused on external measures of success, that I was unaware of subtle changes in our relationship. Within three months, my marriage dissolved, I miscarried twins, and I resigned my position as a hospital department director. From the outside I appeared to be the perfect example of health, but on the inside I was unable to cope.

After spending the majority of my adult life trying to do the "right thing" I was suddenly at the bottom of the barrel. It was from this place of despair that I began to see a bigger message—a blessing in disguise. The difficult experiences ripped away all the false notions that I held so true and provided me a new understanding of life. This was when I realized that health was not just about looking great and having good blood chemistries—it was something much broader and deeper. My journey toward true health and wellness was emerging.

I returned to Dallas, my hometown, to go back to school and get my doctorate. I thought getting a doctorate was a logical next step for me in my career, and since I was reeling from life events it provided a much-needed focus for my life. What I didn't realize was that in the process of studying and researching for my doctorate I would be exposed to a whole new paradigm of health and healing that was congruous with my life experiences.

My first exposure to this new paradigm of health and healing was an "accident." (Of course, now I don't believe in "accidents," just "coincidences.") While attending a fitness convention I was assigned to a breakout session called NIA (neuromuscular integrative action) instead of the one for which I had registered. When I walked into the workshop I instantly thought I was in the wrong place. The presenters were barefoot. I had taught conventional aerobic dance and step classes since 1980, and I had never, ever worked out without my shoes on! To my dismay, the music was soft and flowing. Where was the loud, jangling warm-up music I was used to? Very skeptically, I joined in to what I thought would be such a low-intensity workout that I would certainly have to find something to do later. Surprise!! Not only did my heart rate soar, but so did my spirits. Never before had I felt like this in an exercise class! The movement was expressing the very emotions I was feeling. At one point I found myself gently crying as we did a step that incorporated gentle rocking motions of the arms and side-to-side movements of the pelvis. Years later I would come to realize that, although I had intellectually come to terms with my miscarriage, my body was still holding grief—and NIA allowed that grief to be expressed and my tight muscles to be freed. When the session was all over, I felt like I had showered from the inside out! I was full of joy and peace at the same time. I knew right away that this was something I wanted to teach and literally ran to the exhibit hall to get training information. The rest is history.

NIA was my first step into a world of understanding the powerful connection of mind, body, and spirit. It opened my mind and heart to be curious about how other cultures create health. I learned as much as I could about Chinese medicine, Ayurveda, healing touch, and yoga. Following graduation from my doctoral program I continued to learn. I lived on an ashram to experience a yogic lifestyle. I lived in the rain forest of Costa Rica to study herbal medicine with a group of indigenous women. As I flooded myself with experiences that were quite different from what I once considered the "right" health practices, my life began to shift and my soul began to heal. It was this shift that put me on a new course in life—a course that has given me a deeper understanding of the challenges that people face and a realization that healing is a returning to wholeness that occurs from the inside out.

Deborah Kern, Ph.D., is a keynote presenter and author in the field of holistic health care. She is an adjunct faculty member at the University of Alabama-Huntsville Nursing School, a black belt NIA trainer, a phoenix rising yoga practitioner, and an integral yoga instructor. (256-739-1847, dr.deb@deborahkern.com)

David Gobble

Professor and Director of the Fisher Institute for Wellness and Gerontology at Ball State University

It has always seemed to me to be a high calling to work with and for the health of individuals, organizations, and communities. Since 1972, I have been involved in either public health or academic training programs focused on disease prevention and health promotion. At the start of my career I worked in a local public health department, providing health promotion and education programs for a diverse population, basing my efforts on a mixture of community development and a classic biomedical model of disease causation. The biomedical basis of disease prevention included traditional issues of immunization, sanitation, and what we understood at the time to be critical lifestyle-related issues. I was convinced that I was an expert and possessed valuable knowledge about what was needed in my particular community to improve health and the quality life.

Most of this work was based upon epidemiological assessments and a few local surveys indicating populations in most need of my help. At least, that's what I thought at the time. I felt good doing this work but understood early on that I was having little lasting impact. It was clear that my programs, though well planned, attracted few participants, and those that came were already doing what I thought was the right thing to do regarding disease prevention and health promotion. I assumed that all I needed to do was do more, and work harder, doing the same things, using the same basic approaches, and I would be successful. I defined success as people doing what I thought, or the agency thought, was best for them. I would like to be able reflect and say that I lay awake at night thinking about what was not working and how I needed to understand more about the unique life space of the people I worked with, but that was not really the case. Like most aspiring professionals in the early 1970s, I thought I needed more education and experience doing similar things and I would become more successful.

Well, I got more education, a Ph.D., and more experience, and not much changed. In the late 1970s, while coordinating a graduate program in community health, I began to question what I was teaching and why it was not working to meet people's health and well-being needs. Now I did begin to lose sleep about the validity of what I was doing. I remember reading Don Ardell's book (1977) *High Level Wellness* and Halbert Dunn's (1971) work on defining wellness and thinking that this was more of what I need to be thinking about. I read Ken Pelletier's (1979) *Holistic Medicine: From Stress to Optimal Health* and was convinced that these ideas pointed toward what I needed to be looking at to begin to reach out to more people and embrace a more person-centered approach to health and well-being. Another part of this transformation was Paulo Friere's (1970) work on empowerment. These authors, and many others, supported my evolution toward a more holistic approach as a basis for my work. In essence, I was convinced that people had the right to direct their own health and lives and that I did not know what was best for them. I was convinced that the mind and body were connected in ways that I was only beginning to understand and that empowered individuals could make their lives more meaningful by using a wide variety of methods/techniques. I began to understand that the total environment (home, work, community, and culture) was critical to achieving health and well-being. If I was to stay true to this new understanding, I would need to find a way to either teach new courses

407

in a new major, or leave the university setting and become a consultant. It really did not seem to be a possibility to stay in a traditional health education academic program and promote something so different from my basic academic training and that of the rest of my colleagues.

My first attempt to deal with this emerging realization was in 1982, when I proposed a new Center for Health Promotion at Ball State University, which would operate out of my academic department but have a mission to reach out to the community and would involve an interdisciplinary approach to making the local community a model for community health and empowerment. The proposal was supported by the president and became one of the university's funding priorities in its annual budget request to the state legislature. It did not receive funding from the state, and I was not able to fund it from other sources at the level necessary to impact the community. But it was my first attempt to move in another direction.

At about the same time, I worked with a graduate student on a research project concerning what we were defining as wellness role modeling. The study was eventually published in *Health Values: High Level Wellness* (1983), and it seemed to show that those entering the field of health education did not differ from their collegiate peers regarding lifestyle. It seemed there was a disconnect with the content of what we taught and how we lived. This result reinforced my view that my current focus on the public health model of disease prevention, which guided our curriculum and influenced how we taught and lived, was not robust enough to either capture the factors that influenced health or inspire students and faculty to examine their lives and commit to a holistic approach to life.

In 1985, I was given the opportunity to be a leader on our campus as we examined the potential to do something new with our strong allied health programs. I worked with two other academic colleagues, one from physical education and the other from counseling psychology as we worked with a study committee to examine what opportunities we should pursue. We were able to convince the study committee, and the president, that Ball State University was the ideal place to push forward with a new academic focus that would combine our current resources in allied health and business with the new idea emerging in our society, wellness. With the support of the president and our assistant provost, who coordinated our efforts to move the proposal through the campus community and prepare a final request to the state legislature, we received campus support and state funding to initiate the Institute for Wellness in 1986. We accepted our first master's degree students in 1988 and graduated our first class of wellness managers in 1990.

Now, committing to really deliver an academic program to these students that was different than health education, exercise, and adult fitness was harder than I ever thought. First, I needed to, as academic coordinator, prepare students who would be employable while also putting them on the "cutting" edge of our field. My response during those first few years was to be safe. I stayed close to the traditional allied health disciplines, and our students were well rounded in health education and promotion, fitness, nutrition, and other subjects, reflecting a primary biomedical orientation. I was able to teach one-semester hour seminars, incorporating my emerging understanding of a more comprehensive approach to health that included an emphasis on body, mind, and spirit, and the importance of the organizational context for work and life.

One of my primary partners at this time was a psychologist, Dr. Don Nicholas, who also shared my interest in this broad approach to health. We began a weekly process of meeting and writing and sharing our reading about various ways of promoting health and wholness. This working partnership was one of the highlights of my academic life. We read widely, discussed, and debated the meanings of this literature about health generating versus disease prevention. Two primary organizing constructs formed the basis for our publications and the real foundation for the institute's approach to wellness. First, we were convinced that health truly was a multidimensional phenomenon and that it could only be expressed through a comprehensive analysis of these dimensions. Second, we knew that some overriding principles were in operation that once understood would shed light on health creation. The systems model, first described in biology by Ludwig von Bertalanffy, emerged as we continued to study the complexity of health, and it proved to be the most robust theory for a foundation of wellness and human potential. We also found that Pepper's work on world views was a critical link in making a case for a new way of thinking and writing about wellness instead of disease prevention. Finally, Antonovsky's work (1979) on the origins of health versus the origins of disease showed the way toward a more robust wellness model. The outcome of this work was a critical article published in the *American Journal of Health Promotion* (1991) entitled "World Views, Systems Theory, and Health Promotion." This was our first attempt to share with the larger field our thinking about the opportunities for an emerging field if we adopted a broader view of health and wellness.

Based upon this work, we now began to teach students about health from a much different perspective. We began to explore where health came from and what really maintained health. We exposed students to systems theory, quantum physics, and the best science on mind/body health. We began to expose students to the concepts of meditation and deep relaxation as a basis for health-promoting behaviors. We also emphasized the concept of human variation and the fallacy of normalcy. We were attempting to create an approach to wellness and health that maximized the importance of the individual and his or her potential to live a unique life. We were also emphasizing the critical importance of understanding the environment where health is either created or destroyed. The work of Judd Allen and his father, emphasizing community development and organizational change, was instrumental in our final beliefs in the power of multiple ways to health.

In the early 1990s the concept of wellness across the lifespan began to emerge as a very important part of the systems approach to health and wellness. The institute incorporated a Center for Gerontology, which emphasized the concept of the potential for wellness, regardless of age or outward appearances. This approach emphasized the variable nature of health as we age and how the concept of systems thinking captures the dynamics of the lived experience of unique individuals as they deal with the challenges of maintaining health and dignity. In 1998, the institute changed its name to the Fisher Institute for Wellness and Gerontology to better reflect our emphasis on aging well. During this transition, our students were getting a broad-based education in health and wellness and still receiving a minor in business that would support their efforts to work in various settings as members of management.

The continuing struggle for me is the balance of exposing students to what I consider to be the best science of health and wellness while they go into a job market that looks forward through the "rear-view mirror." Most jobs still rely upon a biomedical model, and few employers are willing to fully invest in comprehensive approaches that support the dignity of the person in the work environment. So I continue to insist that students receive both a strong grounding in the current expectations of the field, which I think are severely limited, and push them to explore the larger potential for both personal growth and individual empowerment. I guess time will tell if this has been the right course.

David Gobble, Ph.D., CHES, has worked in the health promotion and wellness field for over twenty-five years as an educator, administrator, direct service provider, and consultant for a wide range of agencies and organizations. He is currently director of and professor at the Fisher Institute for Wellness and Gerontology at Ball State University in Muncie, Indiana, where he coordinates the nationally recognized master's degree program in wellness management (identified as the foremost program of its kind in the country by the Association for Worksite Health Promotion). His career has focused on the delivery and evaluation of disease prevention and health promotion programs in various work and community settings. (765-285-8158, dgobble@bsu.edu)

HOLISTIC RESOURCES

National Organizations with Conferences

Institute for Noetic Sciences
707-775-3500   www.noetic.org

National Institute for the Clinical Application of Behavioral Medicine
800-743-2226   info@nicabm.com

National Wellness Institute
800-243-8694   www.nationalwellness.org

International Society for the Study of Subtle Energies and Energy Medicine
303-425-4625   www.issseem.org

Association for Humanistic Psychology
510-769-6495   www.ahpweb.org

Omega Institute
800-944-1001   www.eomega.org

Science and Consciousness
505-474-0998   www.bizspirit.com

SCAN
(Sports, Cardiovascular, and Wellness Nutritionists)
719-395-9271   www.nutrifit.org

The Renfrew Center Foundation
(Education and treatment for eating disorders, trauma, anxiety, depression, and
women's issues)
877-367-3383   www.renfrew.org

Journals, Newsletters, and Magazines

Self Healing (published by Dr. Andrew Weil)
800-523-3296   www.drweilselfhealing.com

Robison and Carrier

Alternative Therapies in Health and Medicine
866-828-2962   www.alternativetherapies.com

Journal of Consciousness Studies
44-1392-841600 (England)   www.imprint.co.uk

Book and Audiotape Clubs and Catalogs

Sounds True Audio Catalog
800-333-9185   www.soundstrue.com

One Spirit Book Club
800-998-1979   www.onespirit.com

Hay House, Inc.
800-654-5126   www.hayhouse.com

Image Paths, Inc.
800-800-8661   www.healthjourneys.com

Holistic Program Materials

Life's Odyssey™ Holistic Appraisal and Resource/Counseling Guide
Human Solutions, Inc.
6630 Glendora Ave.
Dallas TX 75230
(469) 232-2324   kmcarrier@sbcglobal.net

Kailo (Consulting, staff training, and prepackaged holistic programming materials
for organizations)
Kelly Putnam
Mercy Medical Center–North Iowa
(641) 422-7141 or e-mail: kailo@mercyhealth.com

Organizations

The Body Positive (Videos, workshops, and consulting on positive body image and
healthy relationships with food for children)   www.thebodypositive.org

Diabetes Care Center (HAES approach for diabetes)
Allen King, M.D., Dana Armstrong R.D., C.D.E.
1119 Pajaro St., Salinas, CA 93901
831-769-9355

The Institute for Relationship Therapy (Books, staying together workshops, and imago therapy training)
Harville Hendrix
1255 5th Ave., Suite C2
New York, NY 10029
212-410-7712   www.imagotherapy.com

Parents Leadership Institute (Parenting workshops, publications, and professional training)
Patty Wipfler
P.O. Box 50492
Palo Alto, CA 94303
415-424-8687   www.parentleaders.org

Re-evaluation Counseling (An international organization dedicated to individual and social healing)
719 Second Avenue North
Seattle, WA 98109
206-284-0311   www.rc.org

Hakomi Institute (Information and training on body-based psychotherapy)
P.O. Box 1873
Boulder, CO 80306
888-421-6699   HakomiHQ@aol.com

Radix Institute (Information and training on body-based psychotherapy)
3212 MonteVista N.E.
Albuquerque, NM 87106-2120
888-77-RADIX (777-2349)   www.radix.org

Centers for Overcoming Overeating (Books, audiotapes, videotapes, and workshops on ending compulsive eating and body hatred)

                                               www.overcomingovereating.com

New York (The National Center)   Chicago
212-875-0442   708-853-1200

New England   Atlanta
508-686-4432 or 404-814-0990   617-341-4885

Breaking Free (Audiotapes and workshops on compulsive eating)
Geneen Roth
P.O. Box 2852
Santa Cruz, CA 95063
408-685-8601   www.geneenroth.com

Ellyn Satter Associates (Books and workshops on child and adult nutrition, feeding, and weight issues)
608-271-7976   www.ellynsatter.com

National Association to Advance Fat Acceptance, Inc. (NAAFA, nonprofit human rights organization dedicated to improving the quality of life of fat people)
P.O. Box 188620
Sacramento, CA 95818
916-558-6880   www.naafa.org

Council on Size and Weight Discrimination
914-679-9160   www.cswd.org

Eating Disorders Awareness and Prevention (EDAP)
206-382-3587   www.nationaleatingdisorders.org

Hugs International, Inc. (You count, calories don't)
800-565-4847 (Canada)   www.hugs.com

International Coach Federation
(888) ICF-3131   www.coachfederation.org

Coach University
(800) 48-COACH   www.coachu.com

Professional Coaches and Mentors Association
(562) 799-2421   PCMA@pacbell.net

Videos

The Losing Game (Video about the nondiet movement)
Albritton TV Productions
202-364-7884

Body Trust: Undieting Your Way to Health and Happiness (Video that teaches people about nonrestrained eating)
800-321-9499

Killing Us Softly
Still Killing Us Softly
Killing Us Softly III
Slim Hopes
(Dr. Jean Kilbourne's powerful videos on media and images of thinness)
Media Education Foundation
413-586-4170

NIA Wave Exercise Videos (neurointegrative mind-body fitness developed by Debbie and Carlos Rosa)
NIA
6244 S.W. Burlingame Ave.
Portland, OR 97201
800-762-5762

The Wave Ecstatic Dance Videos (Nonimpact holistic-based movement developed by Gabrielle Roth)
Raven Recording
P.O. Box 271
Cooper Station,
New York, NY 10276
212-760-1381

Books

Many excellent books are listed at the end of each of the chapters in this book. There are, however, additional books that are very helpful to anyone seeking to develop Holistic Health Promotion programs. Listed below are a few of these for your consideration.

Getting The Love You Want: A Guidebook for Couples
Harville Hendrix, Henry Holt Co., New York, 1988
(Information on healing love relationships)

The No Nag, No Guilt, Do It Your Own Way Guide to Quitting Smoking
Tom Ferguson, Ballantine Books, New York, 1988
(Information on a more compassionate, intrinsically generated approach to smoking less or quitting completely)

Healing Back Pain: The Mind-Body Connection
John E. Sarno, Warner Books, New York, 1991
(Holistic approaches to healing back pain)

Talking Back to Prozac: What Doctors Won't Tell You about Today's Most Controversial Drug
Peter Breggin, St. Martins Press, New York, 1995
(Rethinking the widespread use of drug treatment for depression)

Compulsive Exercise and the Eating Disorders
Alayne Yates, Bruner/Mazel, New York, 1991
(Information on how high levels of exercise combined with restricted eating can interact and lead to unhealthy and addictive exercise and eating behaviors)

Women's Reality: An Emerging Female System In A White Male Society
Ann Wilson Schaef, HarperSanFrancisco, San Francisco, 1992
(Information on how women are reclaiming power in patriarchal societies)

Birth as an American Rite of Passage
Robbie E. Davis-Floyd, University of California Press, Berkeley, 1992
(Information on a holistic approach to pregnancy and birth)

The Wisdom of Menopause: Creating Physical and Emotional Health and Healing During the Change
Christiane Northrup, Bantam Books, New York, 2001
(Information on holistic views of menopause)

Money Harmony: Resolving Money Conflicts in Your Life and Relationships
Olivia Mellan, Walker and Co., New York, 1994
(Information on holistic financial wellness)

The Courage to Be Myself
Carlos J. Valles, Doubleday, New York, 1925.
(The Journey to Find One's Authentic Self)

I Could Do Anything if I Only Knew What It Was: How to Discover What You Really Want and How to Get It
Barbara Sher and Barbara Smith, Delacorte Press, New York, 1994
(Information that helps readers discover what they really want in life and how to get it.)

Awakening Intuition: Using Your Mind-Body Network for Insight and Healing
Mona Lisa Schultz, Harmony Books, New York, 1988
(Information on recognizing and developing intuitive skills)

INDEX

O

P

Y

Z

About the Authors

Jon Robison Ph.D., M.S.

Jonathan Robison holds a doctorate in health education/exercise physiology and a master of science in human nutrition from Michigan State University where he is adjunct assistant professor. Dr. Robison speaks frequently at national conferences and has published numerous scientific articles on a variety of health-related topics. His work promotes shifting health promotion away from its traditional, biomedical, control-oriented focus. He is also involved nationally with the Health at Every Size movement and has been helping people with weight-related concerns for more than 15 years. Aside from his work, Dr. Robison's passions include his wife Jerilyn, his 9-year-old son Joshua, music, humor and racquetball.

Karen Carrier M.Ed.

Karen Carrier has a master's degree in Exercise Science from the University of Houston and spent 15 years working in the area of organizational health promotion. She was part of the original design and ongoing development of the Conoco Inc. employee wellness program, one of the first holistic corporate programs anywhere in the country. She has also been an advocate for the non-diet, size acceptance movement for many years. Karen is currently President of Human Solutions Inc. and an adjunct professor at Nebraska Methodist College. She lives in Dallas, Texas, with her husband Max and their two daughters Lindsey and Madison, and enjoys spending a great deal of time with their two dogs and three horses.

Printed in the United States
115100LV00001B/322/A